Smithsonian

FRONTIERS OF FLIGHT

Smithsonian

FRONTIERS OF FLIGHT

Jeffrey L. Ethell

Smithsonian Books Washington, D.C.
Orion Books New York

Page 1: "a huge jewel," in the words of Charles Lindbergh, the Wright Whirlwind J-5 motor supplied 220 horsepower; pages 2-3: one of the Wright brothers flies their successful 1902 glider at Kitty Hawk, North Carolina; pages 4-5: the space shuttle Atlantis *rides piggyback atop a modified Boeing 747 to Kennedy Space Center, Florida; pages 6-7: the world-spanning Rutan* Voyager *in flight.*

THE SMITHSONIAN INSTITUTION
Secretary Robert McC. Adams
Assistant Secretary for External Affairs
  Thomas E. Lovejoy
Director, Smithsonian Institution Press
  Felix C. Lowe

SMITHSONIAN BOOKS
Editor-in-Chief Patricia Gallagher
Senior Editor Alexis Doster III
Editors Amy Donovan, Joe Goodwin
Assistant Editors Bryan D. Kennedy, Sonia Reece
Senior Picture Editor Frances C. Rowsell
Picture Editors Carrie E. Bruns, R. Jenny Takacs
Picture Research V. Susan Guardado
Special Picture Research Anne DuVivier, Robin Richman
Production Editor Patricia Upchurch
Assistant Production Editor Martha Sewall
Business Manager Stephen J. Bergstrom
Marketing Director Gail Grella
Marketing Manager Ruth A. Chamblee
Marketing Assistant Joyce L. Lombardo
Original Photography Ross Chapple, Terence McArdle
Terence McArdle's photography appears courtesy of Network Projects, Australia and The Discovery Channel. The television series, "Frontiers of Flight," is a production of Network Projects and was directed by John Honey.

Distributed to the trade by Orion Books, a division of Crown Publishers, Inc., 201 East 50th Street, New York, NY 10022. Member of the Crown Publishing Group. ORION and colophon are trademarks of Crown Publishers, Inc.
ISBN O-517 59208-8 (Orion Books)

John "Six-Cylinder" Smith sits at the controls of his Bleriot IX monoplane with a pipe-smoking passenger, around 1910. Smith built engines, including the first air-cooled aircraft radials in the United States.

LIBRARY OF CONGRESS
CATALOGING-IN-PUBLICATION DATA
Ethell, Jeffrey L.
  Smithsonian frontiers of flight / Jeffrey L. Ethell.
  p. cm.
  "...series of flying machines exemplified by those held within the collections of the Smithsonian Institution's National Air and Space Museum"—Introd.
  Includes index.
  ISBN 0-89599-033-4 (alk. paper)
  1. Aeronautics—History. 2. National Air and Space Museum.
  I. National Air and Space Museum. II Title
TL515.E84 1992
629.19'09—dc20   92-28336 CIP

Manufactured in the United States of America
First Edition
10 9 8 7 6 5 4 3 2 1

CONTENTS

INTRODUCTION

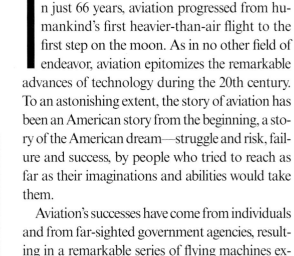

In just 66 years, aviation progressed from humankind's first heavier-than-air flight to the first step on the moon. As in no other field of endeavor, aviation epitomizes the remarkable advances of technology during the 20th century. To an astonishing extent, the story of aviation has been an American story from the beginning, a story of the American dream—struggle and risk, failure and success, by people who tried to reach as far as their imaginations and abilities would take them.

Aviation's successes have come from individuals and from far-sighted government agencies, resulting in a remarkable series of flying machines exemplified by those held within the collections of the Smithsonian Institution's National Air and Space Museum. Through the events surrounding these aircraft and the people who designed and flew them, the reader will now take a trip through a time of human, financial, industrial, and military interactions that stunned the world.

Enthralled by the maneuvers of the Wright 1908 Military Flyer, young Carl Claudy, Jr., watches its historic trials at Fort Myer, Virginia. Seventy-six years later, in April 1984, the space shuttle Challenger *deploys the Long Duration Exposure Facility (LDEF) high above Baja California. Until its retrieval by* Columbia *in January 1990, the LDEF exposed various materials to the harsh conditions of orbital space.*

POWERED FLIGHT

People probably have longed to fly ever since the first true humans began to reflect on the world around them. Birds, bats, squirrels, reptiles, insects and even fish have mocked our yearning to fly, driving dreamers to imagine a host of methods for emulating these creatures. Legendary accounts of human-carrying Chinese kites surfaced almost two centuries before the time of Christ, and such pre-industrial-age thinkers as Leonardo da Vinci designed human-powered flying machines. Yet it was not until the invention of the hot-air balloon that humans first realized the possibility of leaving the surface of the planet. On August 8, 1709, Brazilian priest Bartolomeu de Gusmao demonstrated an unmanned hot-air balloon to the court of King John V of Portugal.

Two French brothers, Joseph Michel and Jacques Etienne Montgolfier, launched their first successful large balloon on April 25, 1783. Its passengers—a sheep, a duck, and a rooster—ascended and descended successfully on September 19, 1783, proving that animals could survive such heights as the balloon achieved in its brief flight.

The first human flight took place on October 15, 1783, when François Pilâtre de Rozier ascended to 85 feet (26 meters) above the ground in the Montgolfier's new balloon, his altitude record limited by a tether. The following month, on November 21, de Rozier and his passenger, the Marquis d'Arlandes, made the first free flight in the same balloon, traveling more than five miles (eight kilometers) in 25 minutes.

Although balloons were unpowered and at the whim of the Earth's air currents, they were, in bold hands, capable of flights of astonishing height and duration. On April 15, 1875, for example, Gaston Tissandier and two passengers took their balloon to the then incredible altitude of 26,000 feet (8,000 meters). The flight ended tragically; although they

Prelude to success: Wilbur Wright lies on the wing of the damaged Flyer on December 14, 1903. The gasoline-powered aircraft stalled on its first takeoff attempt, but it still covered a promising 100 feet in three seconds. Four years of methodical aeronautic experiments and glider flights had brought the two Dayton, Ohio, bicycle makers—and their aircraft—to Kitty Hawk, North Carolina. After three days of repairs to the Flyer, Orville Wright would make the world's first successful, heavier-than-air, powered flight.

carried primitive supplemental-oxygen equipment, Tissandier's passengers died during the flight.

German Count Ferdinand von Zeppelin's huge, hydrogen-filled airship, the world's first successful steerable, lighter-than-air, self-propelled aircraft, first flew on July 2, 1900. But, in spite of such significant breakthroughs, humans still yearned to fly as a bird flies, without the aid of enormous gas bags, to soar and dive under their own control. Unfortunately, this usually led experimenters to attempt to emulate the flight of birds with complicated wing-flapping mechanisms that could not succeed.

In the early 1800s, the science of aerodynamics had been defined by Sir George Cayley, of Great Britain, who investigated many aspects of flight and largely worked out the form that the airplane would take, with fixed wings, cambered airfoil sections, dihedral (the angle between the wing of an aircraft and a horizontal line passing through the aircraft at the point of attachment of the wing), fixed horizontal and vertical stabilizers, and movable control surfaces, including rudders and elevators. He was well aware of the importance of control and thrust to any practical flying-machine design, and he forecast the advent of internal-combustion and even jet engines as the aircraft's prime movers.

Because of the work of Cayley and a few others, by the mid-19th century a firm foundation of aeronautical knowledge existed. Like Cayley, most inventors who achieved any success at all circumvented the lack of efficient power plants by building gliders. Cayley's glider of 1853 was the first aircraft of generally modern layout to make a flight with a man—his coachman—aboard. Immediately after the flight the history-making airman tendered his resignation, protesting that he was "hired to drive and not to fly."

Most early flight experiments were inconsistent and haphazard. However, German engineer Otto Lilienthal combined theory with practical application to produce not only real flying machines but also useful data. Of those who preceded the Wright brothers, Lilienthal took his place with Cayley as one of the most systematic experimenters.

A schooled engineer, Lilienthal was also a true airman who applied flight testing to aerodynamic theory. He combined studies of birds and bird flight with aerodynamic theory and experiments to build and fly 18 types of gliders from 1891 until a crash took his life five years later.

Lilienthal was obsessed with learning the basics of stability and control. He tried wing-tip-steering air brakes and a rudimentary leading-edge, full-span flap. Flying his robust monoplane and biplane gliders, Lilienthal made flights of more than

Aerodrome No. 5, left, a steam-powered model built by Smithsonian Secretary Samuel Langley, flew more than 3,000 feet in May 1896. It was the first successful engine-driven flight. Langley's full-scale aircraft were not as successful. Pilot William Avery, below, built this 1896 biplane glider for the 1904 St. Louis Exposition, and broke his ankle trying to land it.

1,000 feet (300 meters) from his 50-foot (15-meter) artificial hill outside Berlin and the Stöllen Hills near Rhinow, a little to the west of the city. He made studies of propulsion and rudder control and had started to investigate pitch control of his hang-glider-like machines when the inherent control limitations of such gliders made him stall and crash to his death.

American Octave Chanute, a widely known and respected retired structural engineer, published his *Progress in Flying Machines* in 1894, and built a series of biplane hang gliders. Feeling that he was too old to fly them himself, Chanute hired engineer Augustus Moore Herring and others to do the testing. Herring managed to pilot one glider 350 feet (107 meters) along the south shore of Lake Michigan by 1896.

In 1900, Chanute offered aeronautical information to Dayton, Ohio, bicycle-shop owners Orville and Wilbur Wright. The correspondence led to a close relationship among the three that offered much encouragement, if not much useful data, to the soon to be pioneer aviators.

Chanute's Pratt-truss system for bracing the wings of biplanes—carried over from his bridge-building days—was similar to the system eventually adopted by the Wrights. However, Chanute had concentrated on developing automatic stability in his gliders and had paid little attention to the problems of control by the pilot in flight. Nevertheless, the three men engaged in friendly and fruitful debates, and Chanute came to realize, particularly through Herring's flight-testing input, that actual experience in the air must prove the final authority.

Third Secretary of the Smithsonian Institution and respected astronomer Samuel P. Langley became seriously interested in powered flight in 1886. By 1896, Langley's shop had progressed to a pilotless, 26-pound (12 kilogram) scale-model craft, Aerodrome No. 5, that flew three quarters of a mile (over one kilometer), greatly impressing Alexander Graham Bell, who witnessed the flight. Very odd in appearance to the modern eye, the little steam-powered Aerodrome No. 5 owed its configuration of tandem, cambered wings and cruciform tail to designs of British pioneers Thomas Walker and D.S. Brown.

Langley devoted much attention to the finely executed steam engines that powered his model Aerodromes. As with other early flight experimenters, he had little appreciation of the need for mechanisms for actively controlling the flying machine once it was in the air. Relying on Cayley's princi-

German pioneer aviator Otto Lilienthal sails downhill before a crowd of onlookers at Rhinow, Germany. Lilienthal's lift experiments of the 1890s were fundamental to all later aeronautical researchers, including the Wright brothers. Lilienthal was killed in 1896 when he crashed in one of his gliders from an altitude of 50 feet (15 meters).

ples of dihedral for stability, he gave little thought to how the aircraft might be steered. (Cayley had determined that an aircraft with positive dihedral—that is, with wings that slant up from their attaching point on the aircraft—will have positive stability and will tend to continue stably on a course until it is turned by some outside force. The opposite is true for aircraft with wings that slant down from their attaching point. Such an aircraft, with negative stability, will tend to crash unless it is actively and constantly maintained in level flight by a pilot or computer.)

Prompted in part by war with Spain and by Bell's enthusiastic reports, President William McKinley authorized an appropriation to the U.S. Army of $50,000 for the construction of a large, human-carrying Aerodrome. Not only was this the first time anyone had asked to buy a flying machine, it was also the first time an official body had considered flight as a serious proposition rather than a subject for derision. Certainly Langley's status as a scientist, as well as the success of his models, had tremendous bearing on the authorization.

After hiring a talented young engineering student from Cornell University, Charles Matthews Manly, to build the machine, and machinist and inventor Stephen M. Balzer to create a revolutionary internal-combustion power plant, Langley had a quarter-scale model of a human-carrying aircraft flying by 1901. It was the first aircraft to fly with a gasoline engine. Unfortunately, Balzer's full-scale engine was far too heavy and produced but a fraction of the power expected. Manly redesigned it and built what was, in essence, a new engine. Far ahead of its time, this Manly five-cylinder radial engine produced more than 50 horsepower while weighing 207.5 pounds (94 kilograms), including the water to cool it. Such a power-to-weight ratio would not be realized in aero engines again until 1917.

By October 1903, the full-scale Aerodrome was completed and readied for launch from a catapult atop a houseboat in the Potomac River. Manly, who had no previous flight experience, was expected to fly it. On October 7, Manly boarded the craft. He sat sideways, with a steering mechanism

Wilbur Wright soars at Kitty Hawk in 1902. Two years' worth of improvements—including a movable, vertical tail, narrow wings that had been fine tuned in a wind tunnel, and an elliptical elevator—had been incorporated into this machine. The Wrights made between 700 and 1,000 glides in 1902, some covering as much as 600 feet (183 meters). Their glider was a controllable aircraft awaiting an engine.

similar to a ship's wheel and rudder as his only flight control. Upon launch, the Aerodrome's fragile forward wings were pushed out of shape by the force of the catapult, and the craft was fouled in the launch cables. It and Manly plummeted into the river. Both were fished out, Manly uninjured but the Aerodrome somewhat the worse for wear.

By December 8, Manly had repaired the machine, and he tried it again. This time the rear wings failed under the force of the catapult, and Manly became entangled in the wreckage as it went into the water. He barely escaped drowning, and the project was abandoned—along with its excellent engine, which could have had an immense impact on aviation. Manly hadn't even bothered to patent it.

Unfairly derided and humiliated by the press, Samuel Langley retired from any further involvement in aviation experiments. However, he left a legacy for the history of flight: his work inspired the Wright brothers to write to the Smithsonian Institution for information on flight.

Orville and Wilbur Wright had been fascinated with flight ever since their father, Bishop Milton Wright, of the United Brethren Church, gave them a small, rubber-powered flying toy. They were intrigued by the toy's ability to stay aloft, and tried to repair the toy and make others like it. While still young boys they attempted, unsuccessfully, to fly a larger model. By 1885, they began reading about the experiments of Otto Lilienthal. Much later still,

The Wright brothers took the death of Otto Lilienthal to heart: their glider of 1900, above, flies as a kite. Ropes attached to the elevator lever and the wing-warping lever allowed for safe testing of climbs, dives, and turns. The Wrights made progress slowly and carefully; at left, the 1902 glider ready for launch, with Wilbur at the controls. "The machine seems to have reached a higher state of development than the operators," he reported.

they began an orderly investigation into the principles of flight.

Both the Bishop and his wife, Susan, encouraged all five Wright children to explore new ideas and challenges. Although Orville and Wilbur elected to forgo higher education, they were extraordinarily well educated for their own time, or any other, for that matter, and were anything but the "high-school dropouts" of conventional mythology. While still teenagers, they designed and built their own printing press, and began to publish a weekly newspaper. Later, they opened a bicycle-repair shop to take advantage of the cycling mania sweeping America at the time. They did so well that they designed and manufactured their own bicycles, featuring several mechanical innovations.

As adults, Orville and Wilbur—probably sparked by Wilbur—resumed their interest in the problem of flight. In May 1899, Wilbur wrote to the Smithsonian Institution to ask for all documents relating to flight, particularly those of Samuel Langley, stating, "My observations . . . have only convinced me more firmly that human flight is possible and practicable. It is only a question of knowledge and skill."

As had so many before him, Wilbur studied the flight of birds to understand basic aerodynamics. "My observation of the flight of buzzards leads me to believe that they regain their lateral balance,

After achieving the first powered, controlled flight in history, the Wrights returned to gliding for pleasure and education. Here, at Kitty Hawk in 1911, Orville Wright adjusts a wire on glider No. 5. "We had the opportunity of witnessing daily soaring flights of the buzzards, fish & chicken hawks, and eagles," he noted. "Attempts to imitate their flights without a motor have not been very successful."

when partly overturned by a gust of wind, by a torsion of the tips of the wings." Unlike other experimenters of the day, he was more concerned with control than with stability or propulsion. His experience with bicycles made him sensitive to the problems of balance and control. The importance of this interest in active control to the Wrights' success cannot be exaggerated.

By August 1899, the brothers had built a biplane kite with a five-foot (1.5-meter) wingspan, stabilized by a fixed tail plane. The wings could be moved or "staggered" in relation to each other to change the center of gravity for pitch control and they could be warped for roll control. The warping system pulled the outer trailing edges down on one side while pulling the trailing edges up on the other, causing the kite to roll to one side or the other in response to the twisting of the wings. They flew the kite in a strong wind and found that their control systems worked. This was a significant breakthrough. Wing warping, which enabled an aircraft to turn, was the answer to a question no one but the Wrights had yet asked: how do you become a pilot?

After writing to Octave Chanute in 1900, the Wrights contacted the U.S. Weather Bureau to find a suitable testing site for full-scale gliders. They decided on the sand hills of Kitty Hawk, North Carolina, with their steady winds. That autumn they traveled to Kitty Hawk with a single glider, large enough to carry a pilot, that had cost them $15 to build. It had no rudder or fixed stabilizer of any kind, but a forward elevator was incorporated.

Flying their glider, sometimes tethered, like a kite, and sometimes free, as a glider, they quickly discovered that it required a dangerously steep nose-up angle of attack to sustain the glider in the air, even in the strong winds that swept over the dunes. The brothers concluded that this meant the curve of the wing, or airfoil, was inefficient. They decided to use a deeper wing camber, or curve, on their next glider and to increase the wing area as well.

They built two more gliders during 1901 and 1902 and tested them at Kill Devil Hills, both as kites and as piloted gliders. After making a number of flights, some of 300 feet (90 meters), they realized that the 1901 wing design was faulty in some respect; it stalled at an even lower angle of attack than had their first glider, while still not producing enough lift. They went back to Dayton confused and disappointed.

They decided that Lilienthal's airfoil-test data might be in error, and determined to generate their own lift and drag tables. In the winter of 1901-1902, during one of their long discussions, they recalled that other aeronautical experimenters, such as Sir Hiram Maxim, inventor of the machine gun, and Alexandre-Gustave Eiffel, designer of the Eiffel Tower, had used wind tunnels. Soon the brothers had an operational wind tunnel, a large wooden structure set up in their shop. It became their major research tool, enabling them to detect changes in the center of pressure of an airfoil as its angle of attack was changed. With this aid, essential to aeronautical research ever since, the Wrights tested more than 200 airfoil shapes.

Although the Wrights' wing-warping system was a wonderful innovation, its use led them to encounter new problems. When they warped the 1901 glider's wings, one wing would rise and the other would drop as the craft began to bank into the desired turn, but then, suddenly, the uppermost wing would stop, abruptly reversing the turn and causing the glider to stall in a tight circle and crash. The problem was that warping caused one wing to rise because it increased that wing's lift. But the same warping also caused increased drag, slowing the wing until it lost lift and settled. They attempted to counteract this warp drag, or adverse yaw, by installing fixed vertical fins to the rear of the glider.

Flying the 1902 glider with fixed fins, they found that it slipped sideways in turns. In October 1902, they replaced the fixed fins with a single hinged fin that could be controlled by the pilot to act as a rudder, and interconnected it with the wing-warping controls. This innovation enabled the Wrights to control side slipping and to make smooth, coordinated turns, thereby lessening the danger of stalling during turns. Virtually all aircraft since have been designed with a rudder to assist in the coordination of turns and banks.

That year they made between 700 and 1,000 successful glides at Kitty Hawk, testing each modifi-

cation, at times with some real danger, until they had confidence in their design. For the first time in history, a flying machine could be controlled through all three axes of motion: pitch, yaw, and roll. The Wrights became the first aviators to make stable turns. By the close of the season, they knew they had the basis for practical, powered flight.

Through most of 1903, the brothers designed and built the aircraft that would become known to history as the Wright Flyer. The Flyer was a biplane, somewhat larger than any they had built before. It had elevators in front to control pitch and rudder surfaces behind, which, with the wing-warping system, controlled yaw and roll. The pilot lay prone near the center of the lower wing in a hip cradle that, when swung left or right, would warp the wings and turn the rudders with one motion. The elevators were controlled by a stick that tilted the surfaces up or down.

With no suitable engine available, the brothers turned to their mechanic, Charles E. Taylor, who spearheaded the detailed design and construction of a four-cylinder, water-cooled power plant weigh-

Wright glider No. 5 flies with Orville at the controls on October 24, 1911. The brothers' efforts in locating Kill Devil Hills, a spot at Kitty Hawk with strong, steady winds, yielded the fruits of both powered and glider flight. At one point, Orville remained aloft in a 40-mile-per-hour wind for 9 minutes and 45 seconds, a record that remained unbroken until 1921.

ing 180 pounds (82 kilograms), which developed about 12 horsepower.

The Flyer itself had a wingspan of 40 feet, 4 inches (12.3 meters), a length of 21 feet, 3/8 inches (6.5 meters), and a flying weight of about 745 pounds (340 kilograms). Designed to be launched from a trolley on a 60-foot (18-meter) rail, it had two skids instead of wheels. The aircraft was restrained by a cable until the engine was up to full power, then released by the pilot.

Finding little of value in steamship-propeller design, Wilbur and Orville invented the first practical aircraft propeller. They realized that a propeller was nothing more than a rotating, twisted wing, with its lift vector turned to shove the machine forward through the air. Using the airfoil data they had gathered, they created a remarkably efficient design. It was another technical breakthrough that contributed to their success.

The Wrights returned to Kitty Hawk in September, and, by December 14, the Flyer was ready. By a coin toss, Wilbur won the privilege of making the first flight. After engine warm up, he made sure that the engine was at full power and ordered the cable released.

The Flyer moved down the rail on the trolley and was airborne—for a brief few seconds. The nose of the aircraft went up steeply, the wings stalled, and the Flyer settled roughly onto the sand. Wilbur was not hurt, the machine was only slightly damaged, and he was not dismayed. He wrote home that "there is no question of final success." By the 16th, the Flyer was repaired, and the brothers were confident enough to alert the men at the lifesaving station four miles (six kilometers) away of their plan to fly the next day.

The morning of December 17, 1903, dawned with a strong, gusty, 25-mile-per-hour (40-kilo-

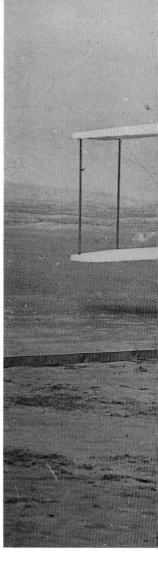

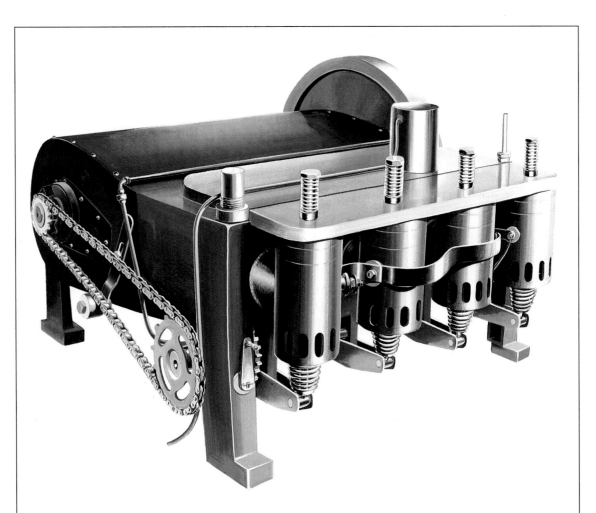

The 12-horsepower Wright motor of 1903, designed and constructed without plans by mechanic Charles Taylor, features four horizontal cylinders. The chain drives the camshaft, which in turn operates the exhaust valves. The air-inlet can, which rests on top of the motor, drips fuel onto a hot plate to be vaporized. A tiny crank controls the ignition, a 26-pound flywheel smoothes the impulses from the cylinders, and bicycle chains drive the two propellers.

In the moment of triumph, on December 17, 1903, Orville takes off while Wilbur watches. The first Wright Flyer proved a handful for the novice pilot: the front elevator, seen tilting up in this picture, was balanced too near its center and positioned too close to the wings. Orville described the flight, during which the Flyer pitched up and down, as "exceedingly erratic."

meter-per-hour) north wind, and with ice on the water puddles. Five people had come from the lifesaving station, and another man and boy had arrived to see what was happening. With an eye as much to historical recording as anything else, the brothers set up a camera to capture the takeoff and asked one of the bystanders to trip the shutter at the right moment.

Naturally, as the Wrights had always ordered their lives in fairness and deference to each other, it was Orville's turn to fly. Shortly before 10:35 A.M., the propellers were pulled through, the engine coughed to life, and he lay down in the hip cradle on the lower wing. As Orville recalled the event:

After running the motor a few minutes to heat it up, I released the wire that held the machine to the track, and the machine started forward into the wind. Wilbur ran at the side of the machine, holding the wing to balance it on the track. Unlike the start on the 14th, made in a calm, the machine, facing a 27-mile wind, started very

slowly. . . . One of the life-saving men snapped the camera for us, taking a picture just as the machine had reached the end of the track and had risen to a height of about two feet. The course of the flight up and down was exceedingly erratic, partly due to the irregularity of the air, and partly to lack of experience in handling this machine. The control of the front rudder was difficult on account of its being balanced too near the center. This gave it a tendency to turn itself when started, so that it turned too far on one side and then too far on the other. As a result the machine would rise suddenly to about 10 feet and then as suddenly, dart for the ground. A sudden dart when about 100 feet from the end of the track, or a little over 120 feet from the point at which it rose into the air, ended the flight. As the velocity of the wind was over 35 feet per second and the speed of the machine against this wind was over 10 feet per second, the speed of the machine relative to the air was over 45 feet per second and the length of the flight was equiv-

alent to a flight of 540 feet made in calm air. This flight lasted only 12 seconds, but it was nevertheless the first in the history of the world in which a machine carrying a man had raised itself by its own power into the air in full flight, had sailed forward without reduction of speed and had finally landed at a point as high as that from which it started.

Dragging the Flyer back to the launch rail, the brothers inspected it and found it to be in excellent shape for another flight. Wilbur climbed aboard, fired it up, and flew it 175 feet (53 meters) in 12 seconds. Orville made the next flight of 15 seconds, covering 200 feet (61 meters). Somewhere around noon Wilbur got airborne and stayed up for an exhilarating 59 seconds, traveling 852 feet (260 meters) before the Flyer, overly sensitive in pitch control, nosed into sand, ending the flight.

Upon inspection, they found that the elevator had been so damaged that they were unable to make the planned long-distance flight to the weather station. Before the machine could be dragged

back to camp for repairs, a gust blew it over, causing extensive damage. It would fly no more.

Although they had been able to control the machine, the Wrights had to fight it through each flight. Every control input had to be changed almost immediately, or the craft would flop into a dive or stall or porpoise up and down. The pilot had to keep the elevator lever and hip cradle constantly in motion. The machine pitched up and down constantly. Flying it was like trying to avert disaster. The experience was exhausting and probably terrifying, and since no one had the background to know it would be any different, the Wrights accepted it as a part of the newly discovered airman's world.

Before leaving the Outer Banks to return to Dayton, the brothers sent their now famous telegram to their father: "Success, four flights Thursday morning. All against twenty-one mile wind, started from level with engine power alone. Average speed through air thirty-one miles, longest 59 seconds. Inform press. Home Christmas."

Wanting to be sure that their achievement was

A painting of the Wright factory in Dayton, Ohio, where the first standardized aircraft and engines were built, depicts a worker in the general-assembly department applying the finishing touches to a 1910 Wright Model B, while two other men cover an elevator and wing with fabric. Unlike earlier Wright machines, the Model B had a rear elevator; a 30-horsepower, four-cylinder, vertical engine; and wheels.

properly reported, Wilbur and Orville wrote a long and meticulously detailed account of what they did and sent it to the Associated Press on January 5, 1904. With the exception of Octave Chanute and his associates, no one seemed to take notice.

During 1904 the brothers established their flight-test work at Huffman Prairie, a 90-acre pasture near Simms Station, eight miles (13 kilometers) east of Dayton. Flyer No. 2 had the same general configuration as the original, but the elevators and rudders were positioned slightly higher to keep them clear of the ground. A new 16-horsepower engine was installed and weight was added under the elevator in an attempt to cure the pitch-instability problem. In order to make takeoffs possible in Dayton's light winds, a weighted catapult was rigged to help accelerate the aircraft to flying speed.

Flight testing was conducted from May 26 to December 9, 1904. By the end of that time, the Wrights had made two flights of more than five minutes each with Flyer No. 2 within the confines of the field, thanks to their ability to make turns. Though the press was invited to witness a flight on two occasions, the engine would not start either time. In any case, most doubted the Wrights had ever flown at all.

During 1905, Flyer No. 3 was tested and flown 49 times, together with No. 2, during a series of trials from June 23 to October 16. Flyer No. 3 had longer front struts than its predecessors, the elevator was enlarged, and the brothers added a second

lever to control the rudder independently. These changes finally cured the long-standing pitch-instability problem that had caused the earlier machines to porpoise up and down unpredictably.

No. 3 bore the brunt of the 1905 testing, logging a total of three hours and five minutes in the air. One flight lasted more than 39 minutes, and covered more than 24 miles (39 kilometers). In its final form, Flyer No. 3 was the world's first practical airplane.

The 1905 Flyer was offered to the U.S. War Department for evaluation, but it was turned down. The War Department remembered the disappointing results with the government-backed Langley Aerodrome. Even the U.S. Patent Office was slow to act upon the Wright patents, not granting them until 1906.

Satisfied with their tests, the Wrights did not fly again until 1908. They wanted to settle the patent issues before conducting a public demonstration of their machine.

Disappointed in the U.S. government's response to their offer, the Wrights investigated the European market in 1907. Encouraged by the response there, they readied a new machine for flight demonstrations in Europe. In the meantime, they took the modified 1905 Flyer to Kitty Hawk, where, on May 14, their mechanic and assistant, Charles Furnas, became the world's first airplane passenger. Later, while Orville stayed in Dayton, Wilbur went to France to demonstrate the new airplane, which

The Wrights stand in front of the 1904 Flyer at their Huffman Prairie test site outside Dayton. Largely a copy of their 1903 machine, the second Flyer exhibited the same stability problems, although, on September 20, 1904, it completed the first circle ever flown by an aircraft. In the summer of 1905, Orville's crash in the third Flyer led to design changes. That October, Wilbur flew the rebuilt 1905 Flyer for 39 minutes. It was the first practical airplane.

came to be known as the Wright Model A.

Wilbur made his first flight in Europe on August 8, 1908, at Le Mans, circling the already famous auto race course there. It is difficult now to imagine the sensation created by this flight and those that followed. Wilbur Wright and his Model A burst into the consciousness of air-minded Europe like a shell exploding overhead. He flew more than 100 demonstration flights. One lasted more than two hours. His audiences had seen nothing before but machines that made short, barely controlled flights, the longest of which lasted but a minute or so. Here was a flying machine that could actually be controlled at will. Here was an American who had truly learned to fly.

Not only did spectators by the hundreds and thousands witness these flights, but Wilbur took passengers aloft on more than 60 occasions. By the end of 1908, total Wright flight time was 36 hours, 20 minutes, more than six times the total of all other aviators combined. Commercial success seemed assured when construction licenses were signed in Britain, France, and Germany.

Although the U.S. Board of Ordnance and Fortification had told the Wrights no money was available for buying an airplane, in 1907 this same board allocated $25,000, or "as much as might be required," to buy a dirigible for the U.S. Army Signal Corps. And the new board president, Major General J. Franklin Bell, had reopened the subject of purchasing a flying machine.

On December 23, Signal Corps Specification Number 486 was issued: "Sealed proposals in duplicate will be received at this office until 12 o'clock noon on February 1, 1908, on behalf of the Board of Ordnance and Fortification for furnishing the Signal Corps with a heavier-than-air flying machine." The general requirements were impressive indeed:

designed to be easily assembled and disassembled so an Army wagon could transport it; carry two people with a combined weight of 350 pounds, and sufficient fuel for 125 miles; reach a speed of at least 40 mph in still air, which would be calculated during a two-lap test flight over a 5-mile course, with and against the wind; demon-strate the ability to remain in the air at least one hour without landing, and that it then land without causing damage that would prevent it from immediately starting another flight; ascend in any sort of country in which the Signal Corps might need it in field service and be able to land without requiring a specially prepared spot; land safely in case of accident to the propelling machinery; simple enough to permit someone to become proficient in its operation within a reasonable amount of time.

The set purchase price of $25,000 had a proviso that 10 percent be added for each full mile per hour of speed over the required speed of 40 miles per hour (64 kilometers per hour), and 10 percent deducted for each full mile per hour under 40. The Wrights proved to be the only successful bidders out of 40.

The Wright Military Flyer had a new 30-horsepower engine and a single instrument, a simple string that hung down in the slip-stream near the pilot and, by its movement, indicated whether the airplane was skidding or slipping instead of flying straight or turning smoothly. It also served as a stall-warning indicator.

When Wilbur departed for what would prove to

Wilbur runs alongside the 1909 Wright Military Flyer and steadies its wing for takeoff at Fort Myer, Virginia, during a demonstration for the U.S. Army. Orville conducted a month-long series of such test flights, which had been interrupted the year before by a crash that injured Orville and killed Army Lieutenant Thomas Selfridge. The 1909 Flyer was equipped with a 25-horsepower motor, longer front struts, and an enlarged elevator.

be his triumphal tour of Europe, Orville had remained behind to complete the military machine and demonstrate it to the U.S. Army. As Orville arrived at Fort Myer, Virginia, with his Flyer, Captain Tom Baldwin's dirigible—or steerable, lighter-than-air ship—powered by an engine from motorcycle builder and racer Glenn Hammond Curtiss, was already under test for acceptance as Signal Corps Airship No. 1. The Wright maintenance shed went up next to the airship's mammoth tent, and people remarked that the post was filling up with "crazy flying people."

At Fort Myer, Orville erected a 25-foot-high (eight-meter) triangular tower, complete with a block and tackle to raise about 1,500 pounds (680 kilograms) of dead weight. This was dropped to catapult the machine down the launch rail and into the air. (The Wrights still considered skids to be more practical than wheels; however, they soon saw that the catapult greatly complicated ground handling, and they added wheels to their airplanes in 1910.)

Orville made his first demonstration of the 1908 Military Flyer on September 3, 1908, followed by several days of very successful and increasingly ambitious flights. On the 9th he established the duration capability and took aloft his first passenger, Army Lieutenant Frank P. Lahm.

During a bad-weather lull, a member of the Acceptance Board, Navy Lieutenant George C. Sweet, asked if he might fly with Orville. The propellers were adjusted for Sweet's heavier weight, but, when flights were resumed on September 17, Army Lieutenant Thomas E. Selfridge took Sweet's place.

With Orville and passenger aboard, the Flyer was airborne at 5:14 P.M. They made four perfect circuits and got halfway through a fifth when a propeller fouled a bracing wire and both broke with audible cracks. The machine glided under control from 150 feet to 75 feet (46 meters to 23 meters), then plunged into the ground, killing Selfridge and placing Orville in the hospital for seven weeks with, among other injuries, a broken hip. It was the world's first fatal powered-airplane crash. The Military Flyer was destroyed.

The Wrights returned on June 3, 1909, with a new demonstration aircraft. Modifications to the rudder and the bracing wires not only increased speed, but separated the props and wires by a wider margin for increased safety. Orville, more or less

On the evening of September 17, 1908, rescuers at Fort Myer, Virginia, scramble to free Orville Wright and Army Lieutenant Thomas Selfridge from the wreckage of the 1908 Military Flyer. The crash—the first fatal powered-airplane accident—took Selfridge's life, and put Orville in the hospital with multiple fractures. These injuries continued to cause Orville such pain that he seldom flew after 1915.

recovered from his injuries, continued as pilot, since the brothers believed that the pilot who had started a project should finish it. Army lieutenants Lahm and Benjamin D. Foulois were assigned as passengers.

Orville conducted a full month of tests, which were not free of peril. At one point, sudden power failure forced him to glide into a tree, breaking the skids and ripping a wing. Demonstrating the military requirement of rapid repair, the Wright team had the Flyer ready to fly again in four hours.

On July 26, President William Howard Taft traveled to Fort Myer and watched the aircraft take off under its own power without the catapult weight. A strong wind helped, with Wilbur running alongside to assure initial guidance. The following day, with Lahm next to him, Orville stayed airborne for one hour, 12 minutes, and 40 seconds to satisfy the endurance requirement, while traveling 40 miles (64 kilometers).

For the required-speed run, a course was set up from Fort Myer to the cornerstone of the Masonic Temple, then under construction atop Shooter's Hill in Alexandria, Virginia, a distance of five miles (eight kilometers). On July 30, the day of the flight, the Army post was swarming with thousands of spectators. Officials held seven stopwatches and a signal balloon was sent aloft at the midway point as a course marker. Telephone and telegraph wires were laid by the Signal Corps to make reports and facilitate flight control.

When Wilbur dropped the signal flag, Orville triggered the catapult counterweight and the Flyer, with Ben Foulois aboard as passenger, quickly climbed to 400 feet (122 meters). Making a 10-mile (16-kilometer) round trip, the attempt was recorded at 37.735 miles per hour (60.376 kilometers per hour) outbound and 47.431 miles per hour (75.89 kilometers per hour) inbound. The 42.583-mile-per-hour (68.133-kilometer-per-hour) average speed earned the Wrights a two-mile-per-hour (3.2-kilometer-per-hour) bonus on the sale price, and they were paid $30,000. This was to include flight instruction for two Army pilots at College Park, Maryland.

The deal went through on November 4, 1909,

Keith Ferris's painting, The Dream Fulfilled, above, captures the thrill of the speed trials of the 1909 Wright Military Flyer on July 30 of that year. Orville pilots from the left seat, while Army Lieutenant Benjamin Foulois sits on the right. The 10-mile course stretched between Fort Myer and Alexandria, Virginia. At right, Army pilot Foulois appears second from right in a 1912 photograph of an Army Wright Model B at Fort Sam Houston, Texas.

and the next day a fledgling pilot promptly cracked up the 1909 Military Flyer. Training was delayed until parts could be shipped from Dayton, but the fact remained that the world's first military aircraft had been purchased and made operational.

The Wrights' success gave hope to many who wanted to see the flying machine mature. Even after the Langley Aerodrome failure, Alexander Graham Bell had continued to support aviation research. Bell formed the Aerial Experiment Association in October 1907, with Canadians Frederick Walker Baldwin and John Alexander Douglas McCurdy and Americans Thomas Selfridge (the same man who would later become the first aviation casualty) and Glenn Curtiss, who was appointed director of experiments. Each of the men had an assignment to build an airplane of his own design at Hammondsport, New York, to take advantage of the Curtiss shops. Though Curtiss had been leaning toward a career as an automobile- and motorcycle-engine builder, he quickly turned to aviation.

Selfridge's *Red Wing* was the first association machine to fly. On March 12, 1908, it traveled 318 feet (97 meters), but it crashed in a heap because it lacked adequate provision for lateral control. Bell

suggested that Baldwin's *White Wing* be equipped with movable wing tips, controlled by the pilot with a shoulder yoke.

Fly the *White Wing* did, the following May, though only in hops. Curtiss was so enthusiastic that he announced the readiness of the Glenn H. Curtiss Manufacturing Company to accept orders and deliver flying machines in 60 days for $5,000 each. There were no buyers, but his ingenuity resulted in the *June Bug*, the Aerial Experiment Association's third machine.

This Curtiss airplane had movable wing tips and some control improvements, together with the same outstanding Curtiss engine that had powered the first two aircraft. After several public demonstra-

A close-up of the cockpit of a late-model Wright flyer reveals the pilot's seat on the right, with two levers that serve to control the elevators, the rudder, and wing warping. On the left is a large fuel tank, below which rests the water-cooled, four-cylinder Wright engine.

tions, Curtiss made a headline-catching flight of 5,090 feet (1,552 meters) in one minute, 42 seconds, in the *June Bug*.

McCurdy's *White Wing* flew successfully with a number of improvements, but, when the association dissolved 18 months after its inception, Curtiss was assigned all American rights to patents and achievements made by all members. He was on his way to challenging the Wrights' aerial supremacy, and within two years he became their major competitor. Orville and Wilbur formed the Wright Company in 1909, backed by $100,000 from a group of financiers. The same year, Curtiss formed the Herring-Curtiss Company with Augustus Herring, who had experience flying gliders inspired by his contacts with Octave Chanute. The Aeronautic Society of New York put in an order for a Curtiss airplane named the *Gold Bug*, for which they paid $5,000. The Curtiss movable wing tips had been replaced with small, movable surfaces mounted between the ends of the upper and lower wings.

From the beginning, Orville and Wilbur viewed Curtiss's inter-wing control surfaces as infringe-ments on their patented lateral-control system. Although hinged lateral-control surfaces, or ailerons, similar in operation to those Curtiss had designed, would replace the Wright wing-warping system on all future aircraft, at the time the Wrights argued that they were simply another form of wing warp-ing. They began a series of legal actions, not only against Curtiss, but also against more than a dozen other aircraft manufacturers in the United States and Europe. The Curtiss Company hired a series of lawyers to defend him.

The courts ruled in the Wright brothers' favor in every case that went to trial, except in Germany. Curtiss kept them from stopping him directly through appeals, legal maneuvering, and the de-termination to set as many aviation records as pos-sible. In 1912, while the patent battle threatened to bring American aviation to a complete standstill, Wilbur Wright died of typhoid fever.

The final battle between Orville and Glenn Cur-tiss took place early in 1914, when the Federal Cir-cuit Court of Appeals ordered Curtiss to cease making airplanes with two ailerons that operated

Pioneer aviator Glenn Curtiss flies one of his early racing planes at Atlantic City, New Jersey, in 1912. Curtiss progressed from motor-cycle racing to flying. This aircraft, like the Wright machines, has a forward elevator; the small, wing-like surfaces between the wings, called ailerons, are used for banking. In a battle that slowed the pace of American aviation, the Wrights sued Curtiss for patent infringement involving the use of ailerons.

At left, Canada's early Aerial Experiment Association (AEA) included, from left to right: Frederick Baldwin; Thomas Selfridge, who died in the crash of the Wright Flyer at Fort Myer, Virginia, in 1908; Glenn Curtiss; founder Alexander Graham Bell; and John McCurdy. (Augustus Post, pictured at far right, was not a member). Between 1907 and 1909, aeronautical experiments with powered aircraft as well as gliders led to multiple Canadian patents, such as the one shown here, which were held by an AEA trustee for the use of the members. Curtiss gained valuable experience in aeronautics through his work with this group.

simultaneously in opposite directions.

Curtiss refused to quit. Henry Ford's lawyer, W. Benton Crisp, had been sent by his employer to help the Curtiss cause. Crisp came up with an ingenious ploy to turn things around: approach the Smithsonian Institution for permission to fly the Langley Aerodrome. Curtiss could then argue in court that the Wright patents were not based on an original invention.

Though Charles Manly had been trying in vain since Langley's death eight years before to obtain such permission, Curtiss was welcomed by Smithsonian Secretary Charles D. Walcott. Not only was the Aerodrome loaned to Curtiss, but Albert P. Zahm, a Curtiss court witness, was allowed to accompany the machine and record the results.

No effort was made to fly the machine as it had been built originally. Curtiss undertook an extensive redesign, including the addition of wings of different form, camber, and bracing, while leaving the general appearance the same. A Curtiss control system was installed, certainly an essential requirement, since the original had no means of lateral control, and stiffening struts were added. The machine was mounted on floats so that it could fly off water.

The Manly engine, with its pusher propellers, was removed, and a Curtiss 90-horsepower OX engine with a tractor propeller was mounted. Even with this extensive rebuild, all the Aerodrome could deliver was a few short hops off the water. Although

In 1910, Orville Wright, above (right), prepares to take railroad magnate Cornelius Vanderbilt III for a flight in a Wright Model B. At right, Wilbur Wright sits at the controls with his sister, Katharine, one of some 60 passengers he took up during his celebrated tour of Europe in 1908. Opposite (left), an English music title sheet fancifully promotes the coming of the aviation age. Opposite (right), a European box-kite-like aircraft follows a Wright Flyer. In fact, Europe was not far behind the Wrights in aviation technology.

other aviators and the courts were not fooled by this questionable effort, Zahm signed a Smithsonian-approved affidavit that the Hammondsport rebuild and Langley's original Aerodrome were "the same machine."

When the Aerodrome was returned to its original configuration and hung in the Smithsonian for display, the plaque beneath read, "The first man-carrying aeroplane in the history of the world capable of sustained free flight." Unable to come to grips with this decision, Orville crated the original 1903 Wright Flyer and sent it to the Science Museum in London. It remained there until a formal retraction was made by the Smithsonian to the Wrights, and it was returned to the United States to a deserved place of honor in the Smithsonian just after Orville's death in 1948.

A definitive court showdown between Orville and Glenn Curtiss never took place. Worn out and

sapped of strength, as much from Wilbur's death as from the courtroom battles, Orville bought up his fellow shareholders' Wright Company stock. He sold everything, including all Wright patents, to a syndicate of New York financiers in 1915, and retired a wealthy man, to tinker for the rest of life.

Wilbur and Orville Wright were the world's first genuine aeronautical engineers. They viewed flight, both in the lab and in the air, as an integrated whole composed of structures, propulsion, aerodynamics, controls, and testing, each dependent upon the others to create a successful flying machine. To this day, flying machines have remained basically unchanged: lift, three-axis control, and efficient propulsion are what make flight possible. The Wright brothers' innate genius, philosophical outlook, intense work ethic, and courage made the airplane a reality.

Intuitive engineers Wilbur (left) and Orville Wright realized the dream of flight, and became the world's first test pilots.

COAST TO COAST

Since America's aviation pioneers were spending more time in court than they were designing aircraft, the lead in development naturally passed from the Wright brothers and Glenn Curtiss to the Europeans. Even so, entrepreneurs moved quickly to keep the miracle of flight before the American public by putting on a series of exhibitions by individuals and by teams formed under the Wright and Curtiss banners. People fell in love with the daring men and women who challenged the sky, and with the airplanes they flew.

Although practical aircraft had now been around for nearly eight years, only a handful of people had ventured into the air. Flight instruction was available at the Wright and Curtiss facilities, but few knew what it took to become a good pilot; even the instructors' experience was limited. The result was a group of pilots with little more than a few hours' flying time attempting incredible feats of aerial daring.

By 1911, Lincoln Beachey, who had learned to fly with Glenn Curtiss, was perhaps the most audacious of the airmen: he flew his Curtiss biplane upside down—on purpose. Air races were dominated by Glenn Curtiss himself, always a lover of speed. Distance and endurance records continued to be challenged, particularly when money was offered as a prize.

Thanks to William Randolph Hearst and his penchant for schemes to boost newspaper circulation, the idea for a coast-to-coast air race was born. During a regional California flying meet in October 1910, Hearst's Los Angeles *Examiner* offered $50,000 to the first flier to cross the North American continent in 30 days. There was no limit on the number of stops, but the flight had to be completed by October 10, 1911. Eight pilots registered for the prize, but almost a year went by before anyone started out.

On September 17, 1911, Calbraith Perry Rodgers takes off from Sheepshead Bay, New York, in his Wright EX at the start of the first coast-to-coast flight. Some 85 days later, Rodgers would wet the wheels of the Vin Fiz Flyer in the Pacific Ocean. "Vin Fiz," visible on the rudder of the EX, was the trademark name for a grape-flavored soft drink marketed by Rodgers' sponsor, the Armour Company, of Chicago.

Many daring men and women took to the skies in the early 1900s to perform crowd-thrilling feats of aerial skill. America's greatest stunt pilot of the time, Lincoln Beachey, photographed above in his Curtiss machine, first flew a plane in the winter of 1910. Beachey became famous for making vertical dives from 5,000 feet (1,524 meters), and then shutting off the engine and landing exactly where he wanted to. On June 27, 1911, to the delight of more than 100,000 onlookers, he performed his "most spectacular flight ever," right, diving under the Suspension Bridge spanning Niagara Falls.

Calbraith Perry "Cal" Rodgers certainly had an adventurer's pedigree. He was the great-grand-nephew of Captain Oliver Hazard Perry, hero of the Battle of Lake Erie, which was fought during the War of 1812, and the great-grandson of Commodore Matthew Calbraith Perry, who opened Japan to the West in 1854. His father was killed by lightning while campaigning against Indians in the American West. Though he had wanted a military

career, Cal's partial deafness from childhood scarlet fever ruled that option out. An otherwise healthy six-foot, four-inch (184-centimeter) 200-pounder (91 kilograms), he turned to sports, particularly football, sailing, horse racing, and fast cars. At age 32, he found that the new field of flying perfectly suited his personality and stamina.

Entering the Wright flying school in Dayton in June 1911, Cal soloed after just 90 minutes of aerial instruction and was issued his pilot's license on August 7. Determined to make this new endeavor his livelihood, he bought a Wright Model B for $5,000, and headed straight for the Chicago International Aviation Meet. With his sights on the Hearst transcontinental prize, he won $11,000, but he knew that wasn't enough to pay for the cross-country flight on his own. Accordingly, Rodgers talked meat-packing millionaire J. Ogden Armour into underwriting the attempt in exchange for publicity for Armour's new grape-soda soft drink, Vin Fiz. Rodgers would paint the drink's name on the wings and tail of a new Wright EX biplane, throw advertising leaflets to the mortals on Earth as he spanned the continent, and get paid $5 per mile to boot.

The obstacles were formidable. Since there were no airports for most of the way across, he would have no source of supply or mechanical help available, no weather reporting, and no instruments or radio. Armour therefore agreed to provide him with a special three-car train to serve as ground accompaniment to the flight and to supply everything needed to make repairs and support the effort in general.

Charlie Taylor, the Wrights' mechanic and the creator of the 1903 Wright Flyer engine, was hired away from Dayton to become the chief mechanic for the flight. Rumor had it that the train also carried a coffin sized perfectly for the pilot—if nothing else, the story made sensational press.

Even though his backing was secure, Rodgers faced a flight of more than 4,000 miles (6,400 kilometers). He would navigate by following railroad tracks as his "iron compass" to the West. With no enclosed cockpit, exposed to the weather and to a 55-mile-per-hour (88-kilometer-per-hour) wind, he controlled his skittish machine from a few boards made into a seat. This truly was an event for the hardiest. By September 1911, only three entrants were still willing to make the attempt for Hearst's prize. The first off was Robert G. Fowler, also a graduate of the Wright flying school, who left Golden Gate Park in San Francisco on the 11th, cheered by a crowd of 10,000. Unfortunately, his Wright airplane wouldn't clear the Sierra Nevada, and he crashed into trees on a rugged slope. The machine, sponsored by the Cole Motor Company of Indianapolis, was shipped to Los Angeles for a 12-day rebuild and another try.

Another entrant, 19-year-old Jimmie Ward, had soloed only a month before he took off from Governor's Island in New York Harbor on September 13. He promptly became lost over New Jersey; after he got back on course over New York State his engine went sour, and he had to land and order a replacement.

On September 17, 1911, just 41 days after getting his pilot's license, Cal Rodgers had the *Vin Fiz*

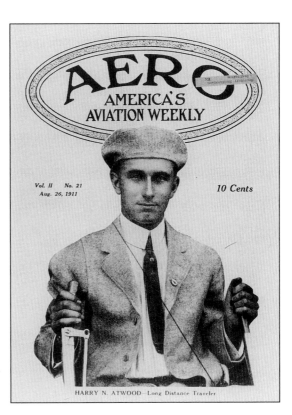

HARRY N. ATWOOD—Long Distance Traveler

Having recently set a new American distance record for a single day's flight—286 miles (460 kilometers) from St. Louis to Chicago in a total of 5 hours and 43 minutes' air time—Harry N. Atwood appears at the controls of an airplane, possibly a Burgess-Wright, on the cover of the August 26, 1911, issue of Aero: America's Aviation Weekly *magazine. Below left, Atwood flies over the south lawn of the White House in a Wright Model B biplane on July 14, 1911.*

assembled and ready at the Sheepshead Bay racetrack on Long Island, pointed toward his final destination of Pasadena, California. A crowd of 2,000 watched as Rodgers strode out to the craft with his hat on backwards, goggles ready, chomping on a large cigar, and clad in padded vest, black-leather riding boots, and black gauntlets. A beauty queen poured a bottle of the grape elixir over the landing skids and declared, "I dub thee *Vin Fiz* Flyer!"

Accepting a four-leaf clover from an admirer, Rodgers mounted the Flyer, lit his cigar, and had the engine started by two men who yanked the propellers. Once the engine was warm, he advanced the spark to full power and lifted off at 4:30 P.M. for the first short leg of his journey. Dutifully keeping to his contract, Cal circled the crowds at Coney Island and dropped Vin Fiz leaflets. He then crossed the East River at the Brooklyn Bridge, and skimmed over Manhattan while thousands cheered him from rooftops and windows. The next day, newspapers were full of accounts of his departure, "daring what no man had dared before in flying directly over the city with its death trap of tall buildings, spires, ragged roofs, and narrow streets."

Rodgers found Armour's three-car train, marked with strips of white canvas, on the track in New Jersey, and followed it. Aboard the Pullman and lounge cars were his wife, Mabel; mechanic Frank Shaffer, who, along with his assistants, would be in charge until Charlie Taylor arrived; and some reporters and Armour representatives. Cal's mother and his cousin, Lieutenant John Rodgers, later a renowned U.S. Navy pilot, would join them shortly. The hangar car, decorated with Vin Fiz slogans, housed Rodgers' Wright Model B, which served as a back-up machine, as well as plenty of spares for the EX and a Palmer-Singer automobile.

To the rousing cheers of thousands of people and the shriek of whistles, Rodgers made a beautiful landing at Middletown, New York, having covered 84 miles (135 kilometers) in 105 minutes with "not a miss of the cylinders and not a swerve of the machine." Hopping from foot to foot to restore the circulation in his legs, he flashed his characteristic, cigar-clenched grin.

That night he told reporters, "It's Chicago in four days, if everything goes right," and added that the next day he would "try for the longest one-day flight ever made. I'll overtake Jimmy Ward at Owego and pass him before night on Tuesday." The rivalry and banter ensured great newspaper sales.

At 6:21 A.M. the *Vin Fiz* was off, but it brushed a willow tree with its rear landing-gear truck. Rodgers leveled the machine and swerved to avoid a hickory tree, only to find a set of telegraph wires in his way. He cut the engine, the elevators caught a tree top, and the machine plunged into a chicken coop. Rodgers emerged with a cut on his scalp and a sprained ankle. The aircraft was a twisted, broken mass, with only the radiator and one gas tank undamaged. It took three days to repair the Wright and get it re-assembled.

Undaunted, Rodgers set off again, paralleling New York's southern border toward Chicago. The realities of pioneering aviation continued to be confirmed with bone-jarring clarity. Engine trouble forced him down at Hancock, New York, where the Wright EX was battered by strong winds. Even following his train, Rodgers got lost and wandered south until he landed at Throop, Pennsylvania. He flew back north, and picked up the westbound route again at Great Bend. After landing at Binghamton, New York, on September 21, he narrowly missed a barbed-wire fence in his efforts to avoid onlookers, who later tried to tear his machine apart for souvenirs. Finally, he made it to Elmira.

On the 22nd, meanwhile, Jimmie Ward's Curtiss airplane suffered complete engine failure, and he crashed into a tree near Rathbone, New York. He was thrown from the wrecked machine, but managed to walk into town and tell the world he was abandoning the transcontinental flight. The third competitor, Robert Fowler, with his rebuilt Wright, again tried to clear the Sierras in California, but once again didn't make it—he'd have to find a more powerful engine.

In Elmira, on September 23, Rodgers damaged the Flyer slightly, nosing it into the ground while trying to avoid trees and telegraph wires. After quick repairs he was off again, but this time the engine lost power when the magneto leads slipped off two cylinders. He managed to get them re-attached in flight and continued on. When the leads worked loose again, he tried to hold them on with

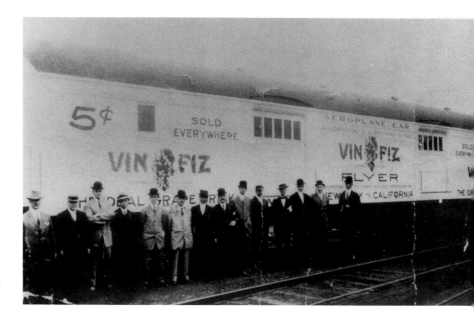

one hand while flying with the other, a nearly impossible feat. He made a forced landing at Canisteo, New York. Later, ignition trouble forced him down on the Alleghany Indian Reservation at Salamanca, where the airplane was torn apart in a crash, causing a delay of four days.

Heading for Akron, Ohio, Rodgers was blown off course by head winds, and lost sight of the railroad. Sunset was upon him, and he had never flown in the dark—for that matter, very few people in the world had ever flown at night. With no city lights to guide him, he waited for the moon to come up and then brought the machine down intact in a pasture full of cows. Sunrise on the 30th found him near Kent and he set off again, navigating around violent thunderstorms with no margin for error.

Armour Company representatives stand in front of the Vin Fiz *hangar car, below, which served both as Cal Rodgers' plane's traveling repair shop and as a billboard for promoting the company's new soft drink. On board the train were several Armour representatives, Rodgers' wife, Mabel, and his mother, as well as "four of the most expert mechanics in the country," spare airplane parts, and "an emergency automobile" to transport the mechanics and equipment to the plane to make repairs.*

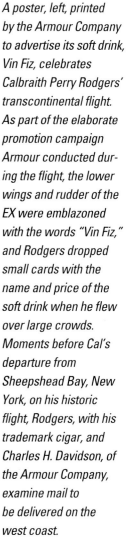

A poster, left, printed by the Armour Company to advertise its soft drink, Vin Fiz, celebrates Calbraith Perry Rodgers' transcontinental flight. As part of the elaborate promotion campaign Armour conducted during the flight, the lower wings and rudder of the EX were emblazoned with the words "Vin Fiz," and Rodgers dropped small cards with the name and price of the soft drink when he flew over large crowds. Moments before Cal's departure from Sheepshead Bay, New York, on his historic flight, Rodgers, with his trademark cigar, and Charles H. Davidson, of the Armour Company, examine mail to be delivered on the west coast.

After breaking a propeller chain, Rodgers came down at Marion, Ohio, for repairs and fuel. Then the engine quit just over the Indiana border. An angry thunderstorm with blinding lighting led to a forced landing at Geneva, Indiana. Although he had been tossed around violently, he found it "a great experience and proved that a motor can go through a heavy rain if you cover the magneto with your gloves, which was not the easiest thing to do."

Rodgers said that rain was not as rough on the pilot as it was on the engine, underscoring just how much these early pilots took for granted the lack of creature comforts afforded by their primitive machines. Raindrops drove like pins into the skin of the hapless pilot, sat exposed in the windstream. The wind-chill factor was amplified and pain became his constant companion. His goggles would sheet over with a thin film of water that blurred vision, and water would penetrate every crevice and crease of his clothing. Soon the moisture chilled Rodgers' body to the point of numbness, and he found that moving the controls took a great effort.

Breathing was difficult, with the 60-mile-per-hour (96-kilometer-per-hour) slip-stream trying to force its way down his throat. And the airplane itself was unstable, requiring his constant and close attention just to keep it in level flight. Even short flights were demanding and hazardous in these early aircraft. To make a long-distance flight called for powers of concentration and endurance—to say nothing of courage—that we can scarcely imagine today. That Rodgers managed to hold his gloved hand over the magneto leads and still fly was a fantastic feat of skill.

Taking off from Huntington, Indiana, he had to wreck the *Vin Fiz* to avoid running into the crowd—both propellers, the left wings, and the landing gear were badly damaged. Strong winds delayed his takeoff from Hammond, Indiana, but at last, on October 8, he landed in Chicago. It had taken him three weeks to fly 1,199 miles (1,920 kilometers).

Aside from the major disasters, every takeoff and landing resulted in some form of minor damage, not to mention parts of the airplane stripped by souvenir hunters, all of which made daily repairs imperative. Without Armour's support, such a flight would have been impossible.

At Grant Park, Illinois, reporters crowded around

Rodgers and asked if he would quit. The deadline for completion of the flight was to expire in two days; clearly the Hearst prize was out of reach. In keeping with his personality and adventurous heritage, Rodgers shot back, "I'm going to do this whether I get $50,000 or 50 cents or nothing. I am going to cross this continent simply to be the first to cross in an aeroplane."

As it was, he was not far from beating the standing distance record of Harry Nelson Atwood, who had flown 1,256 miles (2,010 kilometers) from St. Louis to New York between August 14 and 25, 1911. Wasting no time, Rodgers was airborne from Chicago the same day he landed, although he could not resist flying a daredevil show for the inmates of the state prison at nearby Joliet. To avoid the Ozarks and the Rockies, he headed southwest. By the time he reached Marshall, Missouri, he had covered 1,398 miles (2,237 kilometers), comfortably breaking Atwood's record.

When word went out that the Hearst prize definitely was withdrawn, St. Louis rescinded its offer to Cal of $1,000 for landing in the city. Angered, Rodgers changed his stop to Kansas City. Performing an impressive display of acrobatic flying on October 11, Rodgers swooped into the city and received a roaring cow-town welcome.

Vin Fiz's crashes and malfunctions took a constant toll on airplane, pilot, and mechanics. Above left, Cal Rodgers' mechanics scratch their heads as they contemplate the *Vin Fiz's* engine, which blew a cylinder on November 3 over the Salton Sea in Southern California, forcing him to land at Imperial Junction. Again puffing on his ever present cigar, Rodgers, above, helps mechanic Charles Taylor repair the airplane's wings in Salamanca, New York.

By the 14th, he was off to the southwest for San Antonio, Texas, via Dallas. The public seemed to pay even more attention to him now that the Hearst prize was out of reach, and crowds gathered at each stop to cheer him on. Up to that time, an even 100 people had died in aviation accidents, and Rodgers seemed to stretch the limits of his own luck with each passing day.

After landing in Muskogee, Oklahoma, Cal was greeted by reporters, who, as usual, did not appreciate that his poor hearing prevented him from understanding them. When shaking hands, he often appeared to be "silent" and emotionless, leading a Phoenix, Arizona, reporter to write, "To those who saw Rodgers alight and step from his machine there came a sensation as if they had just spoken to a messenger from Mars."

Pressing on to McAlester, Oklahoma, Rodgers was forced to land for repairs to a cracked cylinder. After getting lost just across the Texas border, he made Fort Worth, then Dallas, while a curious eagle briefly accompanied him .

Shortly after he departed Austin for San Antonio, the Wright engine shook out of its mountings, and Rodgers had to kill the ignition. A later report recounted that he was "...at 3,500 feet. Crystallized piston and intake valves nearly made a wreck. The aviator shut off his engine, volplaned [glided] two miles and made a perfect landing in the only pasture within forty miles." After engine repairs at San Antonio, Cal finally turned west on October 24—he had been unable to turn west before, since he had to follow the tracks of the Southern Pacific Railroad.

Taking off from Spofford on the 25th, Cal spun into the ground, making a complete wreck of the Wright. Incredibly, Charlie Taylor and his crew had grown so accustomed to such incidents that they

In a scene that became all too familiar during its cross-country flight, the crumpled Vin Fiz *rests tail up after crash-landing in a field in Huntington, Indiana, on October 8, 1911. Aborting a takeoff, Rodgers had to bank into a grove of trees to avoid hitting spectators. This time he was not seriously injured, but the plane was badly damaged.*

were able to repair his fourth major crash overnight. But then, at Sanderson, the aircraft was smashed by high winds. Passing Sierra Blanca, the aircraft's engine-cooling pump failed. Rodgers stalled and dropped to the ground from five feet (1.5 meters), destroying the Wright's landing skids. By the time he reached El Paso, it had taken him two weeks and 23 stops to cross the Lone Star State.

As Rodgers flew into Tucson, Arizona, on November 1, his arrival was watched by rival Robert Fowler, who was slugging his way through his second west-east crossing attempt. The two men wished each other well before departing in opposite directions. Fowler eventually would reach Jacksonville, Florida, on February 8, 1912, after persisting for 149 days.

On November 3, the *Vin Fiz* crossed the California border, 178 miles (285 kilometers) from the Pacific. Over the Salton Sea the Wright's engine blew a cylinder, sending steel splinters into Rodgers' right arm and hot oil into his face. Somehow, he managed to bring the aircraft down in the desert at Imperial Junction, where repairs were made both to man and machine. It took a doctor two hours to remove the splinters from the man; it took all night to build an engine, using the one in Rodgers' old Model B, stored in the train's hangar car, and two cylinders from the discarded power plant removed in New York. Pilot and plane were ready the next day.

In trying to find an acceptable takeoff stretch, Rodgers and his crew pushed and carried the airplane four miles through the desert. Once aloft, Rodgers headed for the 6,000-foot (1,830-meter) San Gorgonio Pass. As he went through, the radiator sprang a leak, and then the ignition system started to short out. Heading for the nearest plowed field, he set the Wright down near Banning. Rodgers looked over the battered machine, and he and his mechanics agreed that although the airplane had given just about everything it had, they couldn't quit so close to their goal. Rodgers hopped to Beaumont, where he came down with a broken fuel pipe, then made Pomona for repairs, to the disappointment of the crowd that had been gathering at Pasadena for the final stop.

To coax the *Vin Fiz* into a final leap, Cal and his crew worked to repair the battered machine with the same care they had given it at the beginning of the flight. As Rodgers flew the Wright past Mt. Wilson Observatory, he was spotted, and word was passed to the huge throng of people waiting for him at Tournament Park, Pasadena.

At 4:08 P.M., on November 5, 1911, the crowd went wild as the *Vin Fiz* spiraled down to land. They surged forward past the police to welcome the knight of the air.

Rodgers had flown 4,231 railroad miles (6,770 kilometers) in 4,924 minutes, averaging 51.6 miles per hour (82.6 kilometers per hour) while burning 1,230 gallons (4,674 liters) of gasoline. All that was left of the original aircraft after 69 landings and 15 substantial accidents (not to mention dozens of less drastic mishaps) over 49 days (24 flying, 25 grounded) was one rudder, an engine drip pan,

and, much to Cal and Mabel's delight, a good-luck bottle of Vin Fiz and the strut it was tied to.

The spare parts required to keep the aircraft flying cost Rodgers between $17,000 and $18,000. Although he received $5 a mile for the distance from New York to Fort Worth, then $4 a mile to Pasadena—a grand sum of around $20,000—from Armour, plus some $3,000 to $4,000 in prize money, the Wright EX had cost him $5,000. The trip basically broke even.

Rodgers had hoped to do far better, and even to fund future record flights. After the initial press of the crowd at Pasadena, he placed his hand on his mother's shoulder and said, "Never mind about the money. It didn't amount to much that way— but I did it, didn't I?"

Although Rodgers technically had flown from coast to coast, he made it clear he would not be content until he ran the wheels of the *Vin Fiz* into the waters of the Pacific. Preparations were made by Cal's faithful mechanics for a final short hop.

On November 12, he took off for Long Beach in a very weary airplane. With the ocean but 23 miles (37 kilometers) away, the engine began misfiring badly, and Rodgers landed near Covina Junction to find a broken fuel-feed line. After repairs, and with sunlight fading, he was off again. Before

A triumphant Cal Rodgers enjoys his moment of triumph as Vin Fiz's *wheels touch the Pacific Ocean on December 10, 1911. At Cal's left, lashed to the lower wing, is the crutch he used for support after sustaining a broken ankle in a crash near Compton, California, on November 12.*
Left, the Vin Fiz *executes a turn over farm country. Finding places to land in those early days of flight was not always easy.*

he could make it, the *Vin Fiz* plunged into the ground near Compton. Cal Rodgers was pulled from the wreck with a concussion, a badly sprained ankle, facial burns, and bruises all over his body. The cause of the crash was never determined, but Orville Wright's description of Rodgers seemed to fit better than ever: "He was born with four horseshoes in his pockets."

The next day, while puffing on his ever present cigar, Cal stated, "I am going to finish that flight and finish it with the same machine." A month later, on December 10, 1911, with his crutch lashed to the wing, he landed at Long Beach to a cheering throng of some 50,000 celebrants, and rolled his wheels into the Pacific Ocean, penniless but exhilarated. Shortly thereafter, he was awarded a gold medal from the Aero Club of America.

Four months later, Cal Rodgers was dead. During an exhibition in his Wright Model B on April 3, 1912, over the same beach, a gull flew into his machine, wedging itself between the rudder and tail struts. Cal lost control and crashed just a few yards from shore. He broke his neck and back only a hundred yards from the spot where he had made his triumphal Pacific arrival. In spite of Rodgers' prediction that his record would soon fall, it stood for some eight years, a testimonial to the stature of his achievement.

In October 1919, Army Lieutenant Belvin W. Maynard flew a deHavilland DH-4 in a more direct route from Mineola, New York, to San Francisco in three days, eight hours, 41 minutes air time—less than an hour and a half faster than Rodgers. In less than four years after that, the record would be smashed, and again the idea would be born in the minds of individuals, rather than in government or business bureaucracies.

Army Air Service lieutenants Oakley G. Kelly and Muir S. Fairchild thought an unrefueled transcontinental flight from New York to San Diego would produce spectacular publicity for the Army. During the winter of 1921 and 1922, the two men planned a route, posted it on the wall near the pilots' locker room at McCook Field, Ohio, and promptly became the butt of numerous jokes: there wasn't even a plane in the Army that was capable of making such a flight.

In those days, Army cross-country flights of over 100 miles (160 kilometers) had to be pre-approved by very high authority. Before long, however, when McCook commander Colonel Thurman H. Bane saw the map and asked who had drawn it up, the project took on a life of its own, in spite of the ridicule.

But a major problem remained: that of finding a suitable airplane. American industry had not produced a design capable of making the flight. The only airplane in the world thought to be up to the task was a heavily modified German Junkers JL-6. The Air Service, however, would not buy an airplane built by so recent an enemy. Fortunately, in December 1920, Anthony Fokker had been contracted to build two F IV transports for the U.S. Army. Fokker was Dutch, a neutral nationality during World War I. Nonetheless, with his chief designer, Reinhold Platz, Fokker had turned out some of Germany's most successful wartime fighter designs, including the Fokker D VII.

Both F IVs were crated and shipped to McCook Field in March 1922, and Kelly was assigned as

A gift to the Smithsonian Institution from the Carnegie Museum in Pittsburgh in 1934, the restored Vin Fiz *today hangs in the Smithsonian's National Air and Space Museum. By the end of Rodgers' transcontinental flight, the only original parts remaining were the vertical rudder and two wing struts. Here the airplane appears as it would have to those on the ground as Rodgers flew overhead.*

project officer on the new aircraft. Flying one for the first time on June 1, he knew immediately that it was capable of making the flight. The contract to buy both aircraft at $30,000 each was signed on June 30.

Lieutenant Ernest W. Dichman, assistant chief of the Structure and Airplane Section at nearby Wright Field, volunteered to put the unassembled F IV's wing through maximum static-load tests. Flight tests then were made to plot maximum-altitude ceilings with different loads, which were correlated with time and distance. Without these complicated plots, the pilots would have no way of determining the aircraft's ability to clear the highest points along the proposed route. So thorough was Dichman's report that chief of the Air Service Major General Mason M. Patrick approved the record attempt on August 10.

When Fairchild was injured during flight tests on a reversible propeller, chief of the Flight Test Section Lieutenant John A. Macready, an experienced cross-country pilot, took his place. Macready and Kelly began detailing the plans for the attempt, which would be made at some time in September or October 1922, proceeding from west to east to take advantage of prevailing winds.

The Fokker, renamed the T-2, was modified with a 410-gallon (1,558-liter) fuel tank in the plywood-reinforced center section of the wing, and a 185-gallon (703-liter) tank in the fuselage. A 40-gallon (152-liter) oil tank and a radiator gave the newly overhauled Liberty engine enough cooling and lubrication capacity. The fuselage was gutted to make room for an extra set of controls and a 10-gallon (38-liter) water tank for the radiator, while the heavy glass windows and hinged doors were replaced by celluloid and a light sliding door.

A folding seat was mounted in the pilot's open cockpit to allow the crew to swap positions while in the air. The right side of the Fokker's cockpit was occupied by the engine itself; the pilot sat next to the exposed, roaring power plant, with its bellowing exhaust and clattering valves.

After a series of tests, the T-2 was delivered to Rockwell Field, San Diego, then under the command of one of the Air Service's first pilots, Major Henry Harley Arnold. The runway had been lengthened to 10,000 feet (3,048 meters), the calculated distance it would take the T-2 to get airborne at its 11,000-pound (5,000-kilogram) gross weight. Even then the Fokker's computed altitude ceiling was at ground level. The Army was pushing the very limits of aviation technology.

After a generally favorable weather forecast, the T-2 was moved to the end of the runway and fueled up to 10,695 pounds (4,860 kilograms). On the morning of October 5, 1922, Kelly and Macready flipped a coin to determine who would take the command pilot's seat, up front, and make the takeoff. Kelly won. At 5:53 A.M., the throttle was moved forward to full power, and the ponderous machine staggered into the air.

Still at very low altitude, Kelly turned left to avoid Point Loma and promptly began to settle into the Pacific Ocean. It took careful nursing of the fuel-heavy machine to stop sinking and climb to the 200-foot (60-meter) altitude necessary to start heading east.

Handling the ponderous craft took every bit of the pilots' skill and strength. Not only were the controls very heavy to move, but response was agonizingly slow, so that all maneuvers had to be planned well in advance of their execution.

Neither the forward nor the midships cockpit was an ideal place from which to fly. Although the front seat had the benefit of forward vision, there was virtually no way to see over the engine to the right. Exposure to the elements, not to mention the engine, could become torture. In the fuselage, the back-up pilot had what must have seemed like the experience of flying a whale from inside its belly, with limited vision out the left side and even less out the right. The pilot had no modern instruments to keep the airplane straight and level when flying without visual reference.

Both men faced a constant wrestling match with their overloaded airplane, coaxing what performance they could from it. No one had ever attempted such a task over so long a period of time without rest, but, according to their recollections, neither Kelly nor Macready considered the job to be unusually demanding.

Fifty miles (80 kilometers) out, the Fokker had reached 1,700 feet (520 meters), but fog covered the only way through the rising hills surrounding Temecula Pass. For an hour Kelly tried to make it across the foothills, killing the chances of negotiating the distant mountains by nightfall, and cutting into the fuel needed to make New York.

Reluctantly, the two men decided to turn back for Rockwell. Not wanting to let the circumstances defeat them entirely, they stayed airborne for 35 hours, 18 minutes, 30 seconds, to break the world's airborne-endurance record by almost nine hours. This was more of a testimonial to the stamina of the men than to the machine. However, the Army fliers actually were pleased with the aircraft's performance and fuel consumption. Now they had some realistic experience to apply to the next attempt. It could be done.

After waiting for the next favorable weather forecast, the fliers were off again at 5:57 A.M. on November 3. Kelly was in command, and the takeoff weight was 10,850 pounds (4,932 kilograms), an increase of 155 pounds (70 kilograms). Again they turned to avoid Point Loma and nursed the airplane into a gradual climb. This time, Temecula Pass was clear, and they flew on to the Colorado River. Just after passing the Gila River and locating the Southern Pacific Railway tracks, Kelly shook

U.S. Army Air Service Lieutenant Oakley G. Kelly, earflaps up in the photograph at right, and his copilot, Lieutenant John A. Macready, pose with the Army Air Service's T-2, a Fokker F IV built by the Netherlands Aircraft Company (Fokker), of Veere, Netherlands. In the T-2, on May 2, 1923, they made the first nonstop flight across the United States. Below, the T-2 at Rockwell Field, San Diego, after the successful completion of the nonstop flight from New York.

the wheel, the signal for Macready to take the controls in the rear of the cockpit.

Unstrapping and standing up into the blasting air, Kelly folded the pilot's seat down and made his way through the extremely narrow, triangular tunnel back to Macready, who meanwhile was keeping the aircraft steady with the rear set of controls. As Macready slid out of the seat, holding the wheel, Kelly moved in and grabbed the controls, allowing Macready to make his way forward.

Macready found the constant fight with the controls more than fatiguing. To make matters worse, he had spotted a water leak in the Liberty's number-two cylinder jacket. After passing Deming, New Mexico, he sent a message down a clothesline to Kelly, asking him to switch earlier than

planned so that the two could consult.

Running several calculations, the pilots determined that another hour on their present heading would run them into ever higher terrain, so they turned south, where the land was flatter. Fortunately, each gallon of fuel burned made the T-2 a little lighter and earned a slight increase in altitude as they skimmed the trees.

Down drafts near the Great Divide in New Mexico forced them within 20 feet (six meters) of the brush at just above stall speed. They turned back 10 miles (16 kilometers) to burn fuel, then made a 180-degree turn and struggled up the sloping terrain again.

Leaving the air space over Tucumcari, New Mexico, the men changed places and Macready flew into the gathering darkness. With few visual references he was forced to fly so close to the ground that farmhouses became obstructions. As the weather grew worse, even the railroad tracks were hard to follow, although every now and then the reassuring beam of a train's light would show the way.

After passing over Wichita, Kansas, and on through the night to St. Louis, the two changed places in time for Kelly to take the front controls. He saw the dawn ahead—and more cracked cylinder jackets. As Terre Haute, Indiana, slipped by, Kelly noticed that the cooling-water supply was disappearing rapidly.

Water was squirting from both sides of the engine. Macready turned around, made Indianapolis at 25 hours' elapsed time (2,060 miles, or 3,300 kilometers), and let down for Fort Benjamin Harrison. As he cut the throttle on landing, at 9:15 A.M. local time, the propeller stopped: the engine had destroyed itself due to lack of cooling.

Although bitterly disappointed, the pilots wasted no time in replanning the effort, this time thinking in terms of traveling from east to west. Not only was the distance shorter—2,445 miles versus 2,780 (3,900 kilometers versus 4,320), but, by the time they reached the high Western mountains, the T-2 would be far lighter and able to clear them easily. Since the engine clearly lacked the stamina to fly at full throttle for 12 hours out of San Diego, leaving from New York would allow them to power back one hour out. Though prevailing winds remained west to east, playing the weather would give the pilots some ability to catch favorable winds.

A new Liberty engine was installed, and the T-2 was flown the short distance to McCook Field. Over the winter, the aircraft was readied for a series of record flights. On April 16 and 17, 1923, Kelly and Macready set a world duration record of 36 hours, 4 minutes, 31 seconds, and a world distance record of 2516.5 miles (4,026.4 kilometers). They also set a weight-lifting record, with a single Liberty V-12 engine of 10,900 pounds (4,955 kilograms). Though these feats were recognized in their own right, they actually were intended to gain data for the nonstop transcontinental flight.

In comparing the two long duration flights—the one from San Diego and the maximum effort

out of Ohio—the McCook Field fliers and engineers discovered a crucial difference. The untreated California fuel had an anti-knock equivalent to fuel refined in the East with 20 percent benzol added. Therefore, the pilots insisted that the east to west attempt be made with fuel shipped from California, one of the first applications of gasoline rating by octane.

The Fokker was flown to Roosevelt Field, Long Island, for staging. This time, Kelly requested a professional meteorologist to interpret day-by-day weather information, since the fliers would be basing their plans on forecasts of high- and low-pressure weather systems, something that had never been attempted before. The latest Rand McNally road maps were obtained, studied, and put in order; at that time, there were no aeronautical charts.

As dawn broke on May 2, 1923, and favorable weather was predicted over the entire route, the Fokker was pushed into position and checked over one final time. To reach Tucumcari by the next dawn and check navigation before entering the mountains, the pilots decided to delay the takeoff by two hours.

Kelly took the front, and, as he later recounted to Smithsonian curator Louis S. Casey, the "wheel blocks were removed, full engine power applied, but to our embarrassment the airplane refused to move. The ground crew was then waved in to push

Dutch airman and pioneer aircraft manufacturer Anthony Fokker, seen above at about the age of 21, sits at the controls of his Spin No. 3 airplane. The T-2, one of the more than 40 types of airplane produced by Fokker, appears at right without wing and nacelle. The aircraft's wing-center tank (top), its main cockpit next to the Liberty V-12 engine (center), and the tunnel leading to the back-up pilot's seat (left) are clearly visible. The map depicts Kelly's and Macready's route on the first nonstop, coast-to-coast flight.

on the wheels, and with the combination of man-power and available horsepower we were able to start rolling on the dry, hard, sandy soil."

When the T-2 left the ground after slightly more than half a mile, Kelly saw he wasn't going to clear the electrical wires and trees. He cut the power and set her back down.

That the 10,850-pound (4,932-kilogram) machine did not break when it touched down again at such a great weight is a testimonial not only to Fokker but to Kelly's skill. From his previous battles flying the T-2, he had learned just how far he could push the airplane, knowledge that was a combination of experience and "seat-of-the-pants" instinct and a necessary commodity for survival in the air.

He taxied to the other end for a west-northwest takeoff, in spite of the quartering tail wind he would experience from that direction. The plan was to be airborne before the 20-foot (six-meter) drop off at Roosevelt Field's west end, continue across adja-

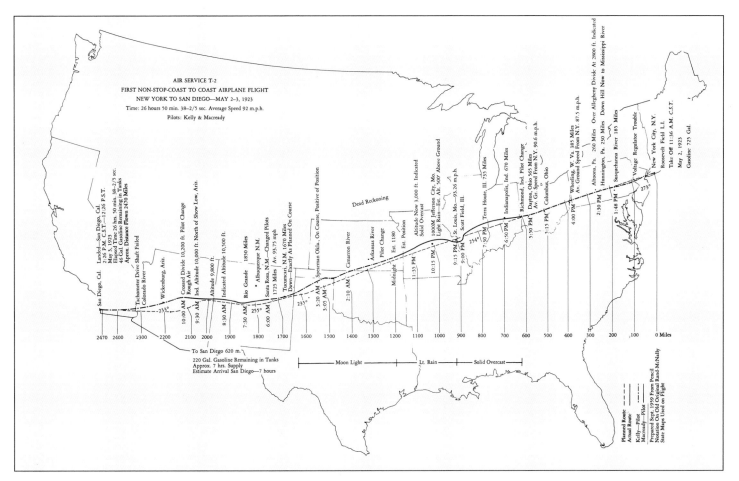

AIR SERVICE T-2
FIRST NON-STOP-COAST TO COAST AIRPLANE FLIGHT
NEW YORK TO SAN DIEGO—MAY 2-3, 1923
Time: 26 hours 50 min. 38-2/5 sec. Average Speed 92 m.p.h.
Pilots: Kelly & Macready

cent Hazelhurst Airfield, and, he hoped, have enough altitude left to clear the hangars at the other end.

At 12:36 P.M., Kelly again pushed the throttle forward, got help from the ground crew to start rolling, and gathered speed. As Macready related in the July 1924 issue of *National Geographic* magazine:

The big monoplane bounced and bounced but did not rise. It was still on the ground when we came to the 20-foot dropoff from Roosevelt to Hazelhurst Field. I was sitting behind, watching the ground go by and the hangars getting nearer.

When we came to the dropoff I wondered whether we would go over the ledge and settle down to the ground. Over we went and settled down, but not quite to earth. . . . The heavily loaded plane could hardly maintain itself in level flight. For 20 minutes over Long Island our climb was hardly appreciable. In fact, for the first few miles we barely cleared the poles and wires.

Kelly flew the T-2 as if it were balanced on the head of a pin. Whenever he saw an open field, he pushed down until they were skimming the grass, thereby gaining enough speed to pull up over telephone wires. The Fokker was too heavy to make any turns, since such maneuvers would cause it to lose lift, stall, and plow into the ground. Agonizingly slowly, the T-2 gained altitude a foot at a time, clawing its way to 1,000 feet (300 meters).

About a half hour out, Kelly noticed that the voltage regulator was discharging, draining much needed power from the batteries. Without the regulator, they would have to land in a few hours, which would bring another frustrating end to the attempt. Kelly shook the wheel for Macready to take the controls in the back.

This usually signaled only a brief period of flying, since all the rear pilot could do for ground reference was look out the left side windows. Much to his frustration, however, Macready had to hold course from the back for more than half an hour without the faintest idea of what was going on up

The large, internally braced, wooden wing, characteristic of Fokker designs of the period, dominates this photograph of the T-2. "It is now reposing in the Smithsonian Institution at Washington, where it belongs," wrote Lieutenant Macready after the flight. "It did its work in excellent shape and deserves a good rest." Only two Fokker F IVs were ever built: one was outfitted as an ambulance plane and designated the A-2, and the other, the T-2, was taken into the service as a transport. Both aircraft were purchased by the U.S. Army Air Service in 1922.

ARMY AIR SERVICE
NON STOP
COAST TO COAST   A.S. 64233

front where Kelly was working on the engine.

Kelly unstrapped, dismantled the balky regulator, reset the breaker points, and put it back together. This was a delicate enough operation on the ground. In a wind-blasted, exposed, noise-filled cockpit, it should have been impossible, yet Kelly pulled it off. He then took the controls back and flew on to Richmond, Indiana, where, at 6:00 P.M., the pilots switched positions.

As Macready settled in up front, the T-2 entered a solid overcast with light rain—miserable conditions for open-cockpit flying. By 9:00 P.M., he caught sight of the sole navigation aid available during the flight, the large searchlight sweeping the sky at Scott Field, Illinois.

From St. Louis to Jefferson City, Missouri, Macready encountered his greatest challenge of the flight:

We had followed the general direction of the Missouri River as light reflected from the muddy water was of considerable assistance as a fixed-point of balance in navigating the airplane at night in poor visibility and light rain. As the Missouri swings to the northwest at Jefferson City it was necessary to take up a compass course striking cross country at about 245 degrees.

Check points are scarce and all towns look alike in western Missouri and southeastern Kansas at night. . . . Picking weather with high and low pressure areas in desired geographic sections of the continent [paid] good dividends with favorable tail winds.

Shortly before midnight, at the 1,200-mile (1,920-kilometer) point, Macready breathed a sigh of relief as the Fokker broke out of the light rain into bright moonlight just after crossing the Kansas border. He was exhausted. At several points he had been forced to fly at 500 feet (150 meters) to keep track of the ground. Without a distinct horizon, Macready had few visual cues to alert him to compensate if the T-2 drifted off course or away from level flight. Furthermore, at this low altitude, a dropping wing, if not caught in time, could cause a steep spiral into the ground. The slightest lack of vigilance or late input on the heavy controls might have spelled disaster.

Storms and rain at night were the most dreaded and difficult aspects of the effort. As Macready later mused, "the experienced pilots of the Army Air Service give us most credit for flying through those long nights and coming out of the darkness in the morning directly on our course. Kelly and I

Lieutenants John Macready (left) and Oakley Kelly display the 737 gallons of gasoline and 40 gallons of oil that fueled and lubricated the T-2 from New York to California. The final take-off weight for the T-2's record 1923 flight was 10,850 pounds (4,932 kilograms). At right, the T-2 flies along railroad tracks during its world-duration-record-smashing flight of more than 36 hours, on April 17 and 18, 1923. American aviation pioneer Orville Wright served as official recorder for the flight, which departed from the same spot in Dayton, Ohio, where he and his brother, Wilbur, had perfected mechanical flight less than 20 years earlier.

take most pride in that feat of navigation."

The men switched positions once again, and Kelly flew to Spearman, Texas, where he got his first positive position check: they were on course at 3:30 A.M., May 3. At 6:00 A.M., after 13 and a half hours of darkness, and with the T-2 in a slow climb, the fliers switched positions. As the sun rose, they were over Santa Rosa, New Mexico, 1,725 miles (2,760 kilometers) from New York.

A careful fuel check over the Rio Grande showed 220 gallons (836 liters) of fuel left, enough for nine more hours. San Diego was 620 miles (992 kilometers) away, about seven hours if the average ground speed of 91 miles per hour (146 kilometers per hour) held up.

At 10:00 A.M., they crossed the Continental Divide at 10,200 feet (3100 meters), the highest point on the flight plan, and changed pilots in the rough mountain air. Nearing San Diego, they switched again so that Macready could have the honor of making the landing.

"Diving down from 8,000 feet with power on," Macready recollected, "we reached San Diego, cocked the T-2 up on the wing to swing down the main street, and passed about 100 feet above the tops of the buildings," and then headed for Rockwell Field.

Macready set the T-2 down without a hitch at 2:26:38 P.M. Pacific Standard Time, after traveling 2,470 miles (3,950 kilometers) in 26 hours, 50 minutes, 38.6 seconds, for an average ground speed of 92.05 miles per hour (147.28 kilometers per hour). "Everyone was excited but Kelly and myself," he recalled. "We had been working in grease and dirt, without rest, for such a long time previous to the flight that we had not had opportunity to think about it [as] an accomplished act."

Nonstop coast to coast. Such a milestone in the still very young field of aviation was difficult for many to imagine. It had happened in barely more than one day's time, just 12 years after it had taken Cal Rodgers almost three months.

A smiling Cal Rodgers, silhouetted at left, took almost three months to fly coast to coast; 12 years later, the Fokker T-2, piloted by Kelly and Macready, would cross the continent in one day.

THE ATLANTIC AND THE WORLD

In a painting by French artist Henry Farré, an Allied seaplane, flying at low altitude, attacks a German submarine in the North Sea during World War I. The limited range of these aircraft made the defense of Atlantic shipping difficult, but the war eventually spawned technology that allowed safe passage for a flight over the Atlantic.

War in the 20th century has levied a heavy toll upon humanity. At the same time, it has been the greatest single impetus for technological development. Nowhere is that more evident than in the innovations that characterized aviation during World Wars I and II. The first flight across the Atlantic Ocean, for example, grew out of war.

When America entered World War I in April 1917, the United States Army and Navy immediately sought to foster closer ties with the Allies in order to determine how the U.S. could most effectively contribute to the war effort against the Central Powers. With aviation still in its infancy, the counsel from European experts on applications for the airplane was contradictory and confusing. A joint U.S. Army and Navy commission was formed in June 1917 to go overseas and study the problem firsthand.

After a short time it became evident that Germany's effective use of the submarine would play a major role in determining Allied strategy. America would have to move its war materiel across the Atlantic by ship, for example, and yet submarines had come very close to severing the oceanic arteries through which American troops and supplies were already pulsing to the Western Front.

Small U.S. seaplanes entered combat that year against submarines from bases in England and France, and other facilities would soon be opened in Italy. Unfortunately, with weapons loaded, the fuel capacity of these machines limited their effective action radius to no more than 100 miles (160 kilometers). And even then their tiny size limited loads to a few small depth charges. Furthermore, these seaplanes had to be shipped across the ocean disassembled, presenting an almost impossible cargo problem. With the U-boat campaign at its height, fewer and fewer ships were available to meet an

A map displays the flight path of the Curtiss NC-4 flying boat, which, in a grueling venture in May 1919, became the first aircraft to cross the Atlantic Ocean. Two similar flying boats—NC-1 and NC-3—also attempted the historic aerial crossing, but only NC-4 was successful, reaching Lisbon, Portugal, on May 27.

ever increasing demand. If a larger airplane could be developed to carry more fuel and weapons and then fly itself across the Atlantic, the U-boat menace could be challenged more effectively.

Although the joint commission recommended immediate development of both lighter-than-air and heavier-than-air machines for anti-submarine combat, it was forced to admit that aircraft of such size and range were beyond the Allies' manufacturing capability.

Despite Admiral William S. Sims's approval of the commission's report on August 25, 1917, Rear Admiral David W. Taylor, chief of the Bureau of Construction and Repair, ordered the design of a flying boat that could fly across the ocean under its own power. Commander Jerome C. Hunsaker, assisted by Commander George C. Westervelt, a

member of the joint commission, was chosen to spearhead the effort.

Pioneer aviator Glenn H. Curtiss, father of the flying boat, instructor for the Navy's initial aviators, and builder of the Navy's first aircraft, was called in as co-designer and builder. Before World War I, he had been asked to design and build the first American twin-engine flying boat, the *America,* created for a transatlantic attempt to claim a London *Daily Mail* prize of $50,000.

Curtiss offered Hunsaker and Westervelt a five-engine and a three-engine version of a flying boat, each with a wingspan of 140 feet (43 meters) and each powered by 400-horsepower Liberty engines. Either version required a crew of five to six. Curtiss's original designation for the aircraft was TH-1, the initials standing for Taylor-Hunsaker.

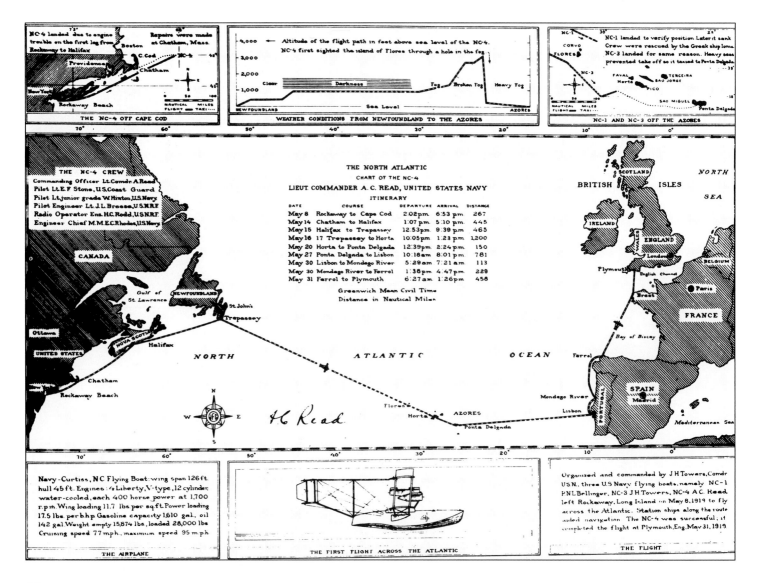

The Navy design group picked the three-engine version, and Commander Holden C. Richardson undertook the detailed design of the hull. Curtiss was given responsibility for designing the wings, tail group, and various smaller items. The contract was signed on November 24, and, on December 21, construction approval was given for four aircraft, with another six to be built later by the new Naval Aircraft Factory.

In the end, deciding on an official designation for the flying boats was a more drawn-out process than designing them. The Curtiss suggestion, TH-1, was never adopted, since the Navy felt that the project was primarily theirs, not Curtiss's, and the initials DWT, for Admiral David W. Taylor, also found no favor. Finally, Navy personnel compro-

mised on NC, for Navy-Curtiss, which suggested the nickname "Nancy," although this never stuck.

Since the aircraft were almost like boats that could fly, the Navy followed practice for individual ships within a class and numbered them individually from NC-1 to NC-4, although they were basically all the same.

As Curtiss's Buffalo, New York, factory expanded under wartime demand for increased production, the NC design work was given a low priority. When an experimental plant opened at Garden City, Long Island, the partially built NC-1 was transferred to this new facility, although it was obviously not large enough for the project. The Navy built a significantly larger shop in a new hangar at Rockaway Naval Air Station, 20 miles (32 kilometers) away.

From left to right, the crew of NC-3: NC flight leader Commander John Towers; Commander Holden C. Richardson, who helped design the NC planes; Lieutenant D. McCulloch; Lieutenant Commander R. Lavender; Chief Machinist's Mate L. Moore; and Lieutenant B. Rhodes.

NC-1 made its maiden flight from Jamaica Bay, New York, on October 4, 1918; the war ended just over a month later, on November 11. There was no longer a use for these big boats, which had cost the U.S. government an average of $125,000 each, even with such government-furnished items as engines.

On another front, even before the war was over, several countries made plans to go after the London *Daily Mail* prize, which had been postponed during the war, for the first aerial crossing of the Atlantic, to or from England. On October 31, Commander John H. Towers proposed to the Chief of Naval Operations that the brand-new NC boats be prepared to make the flight before summer 1919.

Several routes were examined. The aircraft didn't have enough range to fly nonstop from Newfoundland to Ireland or England, so the only practical route was through the Azores and Portugal, then north. As the Navy's plans leaked out, Rockaway, Long Island, and the small division of NCs became the focus of growing world interest.

Assistant Secretary of the Navy Franklin D. Roosevelt visited the Rockaway base and was taken up on a flight. Although the air was rougher than normal that day, and he had to endure the hazards and discomfort of ocean-going, open-cockpit flying, he returned in good spirits. On February 4, 1919, the flight was approved by Secretary of the Navy Josephus Daniels.

NC-1's original tractor-trimotor configuration yielded insufficient power for such a long flight, so NC-2 was modified, and four engines in pusher-tractor pairs were installed. This arrangement proved less efficient than one pusher and three tractors, however, so NC-3 and -4 each were built with a tandem pusher-tractor combination over the hull center line and two tractors outboard. NC-1 then

At left, U.S. Navy sailors tune up NC-4's four, 400-horsepower Liberty engines. The flying boat required three engine changes during its two-and-a-half-week passage over the Atlantic. At right, five of NC-4's six crewmen are visible in this photograph of the aircraft in flight.

was modified to match them.

On the night of March 27, a storm wrecked NC-1's lower-left wing. To keep it flying, NC-2's wing assembly was cannibalized and fitted to NC-1. Five weeks later, on May 5, a hangar fire at Rockaway destroyed NC-1's right wing. With no spare parts available, NC-2's other wing was taken, and she became one of history's first hangar queens, good for dust rather than for glory.

Seaplane Division One was commissioned, along with three of the original four "Nancys," on May 3, 1919, under Navy Commander John Towers. The ceremony was historic, this being the first time the U.S. Navy had commissioned any aircraft into regular service. Towers chose NC-3 as his flagship of the division, while Lieutenant Commander Patrick N.L. Bellinger was given NC-1 and Lieutenant Commander Albert C. Read NC-4. Bellinger planned to make the flight with as little delay as possible, following a route that stretched from Rockaway to Trepassey Bay, Newfoundland (950 miles or 1,520 kilometers), then to Horta, Azores (1,381 miles or 2,210 kilometers), a short hop (169 miles or 270 kilometers) to Ponta Delgada, on to Lisbon (925 miles or 1,480 kilometers), and finally to Plymouth, England (500 miles or 800 kilometers).

At 10 in the morning on May 8, 1919, the three

Nancys lifted off, formed up, and headed for Trepassey. They would take off from there for the Azores on May 16. The clear sky seemed a good omen, but at about 2:00 P.M., off Cape Cod, NC-4's center-rear-engine oil pressure dropped to zero, and then the center-forward engine threw a connecting rod. Read put NC-4 down in the open ocean, and taxied all night—80 miles (130 kilometers)—to Chatham Naval Air Station, at Chatham, Massachusetts, where he put in for two engine changes.

Boats 1 and 3 continued on to Halifax, arriving around seven in the evening. The next morning, serious splits were found in the wooden propellers of both of these Nancys, but there were not enough spare propeller hubs on hand to replace the special hubs used with the faulty props.

The resourceful former commanding officer of the U.S. Navy's wartime Halifax Naval Station, Lieutenant Commander Richard E. Byrd, who had accompanied the flight from Rockaway, recalled that when the Naval station had been returned to the Canadian government at war's end, a number of spare Liberty engine hubs had been on hand. He located the parts, and the Canadians graciously returned them for U.S. Navy duty.

The two boats made Trepassey on the 10th, and

were met by a small fleet of ships that had gathered in support of the effort. Another 21 destroyers were arriving or were already on station, spaced every 50 miles (80 kilometers) all the way from Cape Race, Newfoundland, to Corvo, the westernmost island of the Azores. They served as visual- and radio-communications links with the flight, as well as sources of weather information and potential rescue service.

After being outfitted with its two new engines, NC-4 was held at Chatham by gale-force winds and rain. With the Trepassey departure deadline almost upon them, Read's crew knew that a good-weather "go" would most likely send Towers off with the other two boats. News reports already were labeling Nancy-4 as the "lame duck," and spreading rumors that she would be withdrawn from the flight.

On the 14th, the weather cleared, and NC-4 departed Chatham, reaching Halifax and Trepassey on the 15th, just in time to join the other two aircraft, which were taxiing back from a vain attempt to make the Azores hop. Too heavily laden with fuel, both NC-1 and NC-3 had tried but failed to get off the water. Read had known this would happen, but had kept this information to himself in the hope that NC-4 would not be left behind.

Even after the short flight from Chatham, NC-4 required another engine change and the replacement of three split propellers. Lieutenant James L. Breese and Chief Machinist's Mate Eugene S. Rhoads, both engineers, were to prove again and again how essential they were to the success of the flight. On such long, demanding flights, these airplanes required full-time mechanical attention

On the 16th, NC-4 departed with the other two boats. Engineers Breese and Rhoads kept a close eye on the untried engines. The overnight flight was timed to reach the Azores just after sunrise to afford a daylight landing.

During the night, salt spray shorted out NC-3's running lights, making it very difficult for the other two planes to keep track of her in the dark. Had it not been for the quick thinking of an NC-3 crew member, who used a pocket flashlight as a beacon, NC-1 would have collided with her in midair.

The big flying boats, with their impressive wingspan,

were majestic to behold, but nightmarish to fly. Control effectiveness remained somewhat of a black art, particularly for larger aircraft. Handling an NC in smooth air could be a joy, because of the "locked-in-cement" stability it tended to exhibit. Fighting turbulence, however, when control pressures could climb to more than 100 pounds (45 kilograms), took raw strength.

These pioneer aviators had to be natural athletes—quick and well-coordinated, able to move the controls instinctively, anticipating gusts that could topple the aircraft. Once pushed from its intended course, the NC had to be manhandled back on track with brute force. The wooden control wheels thus were designed to allow room for two sets of strong hands. The open cockpit, blasted by the elements, added to the pilots' difficulties, as did the roar of four engines directly overhead. Deafness was an occupational hazard among early air crew.

The rough air continued through the night, causing the boats to make a "wallowing, plunging" course toward the Azores. Normally, the two pilots aboard each aircraft took turns flying every 30 to 35 minutes in order to avoid exhaustion. Extreme turbulence, however, required the efforts of both pilots, while each crew member watched for the next destroyer. Since NC-4 had the fastest cruising speed, about 75 miles per hour (120 kilometers per hour), she soon outdistanced her companions.

NC-4 sighted the first 16 destroyers without difficulty; the vessels used a combination of burning fuel slicks, searchlights, star shells, and running lights to make themselves visible. Although fog set in before dawn, NC-4 was able to stay above it until around 8:00 A.M., at which point it enveloped the flying boat. Visibility decreased until the pilots found it practically impossible to see the bow.

With no blind-flying instruments (they hadn't been invented yet), the pilot of NC-4 became so disoriented that he put the monster flying boat into a spin from which he barely recovered. Fortunately, radio officer Ensign Herbert C. Rodd managed to pick up radio bearings and weather information from the ships to keep the boat on course.

After 15 hours in the air, cruising at a speed that would barely earn a ticket on a modern highway,

Ted Wilbur's painting of NC-4 in flight depicts Lieutenant Commander Albert Read navigating from the bow, while directly behind him sits Lieutenant Walter Hinton, one of the airplane's two pilots. Handling the NC flying boat generally required the efforts of two pilots, particularly in rough weather, which the Atlantic Ocean served up in quantity.

NC-4 had "run out of ships," and the crew agreed they must be near the Azores. While debating what to do, skipper Read spotted Flores, at the western edge of the islands, through a slight rift in the fog. Pilot Coast Guard Lieutenant Elmer E. Stone and copilot Lieutenant Walter Hinton were ordered to turn east for Fayal and Sao Miguel islands in the hope of making Ponta Delgada in the thinning fog.

When the fog closed in again, they let down in a cove, which they believed belonged to the island of Horta. After settling on the sea, however, with their engines still running, another rift in the fog revealed nothing: they had landed short.

Airborne again in five minutes, NC-4 found Horta just before noon. The pilot and crew had covered more than 1,200 nautical miles (1,440 statute miles or 2,300 kilometers) in 15 hours, 18 minutes, at an average speed of 78 knots (94 miles per hour or 150 kilometers per hour, a knot being one nau-

tical mile or 1.2 statute miles), assisted by a 15-knot (24-kilometer-per-hour) tail wind. No sooner had Nancy-4 set down than a massive fog bank blotted out the port completely.

Meanwhile, after its near midair collision with NC-3, NC-1 had drifted off course in the heavy fog, unable to make contact with the last several destroyers. Not trusting in the accuracy of his navigation based on his Byrd bubble sextant, in the rough air, Bellinger decided to set down on the ocean and get his bearings. The sea was far rougher than expected, and slightly damaged the Nancy. The men found out where they were—only 100 miles (161 kilometers) from Flores—but the flying boat could not get airborne again in the 12-foot (four-meter) waves.

Skipper Bellinger, pilot Lieutenant Commander Marc A. Mitscher, copilot Lieutenant Louis T. Barin, and the other three crew decided to taxi

NC-4's crew included, from left to right: Lieutenant Commander Albert Read; Lieutenant Elmer Stone, who was also the first pilot to serve with the U.S. Coast Guard; Lieutenant Walter Hinton, pilot; Lieutenant James Breese, flight engineer; and Chief Machinist's Mate Eugene "Smokey" Rhoads, assistant engineer. Absent from the photo is radio operator Ensign Herbert Rodd.

their aircraft through the heaving seas toward the nearest destroyer. The pummeling was severe; it was clear they would be lucky to stay afloat.

Miraculously, the Greek freighter *Ionia* appeared out of the fog and hauled the aviators aboard. Although attempts were made to tow NC-1, the towline snapped and the great airplane capsized, broke up, and finally, three days later, sank.

In NC-3, skipper Towers, pilot Richardson and copilot McCulloch (who had made the first flight of NC-1), and the other two crew members found flying above the fog in the bright moonlight a pleasantly memorable experience—until sunrise. Not having checked in with a destroyer since number 13, they were elated to spot a ship on the foggy horizon, and Towers reset course accordingly. What he thought was one of the destroyers, however, was actually the cruiser *Marblehead,* returning from Europe. The flying boat was far off course.

After 15 hours in the air, and with only two hours of fuel left, Towers decided to set down and get a bearing. The landing impact in the rough seas was so severe that the forward centerline engine-support struts buckled, several structural parts failed, and the hull cracked.

The Nancy started to take on water, and, mortally wounded, became a lame surface craft. They were only 45 miles (72 kilometers) from Flores; had they continued on their previous course, they might have sighted Pico, a 7,000-foot-high (2,134-meter-high) mountain, within an hour.

Before leaving Trepassey, Towers had jettisoned the emergency radio transmitter to reduce takeoff weight. Radio officer Lieutenant Commander Robert A. Lavender re-rigged the onboard set and generator. He then could hear the destroyers, but he could not transmit.

However, the radio contact confirmed that they were close to the islands. They also learned that a search for them was being conducted west of Flores, while they were situated south. Towers and his men had to fall back on basic seamanship to save themselves.

One elevator was so badly damaged that it threatened to increase the boat's yawing and eventually to capsize her. After half an hour's effort, they cut it away. The thoroughly soaked fabric covering the wings began to sag and to collect pools of water. Hacking holes in the tough, doped canvas, the crew managed to create a series of drain points.

After 20 hours afloat, NC-3's port wing tip washed away, taking the float with it. Without the float, the wing could dip under at any moment and break off. If one of the wings went, the aircraft would capsize immediately. A crewman was stationed on the starboard wing for almost a full day to keep the port wing out of the water.

At sunrise the next day the island of Pico ap-

peared on the horizon, 40 miles (64 kilometers) away. Even though there was enough fuel to taxi, the danger of disintegration from engine vibration led Towers to decide to drift stern first toward Ponta Delgada, the scheduled second Azores stop. This was a tough decision to make, since it meant another night at sea in waves that were beginning to reach 30 feet (nine meters). The crew was drinking rusty water from the radiators, and eating saltwater-soaked sandwiches and chocolate.

They made numerous efforts to ease the strain on the boat from the relentless seas. A sea anchor quickly broke away. The crew trailed canvas buckets over the sides to help with steering. They poured oil on the water to create a slick, but with an average movement of 12 knots the boat kept drifting away from the oil-flattened area. A sail was rigged, but this caused such a loss of maneuverability that it was quickly hauled in.

At last, on Monday, May 19, the crew sighted Ponta Delgada, and the destroyer *Harding* raced to the rescue of the nearly derelict flying boat. With the harbor in sight, the crew lowered the distress signal, hoisted the national ensign, and turned down *Harding*'s help. They stood atop the hull and sailed into the harbor, still stern first.

Just as she reached the breakwater, the right wing float let go, nearly capsizing the whole boat. *Harding* stood by with a lifeboat, and signaled ahead to have two small boats ready in the harbor to place under the wings as soon as NC-3 was moored.

With three men stationed on the wings to run back and forth with each swell, and the pilots alternating power on the outboard engines, they kept both wings out of the water most of the time. The first of the boats to reach Ponta Delgada, NC-3 and crew made the harbor unassisted, rightfully proud of their accomplishment.

For almost three days, meanwhile, NC-4 rode her moorings at Horta, held prisoner by high winds and seas, rain, and fog. Such conditions didn't stop the local population from showering the crew with flowers and serenading them, while congratulations poured in by radio and cable.

At last, on May 20, NC-4 departed Horta and landed at Ponta Delgada less than two hours later, just a day after the number three boat had limped in to the port. Commander Read of NC-4 had planned to take off for Lisbon the next day, but weather and engine trouble delayed departure for a week.

With the arrival of the *Ionia* and the NC-1 crew, a tumultuous reception for all three crews began— whistles blew, ships in port were dressed out, thousands cheered from ship rails, seawalls, shore, and streets, and a reception was given by the governor as the city called a holiday. Suspense was added to the occasion when word came that two English aircraft would soon depart Newfoundland for England to claim the *Daily Mail* prize.

Although the Navy crews could not receive the money offered as reward, the service did not want to lose the laurels. The next cable reported that one of the British airplanes had cracked up on takeoff, while the other was on its way across. Nothing would be heard of the second plane until weeks later, when its crew arrived in England aboard a freighter that had fished the men from the sea.

The crewmen of NC-4 were up before dawn on Tuesday, May 27. Breese and Rhoads pampered the boat's engines, while radio officer Rodd went over the indispensable radio set. At Read's signal, Stone eased the throttles forward and the Nancy went charging across the harbor in a great V-shaped wedge of spray, lifting off at 8:18 A.M.

Checking the plane's compass, Read found that it was off substantially, apparently due to the im-

pact with the swells during takeoff. The crew therefore encountered some difficulty in following the string of destroyers, but in the end it found each.

Finally, the destroyer *McDougal,* the last ship in the picket line, sent word that NC-4 had passed overhead and was on the way in. The Nancy's crew strained for the sight of land in the deep purple of twilight.

At 7:39 P.M., from the center of the darkening horizon, a diamond sparkle of light flashed: the Cabo da Roca lighthouse, westernmost point of Europe. Minutes later, the flying boat crossed the rocky coast and turned south toward the Tagus River estuary and Lisbon.

Lieutenant Commander Read remembered this

An early advocate of air power and assistant chief of the U.S. Army Air Service, Brigadier General Billy Mitchell actively promoted the record-breaking military flights of the 1920s. Too outspoken in his opinions, Mitchell was court-martialed in 1925, and subsequently resigned from the Army.

moment as "perhaps the biggest thrill of the whole trip. No matter what happened—even if we crashed on landing—the transatlantic flight, the first one in the history of the world, was an accomplished fact." At 8:01 P.M. on May 27, 1919, NC-4's keel settled into the Tagus, and six elated sailor-airmen taxied into Lisbon harbor. As night closed in around them, Read had radioman Rodd send the message, "We are safely across the pond. The job is finished."

On May 30, after two days during which all three NC crews were feted by the Portuguese government and the city of Lisbon, NC-4 left Lisbon. A few hours later, she was forced down off the Mon-

dego River, near Figueira, by a water leak in the port engine, but this was soon repaired.

While taxiing on the river, the seaplane ran aground on a sand bar. On the advice of the port's captain to wait for high tide, and to avoid risking a night landing at Plymouth, Read decided to fly on to El Ferrol, Spain, and to remain there overnight.

On May 31, after a stormy crossing of the Bay of Biscay, during which she missed four of the six destroyers stationed below, NC-4 landed in Plymouth harbor at 1:27 P.M. The crew was received with due pomp by the Lord Mayor at the Mayflower Steps, the point from which the Pilgrim fathers, some 300 years before, had embarked for the New World. The flight had taken an elapsed air time of 53 hours, 58 minutes—and a total time of 24 days—to fly the Atlantic, but it had been done.

In spite of the global attention showered on the six crewmen of NC-4, the public did not see them as heralds of a new day of transatlantic passenger transport. The Navy had started with several airplanes and almost unlimited support on the ocean, and only one airplane and a few men had made it across. This was still a dangerous game requiring near superhuman effort and massive government funding.

For the public, post-World-War I aviation meant barnstorming, daredevil fliers, record-breaking stunts, and the quest to fly farther, faster, and higher. Something even more spectacular would be required to show that aviation had no barriers, some achievement such as, say, the circumnavigation of the world, a proposition that seemed straight out of the pages of a Jules Verne novel.

By the 20th anniversary of manned flight, however, six nations had entered an unannounced race to be the first to fly around the world. When the U.S. Army announced its intention to make the flight, its stated goal was to "point the way for all nations to develop aviation commercially" and to give American aviation a kick in the right direction. Probably at the suggestion of his energetic second in command, Brigadier General Billy Mitchell, chief of the Army Air Service Major General Mason M. Patrick secured War Department approval for the flight in November 1923. Patrick also had the cooperation of the Navy, the U.S. Bureau of Fisheries, and the Coast Guard. Although the finest crews would be chosen and a new aircraft would be designed and built specifically for the effort, the real test would be to provide enough logistical support at all 52 planned stops.

Lieutenant St. Clair Streett planned and dispatched around the globe advance divisions of mechanics, technicians, engines, aircraft spares, crates,

The public admires one of the Army Air Service's Douglas World Cruisers, left, in March 1924, one month before four of the new aircraft—Seattle, Chicago, Boston, and New Orleans—departed on their historic round-the-world flight. At right, women at the Douglas Company in Santa Monica, California, cover a Douglas World Cruiser's fuselage with fabric.

tools, and a host of other items. Captain Lorenzo Snow obtained landing and over-flight approval from the numerous nations to be crossed.

England's Royal Air Force, with its string of worldwide Empire aerodromes and repair facilities, proved to be an invaluable ally. The U.S. Navy stood by to assist on the over-water legs.

When word came down through the squadrons to initiate pilot selection, there began a winnowing process the likes of which would not be seen again until the Mercury astronaut program almost 40 years later. Through the consideration of a series of applications, the number of potential fliers was boiled down to 50, then 25, then 15. Finally, seven names were submitted to Patrick, who then picked four men as pilots: Major Frederick L. Martin, flight leader, and lieutenants Leigh Wade, Lowell H. Smith, and Erik Nelson.

The four aviators were allowed to pick their own "mechanicians" to accompany them and to keep the aircraft in running repair. The final teams were Martin and Sergeant Alva L. Harvey, Wade and Sergeant Henry H. Ogden, Smith and Lieutenant Leslie P. Arnold, and Nelson and Lieutenant John Harding. Five aircraft would be required: four to make the flight and one to serve as a prototype and spare.

After considering submissions from several manufacturers, the Air Service, under Erik Nelson's supervision, selected a small airframe builder in Santa Monica, California, headed by Donald Douglas, to build five World Cruisers to a design based on Douglas's successful DT-2 Navy torpedo plane. The son of an assistant bank cashier, Douglas was 28 years old in 1920 when he opened his aircraft business in the rear of a barbershop with $600 capital. He was, in fact, a genius, having earned a degree from the Massachusetts Institute of Technology in two years. He had designed the Martin bomber while working for Glen L. Martin. When

World Cruiser No. 2, Chicago, rests in a harbor somewhere in Alaska or the Aleutian Islands. One of only two of the aircraft to complete the challenging global flight, it now resides in the collections of the National Air and Space Museum.

his Douglas Company began design and construction of the World Cruisers for the Army's round-the-world flight, it had 112 people on the payroll, and was situated in an abandoned movie studio.

The five aircraft were identical, weighing in at 7,700 pounds (3,493 kilograms) loaded, with a 50-foot (15-meter) wingspan, a service ceiling of 7,000 to 10,000 feet (2,134 to 3,048 meters), and cruise speeds of something like 90 miles (144 kilometers) per hour. The major modifications to the DT-2 involved removing combat equipment and weapons to make room for fuel. Douglas managed to fit a 60-gallon (227-liter) fuel tank in the center section of the upper wing, a 62-gallon (235-liter) tank in each lower wing root, a 150-gallon (568-liter) tank behind the engine fire wall, a 160-gallon (606-liter) tank under the pilot's seat, and a 150-gallon (568-liter) tank beneath the mechanics's seat.

This increase from 115 to 644 gallons (435 to 2,438 liters) of gasoline made the Douglas World Cruiser (DWC) a flying fuel farm with a range of 2,200 miles (3,540 kilometers), but with an average speed of 75 miles per hour (120 kilometers per hour). No human being could sustain nonstop legs of over 29 hours without a great deal of rest in between, which a world flight, if it was to be made in reasonable time, could not afford.

The big, single-engine, two-place, open-cockpit biplanes could be fitted with either pontoons or wheels and with different radiators for tropical- or temperate-climate flying. There was no provision, however, for radios, navigation aids (other than a compass and a crude wind-drift indicator), or equipment to help with blind- and bad-weather flying. The only instruments, other than those for the engine, were a compass, an altimeter, a turn-and-bank indicator, and an air-speed indicator. The crews would have to brave the elements with no protection other than heavy clothing.

The eight men reported to Langley Field, Virginia, for intensive training in first aid, navigation, and meteorology. During their stay, in December of 1923, the pontoon-equipped prototype aircraft was flown in, and each crew member, none of whom had previous float-plane experience, got a chance to fly it off the Tidewater area's rivers and bays.

The DWC was an unwieldy, ponderous machine; with its full capacity of fuel aboard, it required far more muscle to handle than its lighter torpedo-plane sister, the DT-2. The pilots enjoyed the challenge of flying the giant new seaplane, but, with the added weight of the fuel and the pontoons, some of the takeoffs were frightening, involving long wallows through bucking seas before there was enough speed to get airborne.

As with so many early, large aircraft, the DWC's controls were very stiff. The airplane did not have a separate set of instruments for a copilot, so each pilot would have to fly for long periods without relief, unlike the flight regimens of the earlier Navy NC crews and the T-2 pilots. Airplanes were built with a mission in mind. The pilot was taken for

granted, even considered an afterthought, and placed within the machine after everything else had been worked out. Crews accepted this lot as a part of their lives, but the resulting hardships in the air were sometimes painful. In their open cockpits, these men were expected to fly in arctic, sub-zero winds and in tropical heat and monsoons, with little more than a change in clothing to accommodate the extremes.

While the crews got used to the DWC at Langley, Nelson went back to the West Coast to nurse the other four World Cruisers through the production line at Santa Monica. All four pilots tested these new planes as they came off the line, with the last of them rolling out on March 11, 1924. They named them for American cities from the

All four Douglas World Cruisers sit at anchor off Sitka, Alaska, in April 1924. Shortly after this photograph was taken, World Cruiser No. 1, Seattle, crashed into a snow- and fog-enshrouded mountain in the Aleutian Islands and was demolished; miraculously, neither crewman was hurt.

four cardinal points of the compass. Martin chose *Seattle* for No. 1, Smith picked *Chicago* for No. 2, Wade *Boston* for No. 3, and Nelson *New Orleans* for No. 4. The Douglas Company received $192,684 for the four aircraft and spare parts.

Once the planes were ready, they were flown to Sand Point Field, near Seattle, re-rigged with floats, and flown regularly in order to get all the "bugs" out. At the same time, the Navy alerted its pre-planned logistics network to stand by. The Coast Guard made two ships available for the Alaska leg, as did the Bureau of Fisheries. Such inter-service cooperation would prove vital to the Army fliers' safety.

By April 5, 1924, all four aircraft were ready. Major Martin moved the throttle forward on *Seattle*'s 400-horsepower Liberty engine, but he punctured a pontoon on a buoy and the prop dug into the water. After overnight repairs, the four aircraft again lined up on the water.

This time three made it off, but Wade couldn't coax overweight *Boston* off the water, and he was left behind. Unloading a rifle, some clothing, and an anchor did the trick, however, and he followed the flight to Prince Rupert, British Columbia, 650 miles (1,046 kilometers) to the north.

As Wade circled overhead for landing, he saw that *Seattle* lay damaged in the harbor. A combination of high winds and snow squalls had caused Martin to level off while still too high, and the plane stalled in with a mighty splash, breaking the left outer wing struts and guy wires. With the help of local carpenters, new struts were built and the wings were rewired.

On April 13, the four World Cruisers departed Sitka, Alaska, where *Boston* and *New Orleans* had almost been lost to high winds in the harbor. All made Seward, Alaska, safely, but on the leg to Chignik, *Seattle*'s engine crankcase blew. After a frigid night drifting in the harbor at Cape Igvak, Martin and Harvey were towed to Kantak, Alaska, by a Coast Guard cutter for repairs. The others pressed on to Dutch Harbor in the Aleutian Islands to await their commander's arrival. *Seattle* never made it.

Trying to get through blinding snow and fog on April 30, Martin flew into a mountain facing the Bering Sea. Miraculously, neither he nor Sergeant

The Douglas World Cruiser Chicago *in flight. The big, single-engine biplanes could be equipped with either pontoons or wheels, and carried enough fuel for a range of 2,200 miles (3,540 kilometers).*

in eight hours.

Next, the World Cruisers took off for Paramushir, in the Japanese Kurile Islands. They could not fly to the nearest land, the Komandorskiye Ostrova (Commander Islands), because the former Soviet Union had not issued them diplomatic clearance. Nevertheless, as insurance, a Bureau of Fisheries ship was placed in Soviet waters as a back-up lighthouse and refueling vessel. Sure enough, head winds forced the pilots to divert, and they landed near the American ship off Nikol'skoye. A group of non-English-speaking fishermen rowed out to meet them, but, although friendly, they could not invite the fliers ashore without permission from Moscow, which might or might not be granted. Without awaiting the formality, the men were airborne and on their way for Japan the next day.

Navigating by compass, as well as dead reckoning and hoping for correct wind-drift compensation (as they did throughout the entire flight), Smith led the three biplanes into Paramushir, thereby putting the Army Air Service into the record books for the first aerial crossing of the Pacific Ocean. Aided by two U.S. Navy destroyers and the Japanese destroyer *Hamakaze,* the World Cruisers then flew southward over Japan's 4,000 islands to Tokyo.

Making a great S-turn over Japan's main naval base of Kasumiga Ura, the cruisers touched down on the water at 5:36 P.M., June 22, amid loud cheers from about 1,000 officers and bluejackets, several hundred screaming school children waving American flags, and the booming of daytime fireworks.

The commanders of Japan's Army Air Service and Navy Air Service and the American military attachés, the governor of the local province, and other bemedaled and beribboned officials lined up to greet the round-the-world fliers, who, understandably, were unshaven and weather-beaten and dressed in their oil-soaked flying coveralls. In spite of their unkempt appearance, however, the fliers were enthusiastic and ready to press on.

All six stops in Japan were a whirlwind of food, sightseeing, and official greetings. As Leigh Wade recalled, "At one stop, much to our dismay, 28 days of receptions had been planned. We compromised and boiled everything down to three days to give us time for engine changes and repairs." New en-

A giant hoist lifts one of the Douglas World Cruisers out of the water. During the round-the-world flight, another crane collapsed on the World Cruiser Boston *in the North Atlantic, sending it to the deep after it had flown more than three-quarters of the way around the globe.*

Harvey was seriously injured, although the airplane was demolished. Ten days later, they wandered into a fishing village, where, eventually, a destroyer picked them up.

With Lowell Smith as the new flight leader, the three remaining World Cruisers pressed on through Aleutian rain, snow, and sleet across Atka Island, bound for Attu. The wind was so furious in Nazan Bay that it was impossible to board the aircraft, much less fly them. For six days the crews sat out the weather, and then made the next leg—555 miles (893 kilometers)—against screaming head winds

gines were installed—the second one for *Boston*—and then the World Cruisers flew south to Shanghai, where the harbor master, not knowing how much space the aircraft needed, had cleared the river for miles. A record number of vessels became tangled in a monumental traffic snarl.

The pilots fought heavy rains down the South China Sea to Haiphong and Saigon (present-day Ho Chi Minh City) in Vietnam, while the mechanics dealt with an increasing number of problems. Engines were throttled back to reduce their suffering under the demanding conditions, but they over-

heated nonetheless. Exhaust pipes burned out with maddening regularity. Already a month behind schedule, the crews hit the beginning of the typhoon season, which was to test every bit of their skill, and luck.

As the World Cruisers traced the coastline of the Gulf of Tonkin, *Chicago*'s engine overheated beyond limits. Smith reached a small lagoon near Hue and landed while Wade and Nelson circled overhead. They got the signal from *Chicago*'s mechanic Arnold that his engine was so much junk. They then headed to Touraine a few miles away.

With the help of the Vietnamese, Nelson hiked 70 hours back through the jungle to the *Chicago*'s lagoon, and arranged to have the crippled World Cruiser towed upriver to Hue by a native chief who commanded a fleet of war sampans. A new engine, which had been pre-positioned at Saigon, was transported by truck and boat to Hue, where it was installed under extremely primitive conditions. The aircraft made Saigon and rejoined the others.

At this time, with the aircraft at the southernmost latitude of the flight, both men and machines were suffering from the heat and humidity. It was a far cry from the bitter cold of the Aleutians. The high air temperature reduced aircraft performance, which in turn required decreased fuel loads and longer takeoff runs through rivers crowded with all manner of boats.

When the three aircraft landed in Calcutta they had flown 11,232 miles (18,072 kilometers) in 81 days. The pontoons were replaced by wheels, a task which took three days, and other maintenance was completed. Smith broke a rib falling from the upper wing of *Chicago*.

Talking and pleading his way onto *Boston* as a passenger and assistant mechanic on the pretext of compensating for Smith's injury, Associated Press correspondent Linton O. Wells rode the next 2,000 miles (3,218 kilometers) until an official War Department message intercepted the flight in Karachi, denying him permission to continue. The three World Cruisers left Calcutta, and, despite frequent sandstorms and 120-degree F (66-degree Celsius) heat, they made good time across India.

An hour out of Karachi, *New Orleans*'s engine started to blow itself apart as three pistons disintegrated, a connecting rod broke, and assorted pieces were chewed up. Oil was thrown back across the World Cruiser. Nelson nursed the dying Liberty engine and limped into Karachi, with its wonderful Royal Air Force repair depot, on July 3.

Working almost constantly for three days, the crews installed new engines in all three aircraft, and the planes then took off for the Middle East, flying along the barren coastline to Chah Bahar and Bandar-e`Abbās in what is now Iran. Fighting sandstorms over the Arabian desert, the fliers threaded their way through passes in Iran's Kuhha-ye Zagros (Zagros Mountains), which seemed to be full of severe winds, rain, and clouds. They had no choice, since the altitude ceiling of the World Cruisers would not allow them to fly over the range. On July 8, after a bone-wearying 10 hours, 35 minutes airborne, they landed in Baghdad.

Upon making Aleppo (present-day Halab), Syria, the exhausted men were whisked off by their Turkish hosts to a festive dinner party that lasted

U.S. Navy sailors work on one of the Douglas World Cruisers' 400-horsepower Liberty engines. In the course of their record flight, the four aircraft used up 11 of these engines.

A Douglas World Cruiser's open cockpit featured a large steering wheel to control the ailerons and elevators. The leather trim on the coaming offered the pilot some protection from the cockpit rim in the event of a crash.

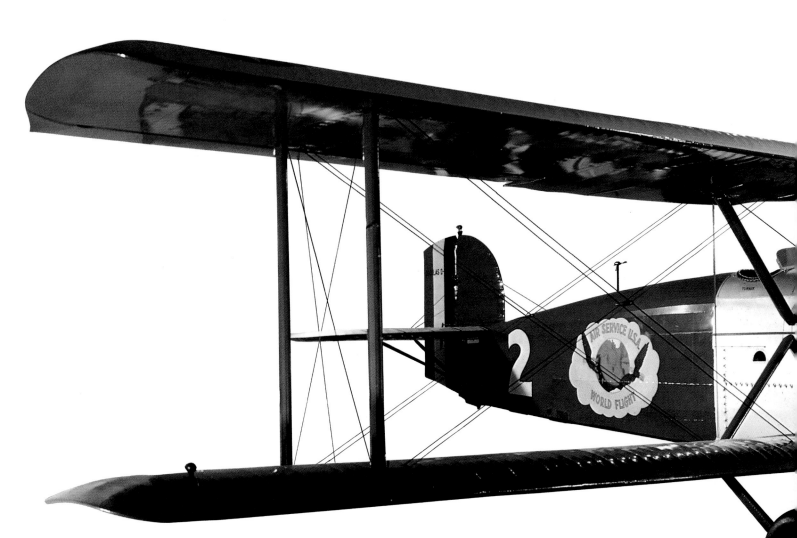

The National Air and Space Museum's restored Douglas World Cruiser, Chicago, *became the round-the-world flight's lead aircraft after World Cruiser No. 1,* Seattle, *hit a mountain in the Aleutian Islands.*

until 2:00 A.M. The more their fame spread, the less rest they seemed to be able to get on the ground. At 6:00 A.M., they crawled into their biplanes and left for Constantinople, where four days of celebration had been planned. The fliers managed to negotiate that down to two.

After stops in Bucharest, Romania; Budapest, Hungary; and Vienna, the flight departed into heavy rain and low clouds for the leg to Paris. The World Cruisers stayed under the overcast and followed the Danube past Linz, Austria, and then threaded mountain passes to Munich, in southern Germany.

After a quick refueling at Strasbourg, France, the World Cruisers were joined just short of the city by a formation of eight French aircraft. In a gesture that endeared them to their new hosts, the fliers bypassed their intended landing at Le Bourget and flew straight to the capital, where they circled over the Arc de Triumph. They dropped a tribute of flowers on the Tomb of the Unknown Soldier, and saluted their departed comrade in arms from

their cockpits before turning back to the airfield.

As they touched down, the crowd erupted with tremendous cheering. It was July 14th, Bastille Day. For an hour, the exhausted Americans made their way through a handshaking mass of people, but there were no beds awaiting them. Instead, they faced a series of receptions, interviews, autographs, radio programs, and, de rigueur, a stop at the Folies Bergére, before they could retire. Upon reaching the hotel they hung a sign with these words on each door: "Please do not wake us until 9 tomorrow unless the hotel is on fire, and not then unless the firemen have given up all hope."

After a short hop to London, the World Cruisers were pushed into the Blackburn Company's facilities for engine changes and remounting of pontoons for the hazardous North Atlantic crossing via Iceland and Greenland, destinations to which no aircraft had previously flown. The U.S. Navy stationed two light cruisers and two destroyers off Scotland as flight guards, then fanned ships out along the route from Greenland to Boston. A rautes out, however, the fliers watched the fog close back in to obscure the sea's surface. They climbed, holding close formation so as not to lose each other. With no blind-flying instruments, the pilots pulled off a miraculous feat, and topped the milky-white clag at 5,000 feet (1,524 meters). But *New Orleans* was gone. Nelson had flown into the others' prop wash (wake turbulence), and had entered what was known as a graveyard spiral.

With no reference to right side up, Nelson had lost control of his big biplane. The World Cruiser punched through the fog-bank bottom with just enough room for the pilot to pull out as he skimmed the water. Mustering incredible courage, he climbed back up through the fog and popped out, but *Chicago* and *Boston* had disappeared. The separated crews feared the worst for each other.

As Nelson continued on to Iceland, he did not realize he was alone: Smith and Wade had turned back for Kirkwall and the crossing fleet's flagship, USS *Richmond*. Smith roared down main street and dropped a scrawled note: CONTACT RICHMOND – START SEARCH FOR NELSON. Then both aircraft set down in the harbor. Shortly after 6:00 P.M. a wireless came through from Nelson that he had continued on and had landed at Hornafjördur, Iceland.

By 9:30 A.M. *Chicago* and *Boston* were off again. At 11:00 A.M., far out over the North Atlantic between the Faroe Islands and the Orkneys, Wade noticed that the oil pressure of his Liberty engine had begun to drop: an oil pump had failed. He set the World Cruiser down on the sea. Smith circled and prepared to land, but he was waved away by the men below who were warning of the rough sea's danger. Smith wheeled away and headed for the nearest Navy picket ship, 100 miles (161 kilometers) away.

An hour later, *Chicago* roared over the *Billingsly* at funnel height and dropped a message on deck. Within seconds, smoke was pouring from her stacks as she came up to maximum speed and turned toward *Boston,* while sending a wireless to alert the flag ship, which joined in.

After drifting for several hours, the stricken World Cruiser was spotted by the *Richmond*. After taking Wade and Ogden aboard, the *Richmond* at-

Lieutenants Leslie Arnold and Lowell Smith stand in front of their ship, Chicago, *right. Arnold replaced Sergeant Arthur Turner as mechanic for this Douglas World Cruiser's flight at the last minute; thus Turner's name still appears on the aircraft's rear cockpit.*

dio chain was organized from Brough via the Orkney Islands, Iceland, Greenland, and Nova Scotia.

The three World Cruisers departed Brough and made Kirkwall in the Orkneys just as a dense fog rolled in. The low-hanging scud refused to break for several days, until, on August 2, a brief clearing allowed the flight to get airborne. Only 10 min-

tempted a tow, but the rough seas had started to take their toll, and so the decision was made to hoist the aircraft out of the water.

[Wade] stood on the ship's deck, watched the crane swing over the side and drop its hook. . . . The lift signal came and the Boston *started rising out of the water. Then all hell broke loose. Five thousand pounds of hoisting gear wrenched off its mooring and crashed down on the plane. The* Boston *was a broken mess.*

She capsized. Aircraft commander Wade made the heartbreaking decision to cut her loose and watch her sink. Without shame, several men wept. To have come so far. . . .

With the team of fliers more than three-fourths of the way around the globe, the War Department would not leave the two distraught men in the lurch. The prototype DWC was ordered to Nova Scotia, where Wade and Ogden could resume the flight with the other two aircraft.

Chicago went on to Iceland, and joined *New Orleans,* and the two World Cruisers hopped to Reykjavík, where the four men had to alter the planned route. A solid field of ice made their original Greenland stop impossible. Although they had plotted a number of alternatives, none was really safe.

After weeks of delay, rumblings of threats to cancel the flight started to come in from Washington.

This was more than the fliers could bear, and so they opted to fly directly to Greenland's southernmost tip, Frederiksdal (present-day Narsaq Kujalleq), an 835-mile (1,344-kilometer) leg with no Naval pickets and only distant ship lanes. If they went down, rescue would be impossible.

Although this would be the most hazardous part of the journey, it wasn't so very different from flying over the trackless jungle of Southeast Asia. The War Department relented, and, on August 21, the two planes once again were off.

The first 500 miles (805 kilometers) of the trip were wonderful, with sparkling weather and excellent visibility, but then that hated enemy, fog, settled in. Too high to top, it forced the two World Cruisers down to wave-top height, where visibili-

At last winging their way along the home stretch, Douglas World Cruisers (left to right) Boston II *(a replacement for the lost original* Boston*),* New Orleans, *and* Chicago *fly across the United States in September 1924.*

ty averaged a mere 150 feet (46 meters). This normally would have been safer than flying so low over land, but a new and extremely treacherous form of mountain now faced them: the iceberg.

Violent, last-second evasive action saved the fliers a dozen times, but the two aircraft became separated and each pilot had to make it on his own. After 11 hours airborne, the four wet, cold, exhausted men reached Frederiksdal and held a celebration. Survival was sweet, and North America lay just 560 miles (901 kilometers) away across Davis Strait.

As the two World Cruisers left Ivigtut, Greenland, for Icy Tickle, Labrador, the seemingly impossible happened: the weather got worse. A couple hundred miles off Labrador, *Chicago*'s fuel pump failed, but Arnold got on the manual wobble pump and kept the Liberty engine running by hand pumping it for two hours. When he thought he couldn't give it one more stroke, he'd look down at the frigid water for motivation. There was also a near collision with a steamship off Cape Charles while skimming along the sea in the fog.

When the two World Cruisers made Icy Tickle, on August 31, the crews were overcome by reporters, photographers, and dignitaries, all of whom knew the significance of the flight's reaching North America, even five months and 14 days after leaving Santa Monica. The haggard faces of the men told of their continuous flirtations with disaster as they made it around the globe, but soon they were removing the pontoons, installing wheels, and overhauling the machines for their final leap down and across the continent.

Enthusiasm reached a high pitch again two days later, when the two World Cruisers left for Pictou, Nova Scotia, and an eager Wade and Ogden, who were waiting with their newly christened *Boston II*. The team once again was intact, though the fliers continued to express regret that Major Martin, Sergeant Harvey, and *Seattle* were not there to share in the glory.

On September 5, three World Cruisers were airborne for Boston, but dense fog, now seemingly a constant companion, forced them down in Casco Bay, off the coast of Maine, in the late afternoon. The cursed mist cleared enough to allow another try on September 6th, and they made Boston and

the cheers of a raucous and well deserved welcome.

After the incredible accomplishments of the flight, crossing America seemed almost easy: after all, it already had been done by several fliers. Surely the hardy World Cruisers and their iron men could do this last leg.

After a stop at Mitchel Field, Long Island, they were off to Bolling Field, Washington, D.C., where President Calvin Coolidge and his cabinet had waited in the rain for three hours to welcome the world travelers. Landing at 14 cities across the U.S., the World Cruisers made San Diego on September 22, and then headed north for Seattle, where sirens blew as the aircraft circled the city.

The official flight was completed on September 28, 1924, as the three aircraft landed at Sand Point Field: *Chicago* touched down at 1:36 p.m., *Boston II* at 1:37:50, and *New Orleans* at 1:38:35. Major Frederick Martin was the first to greet his men. As Lowell Smith climbed down from the cockpit of his cruiser he was asked if he'd do it again. He was quick to reply: not unless he was ordered to. This was no time for false heroism.

The crews had fought disaster, awful weather, heavy airplanes, and mechanical failure continually over the course of 175 days, flying 27,553 miles (44,333 kilometers) and averaging 74.23 miles per hour (119 kilometers per hour), over a total flying time of 371 hours, 11 minutes. They had used up 11 Liberty engines. Making their way through 29 countries, they had lost two aircraft and had walked away from five forced landings, and yet they had not sustained a single serious injury.

Aviation clearly had grown up from barnstorming to genuine accomplishment, thanks to a few intrepid men and the government support behind them.

Opposite, left to right, Army Air Service world fliers Leslie Arnold, John Harding, Lowell Smith, Leigh Wade, and Erik Nelson are greeted in England by Mrs. Stuart McClaren, the wife of an English aviator they had met in the Pacific. Below, U.S. Navy Commander John Towers suits up for an earlier historic flight, that of the first aerial crossing of the Atlantic. Five years later, as U.S. Naval air attaché to England, Towers met the Douglas World Cruiser round-the-world fliers.

Only two weeks after NC-4 had reached Plymouth, England, John Alcock and Arthur Whitten-Brown made the first nonstop crossing of the Atlantic in a twin-engine Royal Air Force Vickers Vimy bomber. Lifting off from St. John's, Newfoundland, on June 14, 1919, they landed at Clifden, Ireland, on the 15th, after a 16-hour, 27-minute flight. The third and fourth nonstop Atlantic crossings were made less than a month later in a round-trip flight by the British dirigible airship R.34, from Scotland to Long Island, New York, and back to England, July 2 to 13. Thirty-one people were aboard.

The ocean barrier thus had been shattered in successive blows during a brief two-month period in 1919. Although the news of these events made front-page headlines, the public seemed to forget about each successive triumph after the furor had died down. Wealthy hotel owner Raymond Orteig was the exception. So taken was he with the potential of aviation that, in 1919, he offered a prize of $25,000 for the first nonstop flight between New York and Paris. It was a goad for yet another seemingly impossible feat, and, indeed, eight years later, despite heroic attempts, the prize remained unclaimed.

By 1926, famed World War I French ace René Fonck had contracted with Igor Sikorsky to prepare for an attempt one of Sikorsky's impressive new S-35 triple-engine airliners. At a cost of $105,000, it was the most expensive airplane in the world. Sikorsky was well aware of what the publicity could do for his company, but he was also meticulous,

and slower than Fonck could stand.

Rejecting Sikorsky's desire for a series of load tests on the fuel-laden, 28,000-pound (12,727-kilogram) machine, which was 10,000 pounds, or 4,546 kilograms, over maximum design weight, Fonck and his crew of three attempted a takeoff from Roosevelt Field, New York, on September 26, 1926. The S-35 lost one of its wheels, refused to get airborne, and then rolled itself into a ball of flaming wreckage. Two of the crew were burned to death. "It is the fortune of the air," Fonck later commented.

USA TO EUROPE NONSTOP

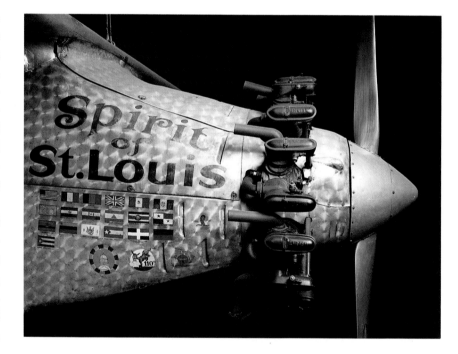

Charles Augustus Lindbergh, right, entered engineering school, but soon dropped out to fly. Once aloft, the "Lone Eagle," as he came to be called, shaped his own curriculum, learned from experience, and tested himself against the sky. Five years later, he piloted the Spirit of St. Louis, *above. The ship was his answer to a merciless test question: how to fly from New York to Paris, nonstop, and survive? Though others died in the attempt, Lindbergh passed with flying colors —those of the United States and the global future of aviation.*

Lindbergh was the 79th person to fly the Atlantic. Alcock and Brown, here nosed over in an Irish bog, were the first to do it nonstop. They reached the Emerald Isle in 1919 after an 1,800-mile flight from Newfoundland. In 1927, Lindbergh was able to cover 3,600 miles. Time and again, such a distance had defeated older, richer, and more experienced fliers.

In April 1927, another overload accident killed Americans Noel Davis and Stanton Wooster when their staggering Keystone Pathfinder stalled on takeoff for a final test flight before heading for Paris. On May 8, another French ace, Captain Charles Nungesser, and his navigator, Captain François Coli, took off from Paris, bound for New York, in their Levasseur PL-8 biplane and simply disappeared, never to be seen again. The rising toll of losses among these transatlantic contenders caught the attention of the public, and Nungesser's disappearance spawned an increasing interest in the three American aircraft being prepared for the flight.

Charles Levine's Wright-Bellanca WB-2 was being readied in an atmosphere of discontent, something that this war-salvage millionaire seemed to create in all his human contacts. Levine had not bothered to apply for the Orteig prize—he had ab-

solutely no need for it—but the continual bickering over who would make the flight, what was needed aboard the aircraft, and the route that was to be followed generated constant delays.

Department-store owner Rodman Wanamaker snubbed the prize as well when he offered to sponsor Navy Commander Richard Byrd and the Fokker F.VII trimotor *America* as a scientific-research flight that would benefit future airline operations. It looked like he was backing a sure bet, since Byrd and pilot Floyd Bennett had flown to the North Pole the year before. After an accident in testing the new aircraft, Bennett was forced to drop out with a broken leg. Air-race pilot Bert Acosta and Norwegian copilot Bernt Balchen were brought on as replacements.

The third aircraft was a real long shot: a small, single-engine Ryan that was virtually a flying fuel tank. It was to be flown by Charles A. Lindbergh,

an unknown airmail pilot who was backed by a group of St. Louis businessmen whom, again, no one seemed to know.

Although more fascinated with mechanics than academics, Charles Augustus Lindbergh had entered engineering studies in 1920 at the University of Wisconsin. After two years, he left to pursue what he felt was his calling—aviation—although he had to start in the lowest-paying, highest-risk aspect of flying, that of barnstorming. After some initial instruction at Lincoln, Nebraska, he became a wing walker and a parachutist for Erold Bahl and "Cupid" Lynch, and then, in Americus, Georgia, he bought a Curtiss JN-4D "Jenny." Underpowered, the Jenny often would stall out with the least provocation. As a result of such special training, a pilot who could master the Jenny most likely could handle any of the era's other flying machines.

After spending more time at the controls, Lindbergh soloed in April 1923, and then linked up with friend Harlan "Bud" Gurney to crisscross the countryside, offering stunts, rides, and thrills. It was an extremely hazardous business, but one of the few in which a pilot could make ends meet—at times almost literally: midair collisions were not uncommon. Gurney recalled that he and "Slim" Lindbergh flew such plane changes as when he lifted a wing walker off Lindbergh's top wing by flying his lower wing tip into the man's hands. The toll on human life became so steady that eventually barnstorming was shut down.

Captain Sir John Alcock (left), and Lieutenant Sir Arthur Witten Brown, in uniform, plan their flight in a Vickers Vimy bomber, above. With a total of 720 horsepower from twin Rolls-Royce Eagle engines, the boxy biplane overcame its antique aerodynamics. Lindbergh's 220-horsepower Wright Whirlwind J-5 was to propel his efficient Ryan monoplane twice the Vimy's distance.

The more Lindbergh flew, the more he wanted to pilot something other than worn-out, low-horsepower, surplus trainers. He knew that the U.S. Army Air Service was the only place in which he could actually get into higher performance machines, so he enlisted as a cadet in the Army Air Service Reserve and received his wings in March 1925. Young Charles made his first emergency bail out that June after a midair collision during gunnery practice. His second emergency jump came the following June when an aircraft he was testing refused to come out of a spin. He managed to escape at a mere 350 feet (107 meters), although the aircraft almost hit him on the way down.

The next year he was flying the airmail, which, like barnstorming, was also a dangerous way to make a living. In April 1926, he started the St. Louis-to-Chicago route as chief pilot for Robertson Aircraft Corporation, flying a surplus DH-4. This called for flying in the poorest of weather and at night, a nightmare at best, with poor airfields, little lighting, no blind-flying aids, and absolutely no heat in winter for the open cockpits. Lindbergh's third emergency jump took place at night in fog, when he could not land; again the abandoned airplane circled him ominously as he descended. His fourth unplanned jump also occurred at night, this time in a snowstorm; he landed on top of a barbed-wire fence.

It was during this period at Robertson, after he had gotten 2,000 hours of flying time under his belt, that he began to contemplate the idea of making the flight that would link the Old World with the New. Sitting in his cold cockpit at night, listening to the engine drone through rain, snow, or fog, he figured the weather over the Atlantic Ocean couldn't be any worse than flying the night mail. As with all his previous aviation goals, he knew he could make the flight—with or without the Orteig prize—if he could line up the financial backing. The real key would be to find the right airplane.

As Lindbergh ran through the choices available, he kept coming back to Giuseppe Bellanca's designs, with their exquisite, efficient airfoils. The Wright-Bellanca WB-2, with its dependable Wright J-5 Whirlwind 220-horsepower engine, seemed to him to be the only single-engine aircraft available that could make it safely to Paris. Although many disagreed with him, he felt that large, multi-engine aircraft were not the ideal choice. First of all, the purchase price and operating costs of these larger planes were far higher than those for single-engine machines; second, flying with two or more engines increased the chance that something would go wrong with one engine, and the remaining engines were not powerful enough to maintain level flight; third, Lindbergh had always preferred flying solo, and for a solo pilot, one engine was enough. He believed in making it to Paris alone.

Lindbergh made a trip to New York to talk to

In 1922, Charles Lindbergh, below, stands before the first plane he flew, a Lincoln Standard Turnabout; Bud Gurney, a friend at flying school in Nebraska, mugs for the camera. Lindbergh and other student pilots of his era often earned their wings in surplus ships from World War I, such as the DH-4, left, and the Curtiss JN-4 "Jenny," right.

Bellanca about the price and availability of the WB-2. The two men liked one another from the beginning: both were loners, with faith in their talent but few backers to help them financially. Charles knew he had a friend in Bellanca, who was as interested in the New York-to-Paris flight as he was, but still the young pilot had no money, apart from his $2,000 life savings.

One of the first men he approached for financial support was his employer, Major William B. Robertson. "Slim came into the office one day and said, 'Bill, I want to fly over the Atlantic Ocean.' 'You're crazy as hell, Slim,' I told him." Nevertheless, Robertson, a veteran flier, knew and respected his chief pilot well enough to share the risk, certainly it was no more chancy than flying in the harsh Midwest winter weather.

"It was another one of those things that we had never feared to tackle," mused Robertson. "So I started using big words right off the bat. I told Slim that if we were to impress anybody, we would have to have a 'prospectus.' It sounded great, so we sat down and wrote one." The Robertson brothers kicked in $1,000 to Charles's savings, and then they approached insurance executive Earl Thompson, who was hard to sell on the idea of flying a single-engine airplane over the ocean, but who was more convinced of the venture's legitimacy after listening to the intense young man.

Harry F. Knight and his son Harry H., both of whom were stock brokers, were approached next, followed by E. Lansing Ray, editor and publisher of the St. Louis *Globe-Democrat,* who came on board after the other city papers declined. Pharmaceutical heir and pioneer balloonist and pilot Major Albert Bond Lambert joined the group, as did his brother, J.D. Wooster Lambert, and banker Harold M. Bixby, who was said to have thought up the now famous name for the aircraft, *Spirit of St. Louis.* These eight men promised the young flier a total of $15,000 to make the flight possible.

Putting his $2,000 into the form of a certified check, Charles returned to New York, at Bellanca's invitation, to formalize purchase of the WB-2, now named *Columbia.* Lindbergh looked forward to flying the airplane home with its new name on the nose.

Strapped for funds himself, as always, Bellanca had teamed up with financier Charles Levine to form the Columbia Aircraft Corporation. When Lindbergh arrived, he found Bellanca still eager to see the young pilot make the flight, but Bellanca's partner, Levine, somewhat less than enthusiastic. Would an unknown airmail pilot be worth as much in publicity as a more famous aviator? Lindbergh was adamant: either he personally would make the flight, or he wasn't interested in buying. Levine suggested they sleep on it for 24 hours. When Lindbergh came back, Levine asked if he'd changed his mind, since that was the only option he had intended all along. Charles was infuriated by Levine's condescending attitude.

Crestfallen, Lindbergh took the train back to St. Louis to relay the bad news. The flight probably was dead without the WB-2. His second choice, the Travel Air firm, turned him down, believing that he probably would fail and that the bad publicity would hurt their sales. Fokker refused to so much as offer a price on a single-engine aircraft, although the company would sell a trimotor for $90,000. Not only was that far above reach, however, but it also violated Lindbergh's faith in using a single-engine aircraft.

Lindbergh was left with but a single company that showed any willingness at all to gamble on an unknown loner: Ryan Airlines, in San Diego. He knew that Pacific Air Transport had used Ryan mail planes on their routes, but that was about all he knew about Ryan's machines. Yet there seemed to be little choice: the competition was heating up. And so, in February 1927, just after his 25th birth-

At Lambert Field, St. Louis, above, Lindbergh appears with three partners, pictured at left, in the Spirit of St. Louis venture. Left to right, from the top: William B. Robertson; Frank H. Robinson; Albert Bond Lambert; J.D. Wooster Lambert; E. Lansing Ray; Harold M. Bixby; Harry F. Knight; Harry Hall Knight; and Earl C. Thompson. These stalwart friends gave the kind of support that money could not buy. When Lindbergh called St. Louis for permission to fly before becoming eligible for a cash prize, Harry Knight replied, "To hell with the money. When you are ready to take off, go ahead."

day, he decided to head out west and see what this small company had to offer.

In San Diego, Lindbergh was immediately impressed with the enthusiasm of Ryan's new president, B. Franklin Mahoney, and with chief engineer Donald A. Hall's grasp of what was needed to make the flight. Although Hall had expected only to modify the existing M-2 mail plane, as the two men talked it became clear that a substantive re-design was in order.

Lindbergh gave Ryan the following basic specifications: a monoplane powered by a 220-horsepower Wright J-5C Whirlwind, good power reserve on takeoff, more than 400 gallons (1,520 liters) of fuel, and the pilot's seat located behind all fuel tanks for safety in a forced landing. Hall then laid out an aircraft of increased length and wingspan, and with

A mechanic prepares the Spirit of St. Louis *for flight. He braces to spin the propeller, which in turn will start the engine. At New York before takeoff, company representatives donated their services to prime the plane for its mission,*

No hands-off buyer, Lindbergh frequently showed up at the factory sheds, and, without being critical, actively participated in the aircraft's design. The plane's most radical feature was the cockpit: its location in the rear, behind the main fuel tank, denied the pilot any forward visibility whatsoever. A Ryan employee who had had extensive submarine experience suggested a retractable periscope mounted in the center of the instrument panel, and Lindbergh accepted it.

During the construction period, Lindbergh devoted himself to an intensive study of navigation and the preparation of charts. During the last four weeks of the plane's building, he spent long days accumulating data for his upcoming dead-reckoning trip across the Atlantic. There were no landmarks or navigational aids; careful attention to

beefed-up load factors for takeoff and flight. After several days, Lindbergh wired his backers in St. Louis that he believed Ryan could provide the aircraft he needed.

On February 28, 1927, an agreement was struck that paid $10,580 for an aircraft with standard instrumentation. The cost of adding a few specialized instruments to it barely left enough for Charles's own expenses. Mahoney agreed to deliver the NYP (New York to Paris) in 60 days. His price was little more than cost, but he recognized the potential publicity value of a successful flight and the rewards it could bring to the small firm.

overhauling the engine and adding a carburetor-heater, installing an Earth-inductor compass, and filling the tanks with California-grade aviation gasoline, shipped east especially for the Spirit.

wind drift through ocean-wave observation, airspeed, and weather conditions would determine the accuracy of his time and distance calculations. The use of a sextant was out, since he saw no way of holding it steady long enough to get a sight. No matter how he viewed it, the New York-to-Paris flight would be a monumental undertaking, something far beyond his experience. To build his stamina, he walked the beaches at night until he was able to stay awake for the period of time he projected it would take him to complete the flight, which was about 34 hours.

With the benefit of a tail wind across the ocean's

3,614 miles (5,782 kilometers), Lindbergh expected to average 100 miles per hour (160 kilometers per hour), so the still-air range of 4,210 miles (6,736 kilometers) on 450 gallons (1,710 liters) of fuel and 25 gallons (95 liters) of oil provided an excellent margin of safety. The great-circle route to Paris, which Lindbergh planned to follow, was divided into 100-mile (160-kilometer) segments, with a planned course alteration every hour to compensate for the curving Earth and for magnetic-variation changes. The aircraft's basic navigation instruments were a turn-and-bank gyro, a drift sight, an air-speed indicator, a magnetic compass, and a Pioneer Earth-inductor compass.

The NYP went through final assembly under Lindbergh's careful supervision, and, again, his careful attention at this stage endeared him all the more to the Ryan workers and employees, and helped to get the *Spirit* built in record time. Construction tasks were spread throughout the small sheds. Once the wings were finished in the upper-attic area, everyone was dismayed to find out they would not make the turns to come down the stairs. Instead, the workers pushed them out a second-story window and lowered them to the ground with a hoist.

Lindbergh started flight testing on April 28. The airplane was very unstable, requiring a fine, almost instinctive touch on the controls. The ailerons were small in order to avoid over-stressing the wing un-

Accidents gave late-starter Lindbergh a window of opportunity. On takeoff for Paris, an

overloaded Sikorsky S-35 trimotor, bottom, had burst into flame. Above right, even with designer Tony Fokker at the controls, America was damaged during a work-up for the Orteig-prize flight, as was the big Bellanca monoplane, above, with, left to right, Bert Acosta, designer Giuseppe Bellanca, and pilot Clarence Chamberlain.

der full load, and consequently the airplane reacted to them sluggishly. With such a large wing and small tail, the Ryan would fall out of level flight with the slightest gust or inattention. So be it: having flown so many marginal aircraft, Lindbergh was not concerned. It was all a part of what pilots expected in the 1920s, and, as Lindbergh himself remarked, the "response is good enough for a long-range airplane."

He and Hall laid out a comprehensive, systematic program to check theoretical versus actual performances. They increased fuel loads successively from 36 to 300 gallons (137 to 1,140 liters), for example, in order to check takeoff distances.

During those rushed days, bad news regarding the other contenders kept coming in: Davis and Wooster killed in their Keystone, Byrd's Fokker seriously damaged, then Chamberlin and Acosta's cracking of the landing gear on Lindbergh's original choice, the Wright-Bellanca. Charles could take no encouragement from the misfortune of his fellow fliers, although he knew they were making overload mistakes that he was trying to avoid.

The pressure on the small Ryan contingent and their pilot reached a peak after the WB-2 was fixed and Chamberlin and Acosta flew *Columbia* to a world endurance record of 51 hours, far more than was needed to cross the Atlantic. Then, on May 8, word came that Nungesser and Coli were airborne from France and heading for New York. At that point, Lindbergh called his backers. Should he give up the Atlantic and try the Pacific instead? The gutsy men from St. Louis encouraged him to stick with his original vision and to proceed according to his carefully laid-out plan. After two days, it became clear that the Frenchmen had disappeared somewhere between Ireland and the U.S.

Although both Hall and Lindbergh would have valued more time for testing, after 23 tests flights and 4 hours, 15 minutes' air time Charles felt he had enough data to head for New York, with one stop in St. Louis, before the competition got the jump on him. On May 10, 1927, Lindbergh departed San Diego and landed at Lambert Field, St. Louis, 14 hours and 25 minutes later. Not only was this an effective shakedown flight for the *Spirit of St. Louis,* but it was a record nonstop flight

over the Rockies at night. Although all kinds of ceremonies in St. Louis had been planned, the backers understood the urgency of the situation and let "Slim" call the shots. Charles spent the night, then departed for New York on May 12, landing at Curtiss Field, Long Island, after 7 hours, 20 minutes.

Between the 13th and the 15th, the *Spirit* made six short test flights out of Curtiss Field, each of which lasted between 10 and 20 minutes. *Columbia* was poised nearby, but Charles Levine's abrasive personality kept getting in the way, and petty squabbles slowed preparations. Byrd arrived with his Fokker, but he would not rush his slow, methodical approach to readiness.

Then fog and poor weather set in, grounding everyone. For almost a week, thousands of spectators mobbed the area to get a glimpse of the planes and their pilots. The unwanted attention and press coverage appalled Lindbergh; he had been totally unprepared for this aspect of the flight.

Late in the evening on May 19, weather forecaster James Kimball gave Charles some hope that the weather would clear. Although Lindbergh had not managed to get much sleep for the past two nights, he had the *Spirit* towed over the back streets to Roosevelt Field in the early morning hours of May 20. No activity in the Byrd or Chamberlin camps was evident. In a gesture typical of pilots of any time, Byrd had given Lindbergh permission to use his 5,000-foot (1,524-meter) grass runway, which had been prepared specially for the heavy Fokker.

Less than a week before Lindbergh's attempt, Lieutenant Commander Noel Davis (left) and Lieutenant Stanton H. Wooster, expert Navy pilots, died in a crash of their trimotor Keystone Pathfinder at Langley Field, near Hampton, Virginia. Like the Sikorsky giant that had killed two of its crew of four, Davis's ship had been loaded beyond design capacity.

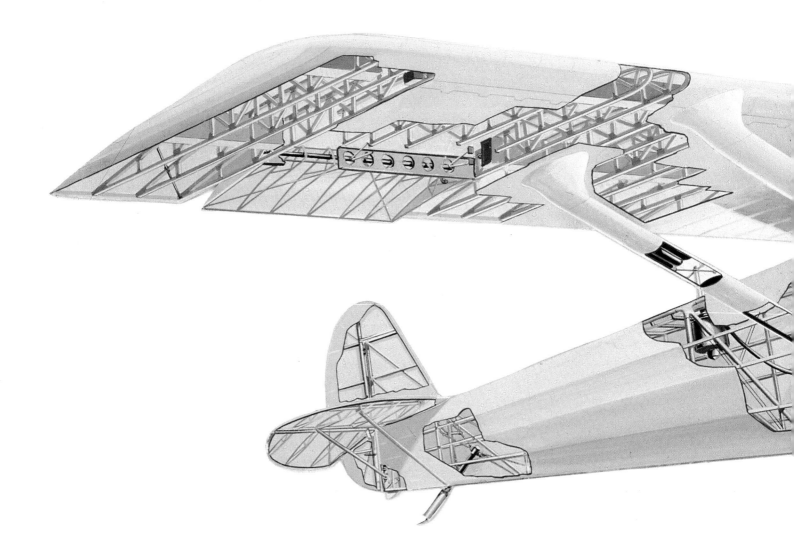

Although clouds were low, with a light rain falling, the winds were light and variable, and Charles had the tanks filled to the top—450 gallons (1,703 liters). He then walked the water-logged runway. It was going to be very close: the soggy ground and lack of a good head wind would work against the plane's getting airborne.

After the engine was warmed up, Lindbergh waved for the wheel chocks to be pulled, and, at 7:53 A.M., slowly moved the throttle up to full power. The *Spirit* barely moved. Loaded to more than its design weight at 5,250 pounds (2,381 kilograms), it began to sink into the mud. Spectators ran up to help, heaving on the wing struts until the Ryan started to move faster than they could keep up with.

Agonizingly slowly, the aircraft gained speed, splashing mud and water into the air as it lurched through numerous puddles. Twice Lindbergh attempted to pull the plane off the ground, but each time it settled back.

With the end of the runway almost upon him, he coaxed the *Spirit* into the air a third time, and with this effort he cleared the telephone wires at the runway's end by 20 feet (six meters). As the aircraft faded into the gloom, Byrd was heard to murmur, "God be with him."

The takeoff, one of the flight's greatest hurdles, had been accomplished, but Lindbergh remained at 200 feet (61 meters) over Long Island, building speed until the rain stopped. Then the clouds be-

Streamlined simplicity marks the Ryan NYP (New York to Paris)— the model designation of the Spirit of St. Louis. *Consulting often with Lindbergh, Donald Hall, chief engineer for Ryan Airlines, designed the craft. Welders fashioned the fuselage of steel*

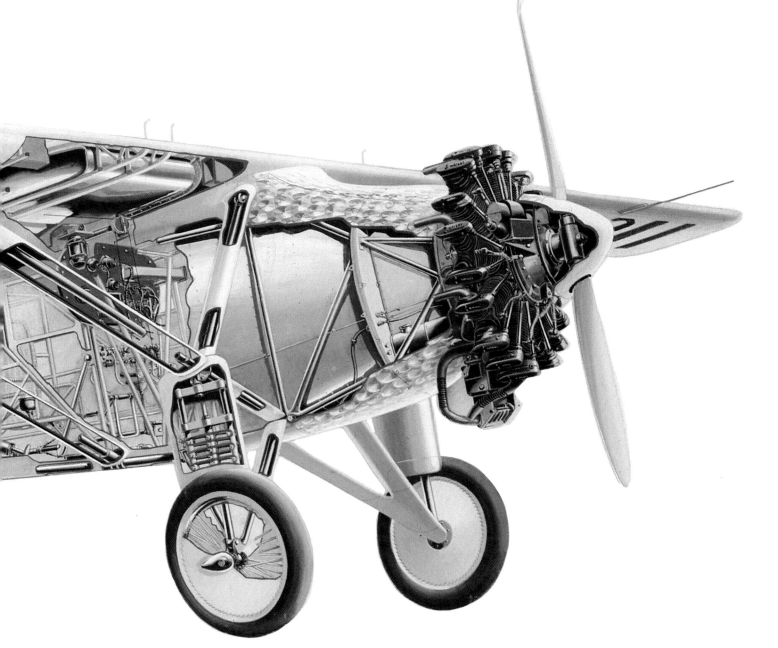

tube while skilled joiners made wing spars and ribs from spruce. Cotton fabric, strengthened and shrunk with acetate shellac, covered all. Bungee cords under tension served as shock absorbers. Fuel was stowed in the wings and in a huge tank behind the engine that blocked all forward view. Farther

back, the pilot sat at his control panel, right, and glanced up at a hanging compass. Its hidden dial was viewed in a small mirror, donated at the last minute by a young onlooker and glued to the panel with chewing gum.

Lindbergh's rugged
monoplane, with its cowl
and gas-tank cover of
turned aluminum, seems
to soar as it hangs at the
Smithsonian today. The
propeller is eight feet,
nine inches long. Too
small tail surfaces sacri-
ficed stability in flight for
a scrap more fuel
efficiency. Lindbergh
totally specialized his
aircraft for its single,
long-distance objective.

gan to part, and the mist gave way to increasingly better visibility. Charles Lindbergh was about to make the first sea crossing of his life.

Picking up tail winds from Cape Cod, he set off for Nova Scotia, some 250 miles (400 kilometers) distant, staying between 20 and 100 feet (6 and 30 meters) above the water and hoping ground effect would give just a bit more help. Then, only three hours out, he began to feel cramped and tired, almost exhausted. Suffering from the effects of being awake for 23 hours before takeoff, he took his first sip of water.

Fortunately, Lindbergh's mind was occupied by the increasing turbulence that was severely flexing the wings of the overloaded *Spirit* and causing him to wonder how long they could take it. Keeping the unstable Ryan under control took every bit of his skill. He elected to reduce speed in order to ease the strain, and promptly ran into a series of storms, with lightning bursting all around him for almost an hour over Nova Scotia. When the wind changed to the southeast, however, the worst of it ended.

The sudden departure of inclement weather, the monotonous droning of the engine, and the trackless ocean stretching before and around him brought on an almost uncontrollable urge to sleep. "My eyes feel dry and hard as stones," he later wrote. "If I could throw myself down on a bed I'd be asleep in an instant." He continually shook his head and body, held his eyelids open with his fingers, slapped his face, pinched himself, flexed his muscles, stuck

his face out into the frigid wind, and stamped his feet. But nothing seemed to work, he recalled. "The worst part about fighting sleep is that the harder you fight the more you strengthen your enemy, and the more you weaken your resistance to him." Paris still lay 2,800 miles (4,480 kilometers) away through the black tunnel of night. Ironically, the only antidote to fatigue seemed to come from engine vibration and the instability of the Ryan, which would fall off into spirals when his attention lapsed, instantly forcing him to take corrective action.

Almost 12 hours after takeoff, the *Spirit* crossed St. John's, Newfoundland, and headed out over the Atlantic into the gathering dusk. Now there would be nothing but water until Ireland. He had been awake for 35 hours.

Although the Ryan was not equipped with radio, having one would not have helped. There was no one to talk to, and radio navigation was virtually unknown. Charles was very pleased with his investment in the expensive Earth-inductor compass, which gave steady, accurate readings regardless of aircraft attitude or vibration. From the waves below he figured he had a tail wind of 30 knots (58 kilometers per hour), which would allow him plenty of latitude in making Paris.

As the light faded, icebergs that looked like weird, dazzling sea monsters appeared to rise out of the ocean's gathering fog. Soon a solid cloud front forced Lindbergh to climb, and two hours from land the *Spirit* was at 9,300 feet (2,835 meters) in a moonless night. Other than the dangerous urge to sleep, Lindbergh felt that so far the flight had been almost too easy. Looking at the stars and feeling alone in the world, he thought of religion, of the infinite expanse of the universe, and of the utter insignificance of humankind.

His reverie was broken as he entered the gathering clouds. Pointing his flashlight at the struts and wings, he noticed ice beginning to form. With no idea of how long he'd be forced to fly in the moisture-laden mist, he drew on his extensive experience flying the night mail and turned around. When he broke out of the icing conditions he resumed course, trying to weave down the canyons and between the soaring pillars of cloud to avoid the lift-killing ice—which, with no forward visibility, was a very difficult thing to do. New York was only 14 hours behind. Should he turn back? The thought was too painful. He would continue.

Slowly, the ice began to melt off the *Spirit*, which had maintained altitude in spite of the burden, thus easing Lindbergh's piloting task. He then noticed that both compasses seemed to be malfunction-

ing, fluctuating as if struck by some sort of magnetic storm.

In spite of these new worries, he felt again the overpowering desire to sleep, to let the airplane go, to drift away from his circumstances. To his good fortune, after two hours of almost complete blackness, the rising moon caught his attention. The clouds took on distinct shapes, shapes he could circumnavigate. Farther ahead, however, he could see a higher cloud formation forming a solid wall to block his path. Again he pondered turning around: could he go through another experience like the last one. Again he pushed such doubts out of his mind. He would go on regardless; there was no turning back.

With his deviations to avoid clouds, his odd compass readings, and his near drifting into sleep, Lindbergh knew that his navigation must be off. As it was, the weather had forced him 90 miles (145 kilometers) south of the great-circle route when he left St. John's. Where had the winds taken him? How much drift actually had taken place during the five hours he had not been able to see the surface of the

Near the takeoff point on New York's Long Island, mechanics check over Lindbergh's plane. Here, specialists from the Wright factory in Dayton, Ohio, consulted with the pilot. They worked to economize fuel consumption through the careful calculation of air-gasoline mixtures during different tasks required of the engine—ignition and warm-up, takeoff, rising to altitude, cruising, and descent.

sea to estimate wind direction and strength?

At this point, he consoled himself with the thought that any European landfall anywhere would do; his future landing spot was a far less serious problem than his drowsiness. "I let my eyelids fall shut for five seconds; then raise them against tons of weight. Protesting, they won't open wide until I force them with my thumb, and lift the muscles of my forehead to help keep them in place." Within a few seconds of Lindbergh's nodding off, the *Spirit* would take over, and gyrate its pilot awake. The airplane's instability was now a godsend, demanding, like a petulant child who throws a tantrum if left alone, that he deal with it.

Six hours out of St. John's, dawn started to creep onto the horizon ahead of the Ryan, never the less he recalled, "the uncontrollable desire to sleep falls over me in quilted layers. . . . This is the hour I've been dreading; the hour against which I've tried to steel myself. I know it's the beginning of my greatest test—the third morning, it is, since I've slept." Always fighting to stay awake, Lindbergh kept saying, "There's no alternative but death and failure."

With a small drink of water and full daylight, he started to pay more attention to navigation. Nineteen hours out of New York, halfway to Paris, the sea remained hidden by the barrier of cloud that lay ahead, so he transferred his efforts to flying by the few instruments aboard, particularly the Earth-inductor compass, which had settled down again.

At the 20th hour, Charles nosed the Ryan into a descent in order to register his first wave-wind-drift check in more than seven hours. As the *Spirit* passed 8,000 feet (2,438 meters), Lindbergh caught sight of the ocean, a heavy sea at the bottom of a well of clouds. To keep the water in sight, he put the aircraft into a steep spiral, pushing the speed up to 140 miles per hour (224 kilometers per hour),

The Spirit of St. Louis wings out from Long Island. Bottom, Lindbergh hugs the water, riding a cushion of air at the surface.

which forced him to throttle back the Whirlwind radial engine. Zooming past the lowest clouds at an altitude of 2,000 feet (610 meters), Charles found he had lost all sense of direction; he soon regained it, however, and determined he had a quartering tail wind from the northwest.

Descending to within 50 feet (15 meters) of the great, breaking seas, he estimated that the wind was blowing at 60 miles (96 kilometers) per hour. Spray was flying off the whitecaps like horizontal rain. If he experienced engine trouble now, he likely would not survive, but at the time he was more worried about his actual position. Having changed course so many times to avoid bad weather, and having no real idea of wind drift, he thought he might have wandered far enough south to hit the Bay of Biscay.

As the clouds lowered and covered the sea again, Lindbergh climbed into increasing turbulence that violently tossed the Ryan about. He had to give absolute attention to what he was doing now, since the *Spirit* was being pummeled by each invisible, hammering fist of bad weather. This should have kept anyone awake, but after an hour the airplane nosed down and dropped a wing without warning—he had "been asleep with open eyes."

Shoving stick and rudder in the correct direction to recover, Lindbergh saw the turn indicator go full left as the airspeed bled off: he had overcorrected and was now in a steep, climbing turn. A violent jolt went through him; he realized he was losing control. Re-concentrating on the instruments, getting himself lined up with deliberate, sluggish movements, he regained level flight. Yet he still could not shake the trance-like state: his conscious mind had stopped functioning.

He dove to within five feet (1.5 meters) of the waves, but did not break out of the fog, so he climbed back up to 1,000 feet (305 meters). Then breaks filled with rain began to appear. At that point, friendly, almost ghostly beings invaded the cockpit, talking to him in hushed human voices. He felt pushed into a different realm. Death was no longer the end, but an entrance into all space, all time.

As Lindbergh left the main storm behind at the end of the 24th hour, he spotted a coastline with

Bottom right, Paris's lights and crowds await Lindbergh at Le Bourget airport. Bottom left, Britishers welcome him to Croydon airport during a triumphant tour. Below, at Le Bourget, the Spirit of St. Louis *upstages Lindbergh at a formal dinner held inside an airport hangar.*

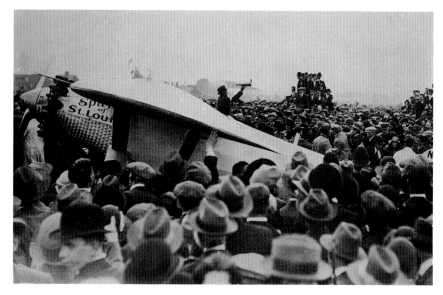

purplish-blue band began to form in the haze, but he refused to become excited over another mirage. If it were Ireland, he'd be two and a half hours ahead of schedule, but the tail wind could have helped. The prospect of sighting Europe instantly blew the clouds of drowsiness away. Unable to resist the urge, he changed course toward what he thought would be the nearest point of land, and then watched craggy shores and rounded mountains form out of the haze.

Now at 2,000 feet (610 meters) he knew without doubt where he was: Valentia Island, in Dingle Bay, on Ireland's west coast, lay before him. After flying 1,887 miles (3,019 kilometers) half-asleep and with almost no references, Charles Lindbergh was a mere three miles (five kilometers) off-course from his intended landfall, an astonishing navigational achievement. Even by modern standards, the er-

hills and groups of trees in what should have been the mid-Atlantic. Was he asleep, hallucinating, totally disoriented—or had he drifted north to Greenland? Just as he reached it, the island evaporated into a sharp, bright horizon. "I'm capable only of holding my plane aloft, and laxly pointed toward a heading I set some hours ago. No extra energy remains. I'm as strengthless as the vapor limbs of the spirits to whom I listen." Hitting himself in the face with his fists as hard as he could generated no pain or response.

"The alternative is death and failure, death and failure," he repeated. For the first time Lindbergh began to doubt himself. Could he endure? After trying every exercise the confines of the cockpit would allow, he stuck his face into the slip-stream, and a glimmer of recovery oozed into his brain. "I've been hanging over the chasm of eternity, holding onto the ledge with my fingertips; but now I'm gaining strength, I'm crawling upward. Consciousness is coming back."

Scanning the horizon, he spotted a small dot: a fishing boat! Thrilled, he flew over it, then turned back to make a low pass. As he approached again he throttled back and yelled, "Which way is Ireland?" There was no response, so he resumed course.

As the 28th hour began, he flew at 100 feet (30 meters), scanning the horizon between squalls. A

Above, an ornate check presented to Lindbergh put to rest his fears that he might have forfeited the Orteig prize due to a late contest entry. Paul Edward Garber accepted the Spirit of St. Louis *for the Smithsonian on April 30, 1928. At top, Paul Garber, historian emeritus at the National Air and Space Museum, visits this national aeronautical treasure in 1992.*

ror was insignificant. Regarding his exhaustion, he wrote, "I know how the dead would feel to live again."

Reaching Paris in six hours seemed an utterly simple task. Getting his charts sequenced and his route set, he was puzzled by the broad expanse of ocean in front of him. In his joy he had turned back out to the sea whence he had come. After a sharp, 180-degree turn, he was back over green Ireland, with its grazing sheep and waving people, and he prolonged his joy by staying low, buzzing small houses, and waving back. It was as if he had had a full night's rest and could fly on forever. The rapidly improving weather enhanced the mood, and brightened the cockpit to match his spirits.

Three hours later, the *Spirit* crossed Cornwall, and then the English Channel, before reaching the French coast at Deauville as the sun went down. To celebrate, Charles ate his first meal since lifting off from Roosevelt Field: a stale meat sandwich that "never touched my tongue like this before." The Seine was easy to spot from 2,000 feet (610 meters). He climbed to 4,000 (1,219 meters); the glow of Paris was a bright beacon.

Circling the Eiffel Tower, Lindbergh turned northeast to Le Bourget airport. He was unsure of the airfield's location, and could not spot its searchlight, so, assuming that he had overshot it, he turned around and caught sight of a cement parking ramp dotted with airplanes.

As he reduced power the aircraft's controls felt strange to him: the *Spirit*'s exaggerated instability at slow speed caught him off guard, and he felt disconnected from his machine. It was as if he had never flown her before. Fear gripped him; he couldn't stall her out after having come this far, but his coordination seemed to have left him.

Maintaining more speed than he needed, Lindbergh still felt as if the aircraft was going to stall as he overshot the floodlights on the field. With two good, solid bounces, the Ryan was down— his first night landing in what he now appreciated was a totally blind airplane. As he rolled out, he realized that any decent landing was a miracle.

Turning to taxi in, he saw to his amazement an ocean of some 100,000 people surging toward him, and he quickly killed the engine. It was 10:22 P.M., on May 21, 1927: 33 hours, 30 minutes, 29.9 seconds and 3,610 miles (5,776 kilometers) from New York. He had been awake for 57.5 hours. Eighty-five gallons (322 liters) of fuel remained, enough for another 1,040 miles (1,664 kilometers).

According to biographer Leonard Mosley, "a souvenir hunter snatched Lindbergh's helmet from his head as he clambered out of the cockpit of the *Spirit of St. Louis* and waved it at the crowd. He was immediately identified by the frenetically happy mob as the flier and borne away on their shoulders." Two French aviators and the Belgian World War I ace Baron Willy Coppens spirited Lindbergh into the hangar, where the *Spirit,* torn and battered by the crowd, was pushed to safety.

After telling the men his worries over lack of a French visa, Charles offered Coppens a crumpled scrap of paper and asked, "Do you know this Paris hotel? I understand it's quite reasonable." That was Charles Lindbergh's last touch with the anonymity that he had assumed would always remain a part of his life.

Because of Lindbergh's courage and stamina, the *Spirit of St. Louis,* a relatively simple airplane, had captured the world's imagination. Technically, its reliable Wright Aeronautical Corporation J-5C Whirlwind engine and Pioneer Earth-inductor compass were responsible for proving that the American and European mainlands could be linked by aviation.

Lindbergh went on to pioneer future airlines' great-circle routes from New York to Japan, via the Arctic Circle, and he worked with Pan American Airways on its first global operations, opening the way for the reality of mass air transport. He had given the world faith in flying. Things would never be the same.

Charles Lindbergh summed up his aspirations with these words: Science, freedom, beauty, adventure: What more could you ask of life? While others of his generation merely dreamed, he made his own luck, achieving his aims by harnessing the power of the future: the great surge of popular interest, as well as military and economic advantage, accruing to those nations that developed efficient aircraft and airlines. Beyond a doubt, the "Lone Eagle" stood apart from the crowd, possibly because of a flood of publicity that robbed his life of privacy. The famous flier was also a great writer; he and his wife, Anne Morrow Lindbergh, inspired many readers.

AIR TRANSPORT FOR ALL

For aircraft designers, the Boeing Monomail of 1930 was the stuff of dreams. Constructed entirely of metal, it featured aluminum girders built up of trusses in wing ribs and spars, to which a stressed skin was riveted. Light in weight, this wing needed no support from external struts or wires. To reduce friction in the air, the wheels retracted into the wing, and an anti-drag cowling around the engine helped boost fuel efficiency. The single wing, underslung and fared smoothly into the fuselage, cleaned up the ship's silhouette. Though streamlined, the Monomail cruised along at just 140 miles (225 kilometers) per hour: engine and propeller technology had yet to catch up with this airframe.

I n spite of the remarkable accomplishments of NC-4, the T-2, and the Douglas World Cruisers in the early 1920s, the general public remained suspicious of the airplane as a form of mass transportation. People preferred railroads for travel within the United States, and Henry Ford's reliable automobiles were popular, too.

The first airlines had been established a few years before the outbreak of World War I. By the early 1920s, governments and entrepreneurs in many European countries and in Latin America had begun creating national and even international air routes, while the United States lagged behind.

Civil aviation in America centered around carrying the mail, mainly in such war-surplus aircraft as the de Havilland DH-4 and a few new single-engine models built by small companies that were trying to break into the airmail market. Transport aviation received a major boost in 1925, when the Kelly Act, supported by the U.S. Post Office, opened the carriage of airmail to private contractors. The first person to initiate operations on two of the eight contract-airmail routes granted by the U. S. Post Office was none other than Henry Ford, whose interest in aviation had been kindled during his backing of Glenn Curtiss in Curtiss's patent fight with the Wright brothers. An audacious letter from William B. "Jackknife" Stout in 1923 rekindled Ford's interest.

A mechanical engineer by trade, Stout had a passion for aircraft design, and was a capable pilot as well. After founding and editing *Aerial Age*, one of the first aviation magazines, he worked in engineering for Packard. During World War I, he served as a technical consultant for the Aircraft Production Board while heading up invention studies for the Army at McCook Field.

Stout's letter to Henry Ford was one of 100 he mailed to Detroit industrialists, asking each for

$1,000 to help him devise and build a new kind of airplane. He brashly concluded each letter with the admonishment that no one should count on seeing his money again. Perhaps attracted by the rather brazen tone of Stout's request, and inspired as well by a thirst for invention and a strong faith in inventors, some 20 investors, including Edsel and Henry Ford, responded to the engineer's offer.

In the end, the airplane that resulted from these investments, the three-place Stout Air Sedan, underpowered with its Curtiss OX-5 engine, could barely fly, but it did feature two advanced concepts: all-metal construction and a cantilever wing with internal but no external bracing. Hugo Junkers had been building such airplanes in Germany since 1915, and Anthony Fokker, of Holland, also had adopted strut-less, cantilever wings in his designs,

but American engineers generally had ignored these innovations.

So, despite its poor performance, the Stout Air Sedan exhibited enough design promise to convince the Fords of Stout's ability, and the Ford Motor Company subsequently supplied a factory building, an airfield, and financial backing for the Stout Metal Plane Company. In 1924, the company built two Model 2-AT (Air Transport) all-metal, eight-passenger aircraft with single, 400-horsepower Liberty engines and with wings designed by George Prudden. Both 2-ATs were tested, and, on April 3, 1925, inaugurated Ford's airline, which carried air freight—principally Ford auto parts—between Detroit and Chicago. Two more 2-ATs went into service in February 1926 when the Ford airline began carrying the mail between Detroit and Cleveland.

Eventually, 11 2-ATs were built, but most were supplied after Ford bought the company from Stout in July 1925—at which time, incidentally, the original 20 investors received twice the amount of their original investment.

The appearance of the Ford Motor Company's logo on the sides of airplanes had a psychological effect on the public that is difficult to overestimate. Ford's genius and the cars he pioneered already had profoundly influenced the development of 20th-century America. Many people believed almost religiously in Ford, in his ingenuity, and in his automobiles, and the public's faith and trust in the automobile magnate now was transferred to airplanes and aviation. Bill Stout was later to say that his greatest contribution to aviation was interesting Henry Ford in aircraft production and mass transportation by air.

In early 1926, at Ford's direction, Stout and his engineering team re-designed the 2-AT and built the first Ford Tri-motor, or the Model 3-AT, with three of the new Wright Whirlwind radial engines. But, as had happened with the Air Sedan, the first Tri-Motor model was a disappointment in both performance and looks. Its failure so angered Ford that he fired Stout as chief engineer of the new aircraft company and replaced him with Harold Hicks. When the small factory burned to the ground, taking the 3-AT with it, Ford started afresh, ordering a new plant and a new design by Hicks and Tom Towle. The new Ford Tri-motor, the 4-AT, flew on June 11, 1926, and soon was followed by a larger, heavier model, the 4-AT-B.

Ford's airplanes, as well as the trimotor aircraft built by Anthony Fokker and already on the market, paved the way for passenger air transport, although at first few owners profited from running an airline solely for passengers. Airmail routes, bolstered by their government subsidies, proved to be the necessary foundation for the American airline industry.

With the wave of national euphoria over Lindbergh's flight to Paris, however, the public at last began to pay serious attention to flying. The Ford name fit right into this turn of events, and further enhanced the public's growing trust. The seventh Ford Tri-motor was flown to Los Angeles in June

1927 to go into service with Maddux Air Lines, and many more followed. In October 1930, Maddux merged with Transcontinental Air Transport to create Transcontinental and Western Air, Inc., the first version of Trans World Airlines (TWA), which emerged to compete with the other large new conglomerates, United Air Lines and American Airways.

In the summer of 1928, Ford came out with a larger version of the Tri-Motor, the 5-AT, which was built with Pratt & Whitney Wasp 420-horsepower engines and an enclosed cockpit and led to the even roomier 5-AT-D, which appeared in 1931. America's first all-metal airliner was now firmly entrenched, with a support infrastructure that mirrored Henry Ford's systematic approach to manufacturing and business operations. Ford also built

"Flying washboards," such as the Ford Tri-motor, opposite, were never-wear-out planes built like bridges and covered with corrugated aluminum. Germans were first to produce metal aircraft, but it took American auto manufacturer Henry Ford to weld such ships into the modern airline corporation. Above, second from right, Ford talks with the pilot of a single-engine Stout 2-AT Air Sedan, ancestor of the Ford Tri-motor.

the first concrete runways in America, erected the first control tower and passenger terminal and hotel, and developed better air-to-ground radio communications and an airway radio-beacon system. He invested in advertisements that touted air travel in leading magazines, and at least indirectly encouraged other investors to invest in aviation. At long last, the American airline industry had fledged; it was still behind Europe's older, more seasoned airlines, but it was catching up rapidly.

Biplanes like the Pitcairn Mailwing (far right) were superseded by big monoplanes, such as the Ford Tri-motor (foreground). The Northrop Alpha of 1930 (second from right), designed by John K. Northrop, first incorporated the stressed-skin multicellular metal wing with a modern, monoplane layout. In 1933, the Boeing 247 (bottom) ruled the skies, then yielded to the DC-3 (center).

One of the Ford industry's more far-reaching programs, and one that significantly affected aviation safety, was its pilot-training school. In January 1929, a Ford announcement proclaimed: "Purchasers of planes are welcome to send their own men to our school for this special training, if they meet the requirements. But we must ask them to consider our decision of their fitness final. So important do we regard this provision that we reserve the right to decline to deliver a Ford plane unless the pilot who will fly it meets with the final approval of the officials of our training school."

In terms of its airplanes, Ford's Tri-motor, when compared to the wire-and-wood, open-cockpit aircraft still common at the time, even looked like it was built like a bridge. Its bracing and trusses resembled those of advanced cantilever structures of steel and concrete, but they were built out of light Alclad aluminum alloy, with corrugated metal skin. The aircraft soon was nicknamed the "Tin Goose." The public's faith in Ford's metal airplane was underscored in March 1931 when Notre Dame's famous football coach, Knute Rockne, was killed in the crash of a wood-and-plywood Fokker F-10 trimotor airliner. Although the cause of the accident was never officially determined, the Bureau of Air Commerce suspected that rot in the plywood of the wings had caused them to delaminate and fail. The publicity that attended the Rockne crash forced wooden airliners out of business almost overnight, leaving the all-metal Ford aircraft to reign supreme for several years.

While Ford's pilot-training school improved safety by wide margins, flying the Tri-motor remained for most pilots a pioneering event, as so few heavy transports were then in existence. Compared to later airliners, the Ford was slow, noisy, and uncomfortable, but it did represent a distinct improvement over its predecessors. Designed to maintain altitude on one engine, it also was inherently stable because of its very large, thick wing. Although the controls were stiff, they were more effective than those of earlier, similarly sized, fabric-and-wood machines. The only serious problem with the Tri-motor arose when an engine failed on takeoff. Without controllable-pitch or "feathering" propellers, a dead engine and its windmilling prop created an immense amount of drag, often leading to a stall and spin, and several fatal crashes were attributed to this cause. Still, most pilots prized the breakthroughs the Ford Tri-motor had pioneered for aviation, and accepted the airplane's risks.

For many pilots hired from companies servicing the airmail routes, flying the Ford was their first opportunity to work in an enclosed cockpit. It must have seemed an incredible luxury: no rain, snow, or sleet to wipe off their goggles, and no howling wind and engine noise. The pilot actually could get up out of his seat and walk back into the cabin while the copilot flew for a while. For these pilots, multiengine safety was a confidence builder, especially when flying over mountains or large expanses of water. And, with the improved controls, a pilot could make small corrections with a single hand, instead of having to wrestle with the wheel two-handed.

The Tri-motor's weight and stability made landings and takeoffs seem effortless, as the aircraft almost glided into and floated off the airfield. Hearing of these new marvels, pilots increasingly began to consider flying for the airlines instead of for flying circuses and airmail companies. The public's image of pilots as daredevils who blithely risked their lives evolved to that of calm, unflappable professionals in snappy uniforms who were keenly aware of their responsibility for the lives of those flying with them.

While the Ford Tri-motor continued to set the standard for airliner comfort and safety, however, many aircraft designers, not entirely satisfied with the aircraft's virtues, scanned for new technology in aviation's many fields to further improve the breed. At Lockheed, for example, John K. "Jack"

Northrop was designing efficient, well-streamlined, internally braced, wood-and-plywood aircraft such as the single-engine Vega, and he came to appreciate that metal structures would be aviation's next frontier. Departing Lockheed to form his own company, he soon produced the Northrop Alpha, a smooth, all-metal, single-engine, four-passenger aircraft that foreshadowed the shape and structure of the modern airliner.

Tested in the California Institute of Technology's Guggenheim Aeronautical Laboratory wind tunnel with the assistance of aerodynamics giant Theodore von Kármán, the Alpha featured a beautifully faired wing-fuselage joint, or fillet, and an advanced NACA cowl that dramatically reduced drag around the engine. The internal structure of its wings and fuselage was composed entirely of aluminum sheet metal, which was folded and riveted into strength-giving shapes and covered with a smooth aluminum "stressed skin" that bound all parts together into an incredibly strong, single unit. Both TWA and National Air Transport (NAT) airlines purchased the sleek new ship for their routes, but passenger-seating capacity—which in the Alpha was only four—remained a hindrance that limited even the advanced single-engine types. An increase in airline capacity, as well as in aircraft size, safety, and passenger trust, clearly would depend on the use of multiple engines.

Although Boeing Aircraft followed the same single-engine pattern as Northrop with its advanced,

Flying in the Ford Tri-motor made thousands of Americans "air-minded." Most important of all, the experience inspired confidence, backed as it was by the maker of the reliable Ford automobiles and by pilots who had been qualified in Ford flight schools. Though fear of flying was far from banished, air travel at last was seen as a practical and survivable adventure, especially after the personal greetings and assurances of captain and crew during routine flights.

retractable-landing-gear Monomail, in August 1931 company president Philip Johnson asked his department heads for recommendations on future production. Assistant sales manager Fred Collins, fresh from a five-month stint as a line copilot with Boeing Air Transport, during which he flew Boeing 80 trimotor biplanes, submitted a 16-page report. In it, he recommended a twin-engine, retractable-landing-gear, all-metal transport that was based to some degree on the company's Army Air Corps B-9 bomber. Responding to the call, chief designer Claire Egtvedt and his team created the Model 247, the world's first modern airliner, designed to carry 10 passengers and thus increase revenues. The engineers at first planned a 16,000-pound (7,258-kilogram) airplane, but, when pilots warned that such a craft would be too heavy to land at smaller airports, they scaled the design down to 12,000 pounds (5,443 kilograms), a decision the company later would regret.

Several months before the prototype was completed, Johnson, Collins, and sales manager Erik Nelson took their "paper" airplane to United Air Lines president Frederick Rentschler. With the

The Boeing 247 and 247D, deployed in a fleet by a group of companies that became United Airlines, made all other air-transport services obsolete. Called the first modern airliner, the 247 flew at more than 170 miles (270 kilometers) per hour, as compared to the Ford's 115. New standards of comfort were also a revelation to travelers of the mid-1930s. At right, Colonel Roscoe Turner stands in front of the famed Boeing ship he raced from London to Melbourne, Australia, in 1934. Today it resides in the National Air and Space Museum.

boldness that characterized his vision for the airline industry, Rentschler ordered 60 Model 247s at a total cost of $3.5 million, a huge sum for the time.

Production got underway in the summer of 1932. On February 8, 1933, the 247, powered by two 525-horsepower Pratt & Whitney Wasp engines, made its first successful flight, entering service with United on March 30, an incredible accomplishment. By the end of June, 30 of the 247s were flying Unit-

prove takeoffs, but these changes resulted in a less efficient cruise performance. Operators could choose one propeller setting or the other, but not both at the same time.

Caldwell engineered further changes in aviation when he showed Boeing and United his drawings for a variable-pitch propeller that would allow the pilot to change the pitch in flight, thus improving the aircraft's performance at both ends of the spectrum. The new propellers were rushed through testing and onto the new 247D models with spectacular results: they yielded a 20-percent reduction in the average takeoff run, a 22-percent increase in the rate of climb, a 5.5-percent boost in cruising speed, and a single-engine-ceiling improvement from 2,000 to 4,000 feet (610 to 1,220 meters). All of the older 247s soon were modified with the new propellers to bring them up to 247D standards.

The speed and comfort of the 247 was a revelation to the traveling public. Cross-country times were slashed by its cruise speed of 160 miles per hour (256 kilometers per hour), as compared to the previous speeds of 110 to 120 miles (176 to 192 kilometers) per hour. The cabin actually was heated, and the traveler sat in plush, upholstered seats with individual reading lamps, noise insulation, and a pleasant interior design. Pilots enjoyed a modern cockpit with the latest in technology from the Pioneer Instrument Company, the same company that had provided Charles Lindbergh with his Earth-inductor compass. A Sperry artificial horizon, a breakthrough in blind flying, enabled pilots to fly in rain, fog, and clouds with some measure of confidence. And the pilot's seat now was adjustable, which reduced fatigue considerably.

Other airlines envied what the new aircraft had to offer. TWA's vice president of operations, Jack Frye, tried to place an order after the first 20 Boeings had been delivered to United, but was turned down flat. Corporately locked into Boeing, United wasn't about to help a competitor. With the assistance of Charles Lindbergh, however, Frye drafted a letter on August 2, 1932, that would be sent to five aircraft manufacturers: Curtiss-Wright, Ford, Martin, Consolidated, and Douglas. In it, he outlined TWA's requirements for a modern airliner: all-metal structure, three engines, 12-passenger ca-

ed routes, and, on July 11, a United 247 made a record, seven-stop, coast-to-coast flight of 20 hours, 30 minutes, handily beating a TWA Ford Tri-motor's time of 26 hours, 45 minutes. The Boeing airliner had catapulted United into undisputed leadership in the airline industry, bringing the company record ticket sales that July.

In spite of its excellent speed, however, the 247 was unable to operate at full gross weight from high-altitude airfields in the Rocky Mountains. Frank Caldwell, chief propeller designer for Hamilton-Standard, the propeller manufacturer under United's large corporate umbrella, recommended adjustments to the 247's fixed-pitch props to im-

Honored instrument maker Elmer Sperry, Jr., teamed up with Boeing and United on the Boeing 247's instruments. His gyroscope-stabilized navigational aids added to airline safety. Many such scientific advances lay just beyond the horizon. They arrived too late, however, to guarantee the 247's monopoly as a speed merchant.

pacity, a high degree of passenger comfort, a cruising speed of 146 miles per hour (234 kilometers per hour), the latest navigational instrumentation, a 1,200-foot-per-minute (366-meter-per-minute) rate of climb to a 21,000-foot (6,405-meter) ceiling, 1,000-mile-plus (1,600-kilometer) range, and 14,200-pound (6,441-kilogram) gross weight.

As airline historian R.E.G. Davies wrote in *Airlines of the United States Since 1914* (Putnam/Smithsonian Institution Press), the ensuing tale "reads almost like a fairy story. Donald Douglas gathered together his team of engineers and designers, decided to enter the competition, and within five days, two of his key men, Arthur Raymond and Harry Wetzel, were on a Santa Fe train bound for New York, where an appointment had been fixed with Frye, and with Richard Robbins, TWA's president,

and technical advisor Charles Lindbergh. From Douglas, Raymond was assistant to James 'Dutch' Kindelberger and Wetzel was vice-president and general manager. . . .

"After three weeks' wrangling, during which time Douglas successfully pleaded its case for two engines, Lindbergh made the toughest request: that the new aircraft should be able to take off on one engine with full payload from any of TWA's aerodromes, and that it should be able to maintain lev-

The cockpit of the Douglas DC-2 airliner appears above, along with a factory test of the DC-1's tail surfaces, weighted with sandbags. Relentless testing was required to make hundreds of advanced features and functions work as one.

el flight on one engine over the highest mountains along the route. Accepting this stringent demand, Douglas got the order. On 20 September, 1932, the contract was signed for the DC-1—Douglas Commercial Number One—at an agreed price of $125,000."

Although both the DC-1 and the Boeing 247 were advanced transports, the Douglas product changed evolution in the aeronautics industry to revolution, thanks primarily to Jack Northrop's multicellular wing structure (which Douglas had gained access to when it bought Northrop's company in 1932), slick aerodynamics from W. Bailey Oswald at the California Institute of Technology, and numerous other technical advances.

The DC-1's first flight, on July 1, 1933, was a heart stopper. As test pilot Carl Cover lifted off out of Santa Monica, westbound toward the Pacific, one engine quit and the other started to run rough. Easing the nose over, Cover found he could make the engines pick up, but with the slightest back pressure on the controls to climb, the engines started to quit again. Thinking fast, he reduced power and landed in a clearing off the end of the runway, just short of the ocean. Almost the entire Douglas plant was out to watch this momentous occasion, and they were horrified as they witnessed what at first appeared to be an inaugural-flight crash.

It turned out that the carburetors had been mounted backwards, so that every time the aircraft entered a climb, the fuel flow was cut off. After turning the carburetors around, the engineers found that the airplane ran like a dream, and Cover's third attempt went flawlessly. With a bit more input from Frye, Lindbergh, and the Douglas team, the single DC-1 ended up as a demonstrator for the modified production version, the DC-2, which flew on May 11, 1934. With the DC-2, the company had a spectacular winner. Deliveries to TWA began the following December.

One week after the aircraft's arrival, TWA opened scheduled DC-2 service on the Columbus-Pittsburgh-Newark run, and, in one more week, began to fly from Newark to Chicago. In just eight days, the Douglases broke the speed record on the latter route four times; by September, TWA retired its Ford Tri-motors. United Airlines soon discovered that its 247s could not compete with the TWA Douglases. Meanwhile, DC-2s started to enter TWA's fleet in numbers, and other airlines wasted little time in buying the new airliner. Trying to hang on with its modified 247Ds, United finally gave up and began retiring its Boeings in favor of the 14-passenger Douglas transports.

Douglas estimated that total development costs for the DC-2 were $307,000. With the first 25 aircraft off the assembly line, the company's net loss amounted to $266,000. The airliner turned out to be the wisest investment Douglas ever made: the company entered the black after the 76th airframe and stayed there for 34 years.

Although a new era in air transport had begun, these modern aircraft still had to earn their wings through some of the worst weather imaginable. Since there was no pressurization or oxygen for the passengers, pilots had to fly below 15,000 feet (4,575 meters); flying "above the weather" at that time was, to a large extent, a myth. The effects of the weather, particularly when flying across some of the American mountain ranges, were sometimes horrifying both for pilots and passengers.

Charlie Myers, who had picked up Eastern Air Transport's first DC-2, learned in short order that the airplane, although an excellent machine, was not a always a miracle worker, even during a standard run. "When I left Atlanta for Newark it was clear. Then, all of a sudden, we were in [bad weather]. We began picking up ice at 5,000 and bang, we were at 13,000! Then, bang, and I was back to 7,000. The next blow sent us back up to 10,000. The engines were loading up [while the DC-2 was] loading down with ice and losing altitude. I got just past the extreme turbulence where it smoothed a little bit, and one engine was sputtering and about to quit. I had a fellow with me, Hank Frieze, an old barnstorming pilot. We couldn't get the ice out of the engines with carburetor heat, and I asked Hank if he remembered what we used to do with the early Wasps when we had ice. See, those engines didn't have heaters on them.

"'You used to lean them out, didn't you?' he replied.

"'Well, what are you waiting for?' I asked. 'Lean 'em out 'till they cry!'

"And he did. He pulled out the mixture control 'till the skipping engine backfired and blew out the ice. Of course, you could blow your carburetor off, too; but we couldn't have been any worse off. I know the passengers were shook up, but I was doing the only thing I could do and didn't have time to explain. The first engine was running again, then the other one started spitting, so I told Hank to blow-out that one. We must have done it a half-a-dozen times.

"I thought we could make Nashville; I had passed Chattanooga because of the weather. I knew the ceilings were down—some of the radio reports said that. The American [Airlines] pilots [on the same run in their DC-2] had gotten down so low they were below some of the hills and had to wiggle out. They did, and were headed back to Nashville. I made a pass and got down below minimums—our minimums were a lot lower than theirs—and I radioed in and said I had to by-pass Nashville.

"The American plane heard me and asked Nashville who we were. Nashville told them we were Eastern, and the American pilot replied, 'If that Eastern pilot can't make it, it's not for us,' and headed for Cincinnati, his other alternate. He was low on gas and didn't know whether he could make it or not. I had plenty of gas, but didn't see a thing 'till I got near Indianapolis. I landed there with a terrific load of ice. My lights were covered over, wings and windshield. I had to bust a side window out so I could see and try to land that thing. We

were on the ground like a ton of bricks; good thing that's a big airport."

Such weather-related troubles aside, American was pleased with its new DC-2s. However, one of the airline's chief attractions had been the overnight luxury-sleeper service it had offered with its twin-engine Curtiss Condor biplanes. Passengers liked the idea of getting aboard an airplane with sleeping berths similar to those on trains and snoozing through a night flight. In the summer of 1935, after a discussion with the airline's chief engineer, Bill Littlewood, American president C.R. Smith called Donald Douglas and asked him if he could modify the DC-2 into a "larger, more comfortable plane which could lure the luxury trade" with sleeping berths.

Douglas, with more work than he could handle in building DC-2s, didn't want to interrupt the production line, but, when Smith agreed to buy 10 of the new aircraft, Douglas said he would give it a go. With its relatively comfortable but slow and outdated Condors, American was losing a great deal of money trying to compete against the much faster, quieter 247s and DC-2s, but Smith was able to convince the U.S. Government Reconstruction Finance Corporation to loan the airline $4,500,000 to purchase the new Douglas sleeper aircraft.

The Douglas Sleeper Transport (DST) project was spearheaded by Fred Stineman, with American chief engineer Littlewood on hand at the fac-

Perhaps as many as 1,000 DC-3s still fly in the 1990s, as opposite. A few will probably carry on to celebrate the centennial of the venerable ship's first flight. The DC-3 started out in 1936 as a DC-2 expanded to accommodate passengers Pullman-style, opposite bottom. Without berths, regular day seating accommodated 21 people. Above, from such production lines in the United States more than 10,000 commercial and military versions of the DC-3 emerged, and many of the same design were assembled abroad. Right, J.H. "Dutch" Kindelberger, the chief engineer at Douglas, stands with Carl Cover, test pilot for the DC-1, -2, and -3 series.

tory for most of the plane's development. The airliner's initial layout featured seven upper and seven lower berths, inspired by the design of the Pullman Company's train cars, with a separate private cabin up front for honeymooning couples. To make the DC-3, Douglas widened the DC-2's fuselage to provide room for the berths, and used the DC-2's nose, landing gear, and wings with longer wing tips—pushing the wingspan from 85 (26 meters) to 95 feet (29 meters)—to handle the increased gross weight of 25,000 pounds (11,340 kilograms). The length of the aircraft increased from 62 to 65.5 feet (19 to 20 meters), and the more powerful Wright R-1820 Cyclone or Pratt & Whitney R-1830 Wasp engines provided a cruising speed of 180 miles per hour (288 kilometers per hour) and a useful load of 9,000 pounds (4,082 kilograms).

The new aircraft was test-flown on December 17, 1935. Smith's vision of the airplane's potential inspired him to ask Douglas to build a daytime version as well, so the original order was increased to 20 aircraft—eight DSTs and 12 airplanes of a 21-passenger version with an extra row of seats in the wider cabin. This latter model subsequently was designated the DC-3.

The resulting aircraft represented a critical turning point in airline history. Not only did the DC-3 boost passenger payload by 50 percent, but the increase in operating cost over that of the DC-2 was a paltry three percent. American Airlines initiated DST nonstop service from New York to Chicago on June 25, 1936, and then received its first DC-3 on August 18. Its new DST Skysleeper service from coast to coast took 16 hours eastbound, and 17 hours, 45 minutes westbound, with no changing of airplanes during the refueling stops. The DC-3s were put to work on the New York-to-Chicago and New York-to-Boston routes.

In 1937, Smith summed up what the DC-3 had done not only for his airline, but for the industry as a whole. "The DC-3 freed the airlines from complete dependence upon government mail pay. It was the first airplane in the world that could make

The cantilever wing of the Smithsonian's DC-3 wraps smoothly around the floor of its roomy fuselage. Refined from the Northrop Alpha's wing, it possessed amazing strength and was virtually "fail safe."

money just by hauling passengers." He was right. The airline industry, including United, which inadvertently had started the process, flocked to Douglas in request of DC-3s. Shortly after the DC-3 entered scheduled service, United president W. A. Patterson was forced to admit that his Boeing 247s were being outclassed, and were losing money as fast as the larger, more efficient DC-3s were making it. United bought a new fleet of Douglas airliners, the first going into service on June 30, 1937, and soon was out of the red.

For almost every major airline now converting to the new airplane, the only limiting factor seemed to be the production rate at Douglas's Santa Monica, California, plant. By 1938, 95 percent of all U.S. commercial-airline traffic was carried on DC-3s; the next year, as foreign airlines continued to buy them, DC-3s plied 90 percent of the world's airline routes.

So ideal were the aircraft's basic specifications that throughout its long production run they were never changed. In July 1936, President Franklin D. Roosevelt presented Donald Douglas with the Collier Trophy, thus honoring the DC-3 as the "outstanding twin-engine commercial transport plane."

From the first, DST's standard equipment included the new Sperry Gyroscope Company automatic pilot, an invaluable aid that lowered fatigue and made long-distance, bad-weather flying tolerable. Design engineers also had installed in the cockpit panel two sets of instruments for pilot and copilot that provided an effective back-up in case of failure, and that enabled pilots to spell each other without having

to strain across the cockpit to see each other's instruments.

Pilots found the DC-3 to be almost a dream, far easier to handle and more stable than the seemingly similar DC-2. They even swore that it "talked" to them as they handled it, and, indeed, the controls did seem to initiate a dialogue, linking pilot and machine as one. Landings and takeoffs were basically free of problems, and, even if one engine quit, Charles Lindbergh's initial insistence that the DC-1 be capable of climbing out on the remaining engine had been carried through to the DC-3.

With practice and experience, pilots could make cushion-soft landings, free of drastic swerves and bounces, which increased passengers' confidence in flying. This in turn enhanced the friendly, luxurious, in-flight club-lounge atmosphere, which featured such amenities as electric razors, good heating and cooling, and meals served on tables with fine silverware, china, and linens. Neither passengers nor pilots need be pioneers any longer; the fruits of more than three decades of aviation development were sweet indeed. Modern airline flying as it is known today began with the DC-3. The world had entered the air age.

A hint of the internal wing construction of the DC-3 appears above. This historic ship, towed through Washington, D.C.'s streets in the dead of night, is bound for its new home at the National Air and Space Museum. The outer wing of the aircraft could be quickly and easily removed for repair or replacement. Donald Douglas, whose company developed the DC series of aircraft, arrives at the Newark, New Jersey, airport in July 1936, only days after the DC-3's debut. The bottom line: the DC-3 flew faster, cheaper, and more safely than any other transport, and made airlines profitable with passenger traffic alone. Previously, government airmail contracts had kept the airlines in business.

Aviation's infancy was nursed on speed. Once freed from the bounds of Earth, people had the potential to propel themselves at speeds that previously had been only the stuff of dreams. In 1909, Glenn Curtiss won the first Gordon Bennett Cup air race, and soon thereafter the new sport of air racing—driven by the spirit of competition and the urge to fly faster, farther, and higher—established itself. Nowhere was the fervor for racing more pronounced than in Europe.

During a meeting of the Aero Club of France in December 1912, the organization's president relayed a message that would have profound effects on aviation technology: "Monsieur Jacques Schneider, head of the great French armaments firm, has advised the aero club that he intends to donate a trophy for a speed race for seaplanes." Schneider then revealed the silver trophy itself, a sculpture of the sensual, winged-female Spirit of Flight, depicted in the act of kissing one of Neptune's sons as he lay on the crest of a wave. Racing pilots came to call the Schneider trophy the "flying flirt."

Racing remained popular up until the beginning of World War I. Although the war advanced aviation technology significantly, the strongly pacifist

sentiment of the postwar era slowed the pace of military innovations. Air racing soon came back into favor, however, and governments that had had trouble raising money for military research funded racing teams to uphold national honor.

As a result, much of the development of fighter planes in the 1920s and '30s was done under the guise of winning races. In his book *Farther and Faster* (Smithsonian Institution Press, 1991), historian Terry Gwynn-Jones stated that "high-speed, closed-circuit competition brought about radical changes in airframe and engine design that saw the airplane progress from wood and fabric biplanes to streamlined, all-metal monoplanes, machines that would triple the world speed record to more than 440 miles per hour."

With seaplanes racing in the Schneider, competition for other aircraft received a shot in the arm in 1920 when American newspaperman Ralph Pulitzer and his two brothers—all three the sons of Joseph Pulitzer, who had established the distinguished awards for literature and journalism—funded a trophy. By the mid-1920s, both races, the Schneider and the Pulitzer, lay firmly at the cutting edge of aviation.

Charles Hubbell's official program cover, left, portrays the thrill of speed, a primary focus of American aviation during the 1920s and '30s. The image of a checkered pylon with one or more airplanes swooping

GOLDEN AIR FRONTIERS

around it captured the spirit of the National Air Races, which tested both pilot and machine. In the 1923 National Air Races outside St. Louis, Lieutenant Alford "Al" Williams, right, flew his Navy Curtiss racer at an average speed of 243.6 miles per hour (392 kilometers per hour) to set new 100- and 200-kilometer closed-circuit world records.

In the United States at the time, the Dayton-Wright, Verville-Sperry, and Curtiss racing designs were the most advanced. Through trial-and-error flight testing, with its inevitable fatalities, speeds increased steadily as designs became more sophisticated. During the years between the wars, many builders chose the "engines-with-wings" approach, which called for brute power with little aerodynamic refinement. This often resulted in high speed at the expense of both effective handling and acceptable landing speeds. It was not unusual, for example, for a pilot to have to battle for an entire race with a shaking, vibrating airplane that was on the verge of coming apart (some did), and then to have to land at nearly 100 miles per hour (161

Lieutenant James H. "Jimmy" Doolittle poses on one of the pontoons of his Curtiss R3C-2, right, after winning the Schneider Cup race for seaplanes at Bay Shore Park, Baltimore, on October 25, 1925. Doolittle went on to set the world's speed record for land planes in 1932 and to earn the Medal of Honor for leading the 1942 "Tokyo Raid" during World War II. His streamlined, black-and-gold Curtiss, above, features engine-cooling radiators built into the wings, and is displayed today in the Pioneers of Flight Gallery at the National Air and Space Museum.

kilometers per hour), a hair-raising landing speed at the time.

In 1921 the Pulitzer rules changed: aircraft now were required to be able to achieve a top speed of at least 140 miles per hour (225 kilometers per hour), and to land at a maximum speed of 75 miles per hour (121 kilometers per hour). This rule eliminated freak racers, and mandated more refined designs from companies that could not hope to compete without government funding. Fortunately, Brigadier General Billy Mitchell was able to convince a skeptical Congress and some rather myopic military leaders that funds allocated for prototype racers would lead directly to new high-speed fighters. History would prove him right.

Glenn Curtiss recognized early on the importance of using racing as a testing ground not only for high speed, but also for the improvement of low-speed performance and of good overall handling. The first results came in the 1921 Pulitzer, when Bert Acosta won first place with one of two Curtiss CRs that had been built with Navy funds. By the time the 1922 Pulitzer was held at Selfridge Field near Detroit, traditional Army-Navy rivalry added considerable spice to the race. Since Curtiss had taken the lead in design, both branches of the armed services were buying racers from his firm.

The Navy bought two CR-2s, which represented refinements of an earlier racer, while the Army

flew two R-6s, which were smaller, more streamlined Curtiss designs with internal wing radiators. The Army placed first and second in the 1922 race, while the Navy came in third and fourth; inter-service rivalry rose to a new level. More importantly, the 225-mile-per-hour (362-kilometer-per-hour)-plus R-6 led to the first Curtiss high-speed fighter, the PW-8.

Meanwhile, the Navy added floats to the CR-1 and CR-2 racers, re-designated them CR-3s, and entered them in the 1923 Schneider Cup race. The results were spectacular: Navy pilots David Rittenhouse and Rutledge Irvine took first and second place, putting America on top in this race for the first time and establishing the Curtiss revolution in advanced design.

Air racing had opened a door to the future, and the breakthroughs of each event were like those of the early space shots some 40 years later. Five-hundred-horsepower V-12 engines roared and snarled through short exhaust stacks, providing a spine-tingling experience for crowds—and pilots. Flying a Schneider or Pulitzer racer shoved pilots out into an unknown realm, one that later would become the domain of the professional test pilot.

Aside from racers, no other type of airplane could average 200-miles-per-hour (322-kilometers-per-hour) lap speeds or pull seven Gs (from the term in physics for a gravitational constant, which increases with acceleration) in a pylon turn, but these specialized machines also were unforgiving of tech-

nical mistakes and malfunctions as well as of human weaknesses. After winning the 1922 Pulitzer at 205.8 miles per hour (331 kilometers per hour) in his R-6, for example, exhausted Army Lieutenant Russell Maughan remarked, "I was stunned more or less at each of the fifteen turns. On the straightaway I came to." He was referring to the blackouts that were caused by the blood's being drawn away from his brain by high G-forces in the turns. In the 1924 Pulitzer, Captain Burt Skeel was killed when the laminated wood prop on his R-6 flew apart and the racer broke up in midair.

Even if nothing went wrong, flying a racer was a demanding job. As speeds went up, the controls stiffened, and pilots often had to use both hands on the stick to exert enough force for effective control. With the massive, in-line engines up front, visibility was poor. A pilot often had to choose between speed or vision; he couldn't have both.

Four days after the 1922 Pulitzer, General Billy Mitchell climbed into a Curtiss R-6 and went after the world's speed record, which had been held by the French since 1909. He broke it handily, clock-

The silver Schneider Trophy, at left, donated in December 1912 by French aviation enthusiast Jacques Schneider "for a speed race for seaplanes," depicts the Spirit of Flight bestowing a kiss upon one of Neptune's sons. Below, workers assemble the Curtiss CR-1 (A6080) and CR-2 (A6081) for the U.S. Navy at the aircraft company's Garden City, New Jersey, plant in 1922.

Lockheed's managers listen intently as designer John K. Northrop, above (left), discusses the blueprints for the company's new airplane, the Vega, in 1927. Gathered in front of a Vega fuselage, from left to right, are Tony Stadlman, Gerald Vultee (in fuselage), Ben Hunter (upper right), Allan Lockheed (far right), and Kenneth Jay. The sleek Vega featured a semi-monocoque, or shell, fuselage structure with internally braced wings.

ing 224.4 miles per hour (361 kilometers per hour).

The next year, the Navy poured its money into beating Army, funding Curtiss to create the R2C-1, which featured a more powerful D-12 engine and an all-metal Reed propeller. After a few test flights, Curtiss knew it had a winner: company test pilot Harold Brow and Navy Lieutenant Alford "Al" Williams pushed it past 240 miles per hour (386 kilometers per hour). They took first and second in the 1923 Pulitzer, with Williams averaging almost 244 miles per hour (393 kilometers per hour) for the win. Having spent its annual budget allotment on bombers and observation aircraft, the Army was forced to compete with the previous year's R-6. But in just one year, Curtiss had pushed technology far ahead, even far enough to win the Schneider Trophy seaplane race as well.

On November 4, Williams set a new world speed record of 263.3 miles per hour (424 kilometers per hour). Brow promptly went up the same day and broke it at 265.69 miles per hour (428 kilometers per hour). The next day, Williams was airborne again, and, pushing the airplane dangerously, reached 266.59 miles per hour (429 kilometers per hour), breaking the record again.

Having spent what it considered to be enough money for the time being, the Navy bowed out of

competition for the next racing season. As a result, the 1924 Pulitzer-winning Verville-Sperry aircraft's top speed was almost 30 miles per hour (48 kilometers per hour) slower, although the airplane's retractable landing gear and monoplane, cantilever wing were visions of things to come.

The services pooled their funds for 1925, with the Navy contributing the most. Together they contracted Curtiss to build its ultimate racer, the R3C, a refinement of the R2C. The new Arthur Nutt-designed Curtiss V-1400 engine generated 560 horsepower within a smooth airframe whose thinner, reinforced wings were capable of sustaining over 12 Gs.

The first R3C rolled out on September 11, and was flown by Al Williams. There were problems from the moment the racer shed its aluminum-wheel fairings. When Lieutenant James H. "Jimmy" Doolittle, the McCook Field Army test pilot assigned to the project, took the aircraft on its first high-speed run, he felt the lateral control change without any input from him. Looking out at the ailerons, he saw the left upper wing starting to buckle under the load. He pulled the throttle back, landed immediately, and the new racer was repaired. On another flight, the propeller spinner split, and half of it crashed back through the prop and into the wing radiators and tail. More repairs.

The last Pulitzer Trophy race was flown on October 12, 1925, at Mitchel Field, Long Island. Since single Navy and Army R3Cs provided the only new competition, a separate heat was organized for the four standard Curtiss fighters, which flew about 75 miles per hour (121 kilometers per hour) slower. Not only were speeds lower; the crowd did not get to see the Army-Navy battle they expected: the Army's R3C-1, with Lieutenant Cyrus Bettis at the controls, won first place at 248.9 miles per hour (401 kilometers per hour); Al Williams brought the Navy R3C in at eight miles an hour (13 kilometers per hour) slower.

The remaining R3Cs were fitted with floats and re-designated R3C-2s for the Schneider Cup, which was set for October 26 at Bay Shore Park, Baltimore. Since the previous year's race had been canceled, expectations were running high for Navy pilots George Cuddihy and Ralph Ofstie, as well as for the Army's Jimmy Doolittle. Unlike most other pilots of the day, Doolittle had an engineer's eye for flying: he capitalized on an aircraft's strong points and minimized the potential effects of its deficiencies.

As the race got underway, it became clear that Doolittle was outflying his competitors by gaining speed around the pylons, where high Gs in the almost 90-degree-bank turns slowed the aircraft down. Doolittle would dive around the pylon, hold a tight, constant-G turn, and then convert his diving speed into level-flight speed on the straightaway, where, even with neutral elevators, the R3C-2 had an inherent tendency to climb. Doolittle won the race at an average speed of 232.57 miles per hour (374 kilometers per hour), while the number-two slot was captured by British test pilot Hubert Broad in a Gloster III-A at 199.17 miles per hour (321 kilometers per hour). The next day, Doolittle set a world float-plane speed record of 245.713 miles per hour (395 kilometers per hour).

Although the first half of the 1920s had borne much fruit in racing research, military spending for such aircraft dwindled later in the decade. The Pulitzer race for 1926 was canceled. The Navy tried to develop modified R3C-3s and R3C-4s, with more powerful Packard and Curtiss engines, for the 1926 Schneider Cup, but the aircraft never made it past the testing stage. The day of these elegant biplane racers was over, and the era of the monocoque monoplane was about to begin.

When Jack Northrop designed the Vega monoplane for Lockheed, he wanted to create an advanced aircraft that not only could break records but could offer a superior means of transportation. Though the sleek Vega was made of wood, its strong monocoque fuselage and efficient cantilever, monoplane wing made it a very popular airplane for record flying from 1928 until the mid-1930s.

The greatest of the Vega pilots was an eighth-grade dropout and former oil-field roughneck named Wiley Post, whose unique combination of flying skill, romantic appeal, and brilliant self-taught engineering would result in his producing a number of aviation breakthroughs. In the short span of five years, he conducted human-factor research on the relationship of biological rhythms to pilot proficiency and fatigue; pioneered high-altitude research flying; flew around the world twice, once solo; invented and tested the first full-pressure suit, the forerunner of the space suit; and discovered the jet streams. No other human being was more instrumental in bridging the gap between the romantic, open-cockpit era and that of calculated, scientific flying.

Overcome with an early yearning to fly, Post became a barnstorming parachutist and received some flight instruction along the way while working in the oil fields. After soloing a Canuck, as the Canadian-built Jenny was called, in 1926, he seemed headed for a new career when a serious injury oc-

One of the great prizes of the National Air Races, the Bendix Trophy was established in 1931 by American inventor and industrialist Vincent Bendix for winners of the Bendix Transcontintental Air Race.

curred that threatened his bright future: a metal chip, thrown from a defective bolt during an oil-rigging job, entered his left eye, which became infected and had to be removed. For most 28-year-olds, this would have meant an end to flying, but, while recuperating, Post taught himself to judge distances using only one eye.

Using $200 from the $1,698.25 he received from workman's compensation to buy a damaged Canuck, Post repaired the plane, offered flight instruction and passenger hops, and then started barnstorming with a friend who owned another Canuck. In 1927, he met 17-year-old Mae Laine, and they eloped. Married life became particularly tough when Post wrecked the Canuck and couldn't afford to have it repaired.

Fortune intervened in 1928 when Wiley, in the process of hunting for a job, met Powell Briscoe and F.C. Hall, oil-business partners who were looking for a plane and pilot that together would enable them to beat the competition to potential drilling sites. The fact that Post had only one eye didn't seem to affect the oilmen in the least, and soon Wiley was flying a three-place Travel Air biplane across the Midwest. The small company prospered from this early application of business flying, and late that same year Hall bought a new, streamlined Lockheed Vega with a comfortable, enclosed cockpit and a spacious cabin. Hall named the airplane *Winnie Mae*, after his daughter.

Unfortunately, the stock-market crash of 1929 forced Briscoe and Hall to sell the speedster, and Post once again found himself out of work. When he returned *Winnie Mae* to Lockheed, however, he landed a job with the company as a salesman and test pilot. His exposure both to a talented aircraft-design team and to methodical test flying was invaluable, and it opened his mind to aviation's future possibilities, including those that might result from Jimmy Doolittle's blind-flying experiments with gyroscopically stabilized instruments.

In June 1930, Hall asked Post to come back to the company; this time Post brought with him an improved Vega 5C with a 420-horsepower Wasp engine, christened as the second *Winnie Mae* and painted all white with blue trim. The newer, faster

Artist John Batchelor's cut-away view of Lockheed's Vega 5C Winnie Mae *reveals its spruce-veneer-plywood semi-monocoque fuselage, its centrally located gas tanks, and its internally braced wing design. In June 1931, accompanied by Australian navigator Harold Gatty, American aviator Wiley Post piloted* Winnie Mae *to its first around-the-world record, circumnavigating the globe in 8 days, 15 hours, and 51 minutes.*

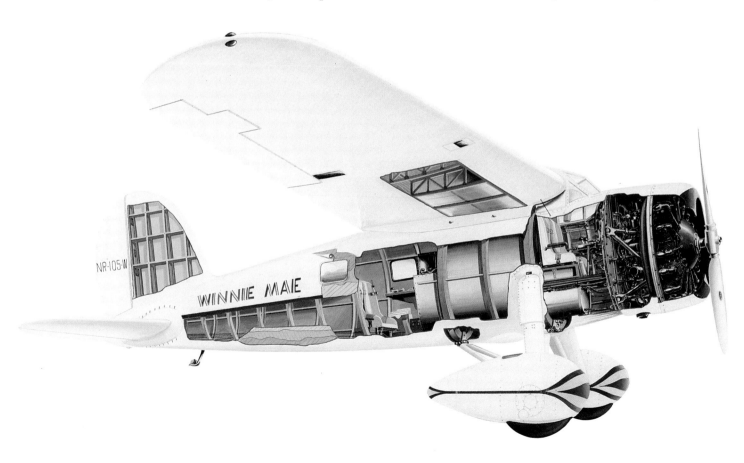

Lockheed gave Post a taste for big-time aviation. Although he had been flying for only three years, he had amassed quite a lot of experience. With typical boldness, Wiley asked Hall if he could enter the nonstop air race between Los Angeles and Chicago—a part of the 1930 National Air Races—and then continue on to New York to try to break the coast-to-coast speed record.

Hall must have been a somewhat unusual employer, brought up as he was in the hardscrabble world of oil speculation when risk was a way of life. In any case, he thought the nonstop air race was a great idea. Post set about modifying the Vega with additional fuel tanks and a special supercharger for improved high-altitude performance, and Australian navigation expert Harold Gatty laid out the course.

A few minutes after takeoff on the big day, the magnetic compass failed, and Post lost 40 minutes trying to find his way back on course. Navigating entirely by watching the ground, he went on to win the 1,760-mile (2,832-kilometer) race in nine hours, nine minutes, four seconds, at an average speed of 192 miles per hour (309 kilometers per hour), and took home $7,500.

The compass malfunction ruled out Post's proposed dash to New York, but Wiley went home to make another request of Hall: instead of making another try at the transcontinental record, what did Hall think of the idea of an around-the-world record flight to promote the future of global airplane-passenger service? The German *Graf Zeppelin* airship had circled the globe in 21 days in 1929, so why not wrap up the world in eight days in *Winnie Mae*?

In early 1931, Post and Harold Gatty planned the flight in detail. This time the two would fly together. Gatty, a master navigator and a graduate of the Royal Australian Naval College, engineered a drift meter and ground-speed indicator from clock parts and gears that worked so well that it later became standard equipment for the military services. Post concentrated on the flight instruments, and, with the help of Jimmy Doolittle, grouped the rate-of-climb, artificial horizon, directional gyro, and the turn-and-bank indicators for faster scan and decreased fatigue. A duplicate set, with the drift meter and "master" aperiodic compass for Gatty's use, was installed in the back.

Unlike many other time-distance-record pilots of the day, Post believed that physical and mental conditioning was crucial, particularly, in this case, as he would be the only pilot aboard and would not be able to leave the controls. He worked on making himself relax without falling asleep, and then, a few weeks before the flight, he started sleeping and eating at different times each day to accustom his body to interrupted schedules and differing time zones. He sat for hours, sometimes all night, in the parked Vega, logging the deterioration in his capabilities and the effects of cat napping. As he later wrote in his book, *Around the World in Eight Days,* "I knew that the variance in time as we progressed would bring on acute fatigue if I were used to regular hours." Post was the first aviator to investigate this body-clock phenomenon that was later to be known as "jet lag."

After a shakedown flight from California to New York, Post and Gatty waited in poor weather for weeks, finally departing Roosevelt Field early on the morning of June 23, 1931. After a refueling stop in Newfoundland, the two headed out across the Atlantic and 1,900 miles (3,057 kilometers) of poor weather. For hours, Post flew blind, using nothing but his instruments, thus proving their worth conclusively.

These poor flying conditions were a preview of things to come. Not only did the two men at times get lost in the bad weather, but fatigue often clouded their judgment, leading to such critical and potentially disastrous lapses as departures without enough fuel to reach the next destination.

The long legs across the Soviet Union were plagued by weather so bad that it often forced them down to tree-top level and to landings in fields in which *Winnie Mae* would become mired in the mud. Post recalled the 2,400-mile (3,861-kilome-

Wiley Post's 1930 National Aeronautic Association (NAA) sport-flying license bears the signature of American aviation pioneer and association chairman Orville Wright. The NAA sanctioned and certified the results of Post's record-breaking outings, including his 1933 solo around-the-world flight of 7 days, 18 hours, and 49 minutes in Winnie Mae. *Post was the first to investigate the effects of the body-clock phenomenon we now call "jet lag."*

ter) segment from Asia to North America "as the really dangerous section of the journey," with dense fog and treacherous mountains sticking up between a layer of clouds. Battling this weather and terrain for 16 hours and 45 minutes, they finally crossed the Bering Sea and landed on a soft beach just east of Nome, Alaska, their fuel tanks nearly empty.

After pumping 100 gallons (379 liters) aboard for the flight to Fairbanks, Post tried to get airborne, but the soft sand nosed the Vega over and the propeller tips bent. He used a rock, a hammer, and a wrench to straighten the blades, and, after a close call in which the prop grazed Gatty during run up, they were off.

After a brief stay in Fairbanks, they punched through torrential rain across Canada and landed at Edmonton, which Post described as "a swamp." Concerned about the possibility of another nose-over, Wiley was advised by a local airmail pilot to take off from the city's main street. While the two Americans grabbed some sleep, the city fathers removed power and phone lines, and the next morning the Vega roared down Portage Avenue past a cheering crowd and flew on to Cleveland.

After 30 minutes on the ground to refuel, Post and Gatty departed on the final leg to Roosevelt Field. They landed on July 1, 1931, having circumnavigated the globe in 8 days, 15 hours, 51 minutes, and having covered 15,474 miles (24,898 kilometers) and logged 107 hours, 2 minutes in the air.

Although Post attempted to deflect praise—"we didn't advance the mechanics of aviation one inch," he opined—the flight exhibited just what an airplane could do with modern equipment. Airlines would follow Post's lead quickly, eventually transforming long-distance flying into a common everyday experience.

As supportive of Post and his venture as F.C. Hall had been, he and Wiley now argued over Post's use of the company plane for personal promotion. Things settled down when Post bought *Winnie Mae* for $21,000, but Hall then bought another Vega and hired pilot Frank Hoover to challenge the Post-Gatty world flight record.

The Great Depression rendered 1932 a lean year for record flying: Hoover's flight was never made, and, without Hall's support, Post was limited in what he could try. Nevertheless, Wiley was determined to make another world flight—this time alone. Borrowing himself into significant debt, he set about modifying his aircraft.

Post knew that fatigue was his greatest enemy, so he approached the Sperry Gyroscope Company and persuaded them to supply, at no charge, the prototype of its revolutionary new "robot" automatic pilot, which was nicknamed "Mechanical Mike," to spell him at the controls. He also engaged in some sweet talking with the U.S. Army Signal Corps, and gained access to the new radio direction finder (RDF), which could home in on any broadcast station in the world. Navigation now would be a far simpler task than before.

During his preparations, an accident that almost destroyed *Winnie Mae* gave Post an opportunity to modify the machine extensively during its rebuild at Braniff Airlines. The aircraft's total fuel capacity was increased to 645 gallons (2,442 liters), and, under Pratt & Whitney's sponsorship, the

Wiley Post (left) and Harold Gatty wave to the crowd during a parade through the streets of New York on July 2, 1931, after successfully completing their circumnavigation of the Earth. At right, Wiley Post awaits favorable takeoff weather for his 1934 attempt to break the altitude record of 44,819 feet (13,661 meters). The pressure suit he wore consisted of three layers—long underwear; an inner, black-rubber air-pressure bladder; and an outer cloth layer—and could withstand up to seven pounds per square inch of pressure. On his knee he holds the specially designed helmet that would provide him with oxygen at high altitudes. Above right, having jettisoned her landing gear, Winnie Mae was free to climb higher than any aircraft had gone before. A metal-covered, spruce landing skid, tailor-made for these flights, runs along the bottom of the fuselage.

Wasp engine was rebuilt with cylinders that produced higher compression, a new carburetor, fresh magnetos, an ignition harness, and a controllable pitch propeller for improved takeoff and climb performance and better fuel consumption.

Post now had what amounted to a newer, more modern airplane, but he was also flat broke, with no money to make the flight. Fortunately, a group of Oklahoma City businessmen rounded up 41 people and companies to back their city's adopted son's solo flight with money and services, including free fuel, oil, and grease from the Socony-Vacuum Company, which later became Mobil Oil, and a letter of credit from the Texas Company, which was to become Texaco.

Although rival pilot Jimmy Mattern was preparing his own Vega for a solo world flight, Post would not be pushed into leaving before he was ready. Mattern was the first to be off, departing on June 3, 1933, but, in Siberia, he barely survived a forced landing and a harrowing rescue from one of the world's most remote regions.

At 5:10 A.M. on July 15, 1933, *Winnie Mae* lifted off from Floyd Bennett Field, New York, bound nonstop for Berlin. Disregarding the habit of the more flamboyant fliers of the era, Post wore a double-breasted, dark-gray suit, a white shirt, and a blue tie, and he sported a new white eye patch. Wiley had adopted the trademark patch after his glass eye had become chilled during the 1931 flight, and had caused him to have headaches.

In very short order, "Mechanical Mike," the autopilot, and the RDF proved to be wonders. Post was able to maintain course through very bad weather with the two devices, and he touched down at Berlin's Tempelhof airport after 25 hours and 45 minutes. Post was the first pilot to fly the 3,942 miles (6,343 kilometers) between the two cities nonstop. Greatly fatigued, he nonetheless left for Novosibirsk just over two hours later, but a lack of maps and a malfunctioning autopilot forced him to turn back and land at Königsberg for the night.

Continuing on to Moscow, where rudimentary repairs to the Sperry robot were made, Wiley then pressed on to Novosibirsk and worked his way across the Soviet Union. The toughest leg of the flight was between Khabarovsk and Fairbanks. Deep fatigue and severe weather forced him to fly on instruments for seven hours nonstop. He later said that, without the autopilot's help, completing this leg would have been close to impossible. Since Mechanical Mike did such an excellent job of flying, Post was able to doze off at times in order to revive himself. Nevertheless, Wiley had to prevent him-

Reminders of its many record-setting flights decorate Winnie Mae *'s fuselage. The historic Lockheed, together with its removable landing gear and pilot Wiley Post's pressure suit, came to the Smithsonian Institution in 1936.*

self from dropping into a deep sleep, and to this end devised an ingenious alarm clock. He held a wrench that was tied by a string to one finger. When he fell asleep, the wrench would fall and jerk the finger, jarring him back to consciousness. He'd check engine instruments, course, and time, and then reset the alarm and doze off again.

The RDF began to fail, causing him to wander off course, and Post finally set down at Flat, Alaska, as exhausted as he'd ever been. To make matters worse, the crude, 700-foot (213-meter) landing strip had a ditch at one end that caught the Vega as it rolled out, collapsing the right landing-gear leg, throwing the nose into the ground, and bending the complex Smith propeller. What should have been the end of the flight, however, became a rally of support from fellow aviators, who flew up a new prop and, with the help of the local mining company, repaired the Vega, while Post got some much needed sleep.

The next day, Wiley left for Fairbanks, where he took on fuel and then flew on through more bad weather to Edmonton. This time the field was dry; he didn't need to use the main street for takeoff. On the last leg of the flight to New York, Post let Mechanical Mike do most of the flying while he navigated with the RDF. More than 50,000 people were waiting for Post and *Winnie Mae* as they touched down in the growing darkness on July 22, 1933. Wiley Post had flown around the world alone in 7 days, 18 hours, 49.5 minutes, demonstrating

how indispensable the automatic pilot and radio navigation could be to aviation.

Post knew his faithful Vega was being left behind in terms of aviation technology, but he still wanted to enter it in the 1934 MacRobertson Race from London to Melbourne, a race that would feature specialized racing types and the new Boeing 247 and Douglas DC-2. He theorized that if he could cruise above 30,000 feet (9,144 meters) he could attain faster true air speeds in the thinner air of the stratosphere by tapping into the more than 100-mile-per-hour (161-kilometer-per-hour) jetstream winds, which had not been proven to exist. Shortly after his second round-the-world flight, Post had predicted that future airline passengers would fly in pressurized aircraft at 500 miles per hour (805 kilometers per hour) in the upper atmosphere, and also that, before much longer, people would leave the atmosphere altogether to fly in space.

Since *Winnie Mae*'s wooden-fuselage shell could not accommodate a pressure cabin, Post chose the next most logical solution: to dress in a fully pressurized suit. At Jimmy Doolittle's recommendation, Post approached the B.F. Goodrich Company in April 1934 to seek their help in developing a rubberized flying suit that could maintain the pilot at an atmospheric pressure equal to that at 5,500 feet (1,676 meters), regardless of how high the airplane flew.

The suit, which was sewn in two parts that were joined at the waist, was ready in June, but, during an unmanned static-pressure test in the Wright Field, Ohio, high-altitude pressure chamber, it burst. A second suit was made, but it fit Post so closely that he had to be cut out of it, which ruined it completely. Adopting a new approach, Post and Goodrich employee Russell Colley combined elements from both failed suits into a single-piece suit. A rubber inner garment was covered with a three-ply outer shell to which an aluminum helmet was attached with butterfly nuts, so that the suit resembled a deep-sea diver's rig. A single porthole of glass afforded limited visibility. The only way to get into the suit was through the neckhole, but Post found this an excellent compromise for his purposes.

Initial tests at Wright Field, which were held under conditions of strict secrecy, proved that the suit could hold a steady pressure of seven pounds per square inch. A high-pressure, liquid-oxygen tank supplied both breathing oxygen and pressure for the suit. While a nervous Mrs. Post waited outside, Wiley made his first tests in the suit in the Wright chamber on August 27 and 28, 1934, to simulated altitudes in excess of 20,000 feet (6,096 meters). The suit proved so remarkably effective that the Army kept its details secret in order to use it as the basis for further research.

In the meantime, *Winnie Mae,* sponsored by Phillips Petroleum, TWA, and others, had been modified yet again for Post's new venture. The aircraft's Wasp engine had been retrofitted with a sec-

ond supercharger, enabling it to generate all 450 horsepower up to 35,000 feet (10,668 meters), and to climb to a maximum of 50,000 feet (15,240 meters), an unheard-of altitude at the time. And Lockheed had designed a landing gear that could be jettisoned and free the aircraft of substantial drag; Post could land power-off on a new skid that ran along the bottom of the fuselage.

On September 5, Post went flying in his new suit. *Winnie Mae* reached 40,000 feet (12,192 meters), close to the world's altitude record, over Chicago.

Unfortunately, the need for further modifications to the Vega took Post out of the running for the MacRobertson Race. He chose the best alternative: a U.S. coast-to-coast flight above 30,000 feet (9,144 meters). During more tests in early December 1934, he reached 48,000 feet (14,630 meters), and later probably reached 50,000 feet (15,240 meters), but the recording barograph failed and the record could not be confirmed. It was during these flights, which were conducted over Bartlesville, Oklahoma, that he confirmed the jet stream's existence.

After an initial attempt that was scuttled by engine failure resulting from sabotage by a jealous rival, Post lifted off from Burbank, California, on March 15, 1935, and flew to Cleveland, which was as far as his oxygen supply would take him. Cruising between 30,000 and 40,000 feet (9,144 and 12,192 meters), Wiley picked up the jet stream and averaged a fantastic 279.36 miles per hour (450 kilometers per hour), more than 100 miles per hour (161 kilometers per hour) above the Vega's normal cruise speed. At certain times he hit a ground speed of 340 miles per hour (547 kilometers per hour).

Post tried twice more to make it all the way across the United States in the sub-stratosphere, but mechanical failure stopped him on each attempt. Faithful *Winnie Mae* had given her all, and there was no more to pull from her tired, worn, and outdated frame. In June 1935, assisted by a Congressional grant, Post donated the Vega and the world's first pressure suit, the forerunner of modern space suits, to the Smithsonian Institution.

The implications of Post's high-altitude flights for aviation's future were immediate and far-reaching. Not only was the utility of pressurization proven, but the effects of high altitudes on engine ignition

and radio equipment were encountered for the first time, leading to extensive re-design of these and other parts.

Not one to sit around, Post now planned another round-the-world flight in the opposite direction, this one to be flown in a hybrid aircraft made from a Lockheed Orion fuselage, a Lockheed Sirius wing, and Fokker trimotor floats. Humorist Will Rogers, long an aviation booster and a close friend of Post, accompanied him on the flight as they headed northwest out of California. The aircraft turned out to have a nasty habit of nosing down at low speed regardless of how much opposite pressure the pilot put on the control stick. Like so many other pioneering aviators in similar situations, Post simply put up with this quirk; almost every airplane of the era had some dangerous tendencies.

On August 15, 1935, as the aircraft left a small lake near Point Barrow, Alaska, the engine quit and the plane immediately dived into the water, killing Post and Rogers. It was a tragic end for two great men.

When oil-drilling-equipment tycoon and film maker Howard Hughes turned to aviation, he brought an insatiable desire to learn, to innovate, and to conquer. As with other interests in his life, he focused on it so intently that virtually everything else around him disappeared. This singular drive, combined with his eccentric personality, ideally suited him for aviation's golden age.

An excellent pilot, Hughes also had a feel for mechanical engineering and aviation design. His thirst for speed was whetted initially when he aerodynamically modified a civil version of the Boeing P-12/F4B fighter so that it could reach speeds of 225 miles per hour (362 kilometers per hour). On January 14, 1934, he entered and won his first air race, the All-American Air Meet, in Miami.

Though the Boeing was a sterling performer, Hughes was well aware of its design flaws: a fixed landing gear, biplane wings, strut and wire bracing, and an open cockpit. Aviation was undergoing rapid changes at the time, but no single plane embodied all the design improvements that appeared on several different machines. With no hesitation, Hughes determined to build the fastest land

plane in the world.

Perhaps Hughes' greatest talent was finding talent, and, during the Depression, many people were out of work. Hughes picked recent California Institute of Technology graduate Richard W. Palmer to be in charge, and gave him the freedom to bring on some of his Cal Tech friends. Hughes also hired Glenn Odekirk, a topnotch mechanic who had worked on his film *Hell's Angels,* to oversee the plane's actual building.

Once the team was in place, Hughes held impromptu sessions to explain what he wanted: a plane that would fly faster than anything else on the planet. Everyone agreed that Howard knew how to communicate what he was after, and his employees were delighted to try to match their skills to his challenge. He would often call them in the middle of the night to talk over some of the most esoteric aspects of design or construction.

Using advice from aerodynamicist John Stack of the NACA's Langley Research Center and the wind tunnel at Cal Tech, the team tested a series of wooden aircraft models, each requiring

Movie mogul and business executive Howard Hughes poses by the borrowed Northrop Gamma that he flew from Burbank, California, to Newark, New Jersey, in 9 hours, 27 minutes— a new record—in January 1936. Later, in this same aircraft, he set new record flying times from Miami to New York and Chicago to Los Angeles.

Hughes' approval, until a final design was chosen. The winner was like nothing else flying.

As construction began, and then progressed in a sealed-off hangar section of Burbank's Grand Central Airport, the complete secrecy demanded by Hughes whetted the public's appetite. What did this mystery ship look like? Was it just another Hughes infatuation?

In the 18 months it took to build the Hughes H-1, Dick Palmer and Glenn Odekirk literally made aviation history. When it was rolled out in August 1935, the H-1's innovations were obvious from any angle. All rivets and joints were flush with the aircraft's skin, while flat-head and counter-sunk screws were used on the plywood wings. Gently curving wing fillets between the wing and fuselage helped to stabilize airflow, reduce drag, and prevent potentially dangerous tail buffeting. A tightly fitted, bell-shaped engine cowling reduced airframe drag while improving cooling for the 1,000-horsepower, Pratt & Whitney Twin Wasp Junior engine. The landing gear retracted into the wings so closely that the landing-gear-fairing doors were hard to find. The ailerons were designed to droop 15 degrees when the flaps were lowered to improve lift along the full length of the wing, providing excellent slow-speed safety and handling.

Although Hughes Tool Company officials were horrified at the prospect, and both Palmer and Odekirk tried to talk him out of it, Hughes was determined to do his own test flying. It was his air-plane, he had paid all the bills, and there was no arguing about it. On August 18, 1935, Hughes lifted off of Mines Field in the H-1 and cruised over Los Angeles for 15 minutes, pushing the machine up to 300 miles per hour (483 kilometers per hour) with no great effort. When the news leaked out, everyone was sure he would enter the plane in the National Air Races over Labor Day. With his typical flair for mystery, however, Howard let the races go by without a word. His sights were set on an assault of the world's land-plane speed record of 314 miles per hour (505 kilometers per hour), which was held by the French.

The H-1 was moved to Martin Field, a small airstrip in Santa Ana set amid flat orange groves. The National Aeronautic Association had set up the three-kilometer course to run north to south over an adjacent bean field. Three judges were picked—famed aviator Amelia Earhart, Hollywood pilot Paul Mantz, and NAA official Lawrence Therkelson—to witness the four speed runs, from which the average top speed would be calculated.

After an aborted attempt on September 12, Hughes returned the next day and set an official speed record of 352.322 miles per hour (567 kilometers per hour). As he pulled off the course from the last run, apparently unaware of how much fuel he had burned, the engine sputtered to a stop. Although the H-1 had an auxiliary fuel tank, Howard did not switch over to it. He had to make some fast decisions, which boiled down to bailing out or bel-

Ground crewmen at Floyd Bennett Field, New York, in January 1936, move the Northrop Gamma in which Howard Hughes beat air racer Roscoe Turner's cross-country record by 36 minutes. Not satisfied with this performance, Hughes had his own H-1 racer modified for yet another record-setting attempt.

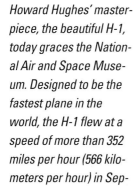

Howard Hughes' masterpiece, the beautiful H-1, today graces the National Air and Space Museum. Designed to be the fastest plane in the world, the H-1 flew at a speed of more than 352 miles per hour (566 kilometers per hour) in September 1935. It was fitted with new, moderate-aspect-ratio wings, as seen here, and, on January 19, 1937, it crossed the country in 7 hours, 28 minutes. Below, Hughes sits in the cockpit of the H-1, which, with its engine cowling removed, shows off its Pratt & Whitney Twin Wasp Junior radial engine, capable of delivering up to 1,000 horsepower.

lying in. Not wanting to lose his pride and joy, he opted to put it down in a beet field.

With consummate skill, Hughes touched down with wheels up and slid to a stop, incurring only minor damage to the H-1 and no injury to himself. A less experienced pilot might have been tempted to lower the landing gear. Had Hughes done that, the aircraft might have flipped over onto its back and been heavily damaged, if not destroyed, and the pilot might have been killed. When told he had broken the record, Hughes turned back to look at his crippled bird and said, "It'll go faster."

With the H-1, Howard Hughes changed his image from that of a millionaire tycoon and Hollywood movie producer who only played with airplanes to that of a serious aviation innovator and visionary. So far ahead of its time was the H-1 that in it can be seen all the basic principles that were designed into the great World War II single-engine fighters. To his fame the world now added respect, but Hughes was careful to place the credit with the design team and the builders, who, he said, had built him "a perfect machine."

Howard had still bigger plans: he wanted to break the transcontinental speed record of just over 10 hours that was held by crack racing pilot and showman Roscoe Turner. As had Wiley Post before him, Hughes knew high-altitude flying held the key to higher speeds. Following a hunch that air-speed indicators became inaccurate in the upper atmosphere, he set up a series of experimental runs with the H-1.

Laying out a 72-mile (116-mile) course from Mt. Wilson Observatory, near Los Angeles, to San Jacinto Peak, near Palm Springs, Howard stationed Hughes Aircraft employees at designated points to record his speeds. After flying the route at 15,000 feet (4,572 meters) and comparing the recorded times with his air-speed instrument, he found that the instrument read a good 15 miles per hour (24 kilometers per hour) slower. There was no doubt in his mind that he could break Turner's record with little effort, but his real interest was in what the flight could do for the future. Could an airliner carrying people in the sub-stratosphere make it coast to coast on less fuel and at less cost than current aircraft? Hughes wanted to test the theory

himself, just as Post had.

Unfortunately, he could not do it with the short-range, short-winged H-1 racer. After talking accomplished female pilot Jackie Cochran into leasing him her Northrop Gamma Bendix racer and installing a new, more powerful engine, Hughes flew from Burbank, California, to Newark, New Jersey, on January 13, 1936. Using oxygen above 15,000 feet (4,572 meters), he found he could top most of the weather and the mountain ranges between the coasts. He broke the record with a time of 9 hours, 27 minutes, 10 seconds, but that was only 36 minutes faster than Turner's flight. Before Cochran finally got her airplane back, Howard had set two more records—from Miami to New York and from Chicago to Los Angeles.

But Hughes wanted to do more than just squeak by the existing records. Clearly there was nothing available that could match the H-1, so why not modify it? He asked his Hughes Aircraft team to modify the "beautiful little thing" for a transcontinental dash, and they did: longer wings were built, fuel capacity was increased, a sliding canopy was fitted to enclose the cockpit, an oxygen tank was added, and numerous other refinements were made.

Renamed the *Winged Bullet,* the H-1 was rolled out of its Burbank hangar in the early morning hours of January 19, 1937, and filled with 280 gallons (1,060 liters) of fuel. In spite of cloud cover over most of the U.S., Hughes decided to set off at 2:15 A.M. to take advantage of very favorable tail winds. Once settled into cruise speed and on oxygen, he was very happy with his 330-miles-per-hour (531-kilometers-per-hour) speed. Then near disaster struck with the occurrence of something that would become an insidious enemy of later pilots: his oxygen mask malfunctioned, and Hughes began to suffer from hypoxia, or the lack of enough oxygen to function normally.

As he later told newspaper reporters, his "arms and legs were practically paralyzed," and he had the "helpless, hopeless feeling" that he was losing consciousness. Mustering his resolve, he pushed the stick forward and dived into the oxygen-rich lower atmosphere, almost immediately regaining his mental acuity. In spite of the slower speeds at the lower altitude and the realization that he had a dead radio, Howard pressed on and made Newark in 7 hours, 28 minutes, 25 seconds for an average of 332 miles per hour (534 kilometers per hour). He not only had topped his own record, but had set one that no one else would break for seven years.

The flight earned Hughes the Harmon International Trophy for the world's outstanding pilot; it was presented to him by President Franklin D. Roosevelt. Howard had plowed fresh fields in the sky, and, despite his quirky personality, he never again was considered anything but an aviation visionary.

Flying the all-metal, twin-engine Lockheed 14, Hughes went on to smash Wiley Post's round-the-world record in July 1938. His company, Hughes Aircraft, expanded throughout World War II and established itself as a major aerospace company in the postwar era, particularly in the development of helicopters and fighter-weapons systems. The stamp of Howard Hughes' vision, personified in the H-1, has remained a significant aspect of American aviation history.

Although the Hughes H-1 often was referred to as a racer, it never took part in the closed-course pylon and cross-country races that made America's golden age of aviation so thrilling. By the early 1930s, the National Air Races had become the primary testing ground for aviation innovation and development, drawing both civilian and military contestants. Dozens of aerobatics displays, including the first military formation teams, could be seen at air shows around the country, and the latest in aviation hardware was always on display at Cleveland, the hub of the racing scene.

With the 1929 Nationals came a significant change. For the first time, civilian entries beat out their military counterparts. That year, Doug Davis, flying the Beech *Mystery Ship,* came in first at 194.9 miles per hour (314 kilometers per hour), and Roscoe Turner, in a production Lockheed Vega, captured third, leaving the Curtiss Hawk fighters behind, though one did take second. The military had not bothered with racing since 1925, and it showed. They were being outclassed at their own game, mostly by a bunch of unschooled grease monkeys with plenty of vision and very little money.

In 1930, Nationals organizer Cliff Henderson talked Cleveland manufacturer Charles Thompson into sponsoring a new closed-course, all-out, speed-race trophy worth $10,000 in prize money, which was a lot of money for the Depression era, and which was offered along with $90,000 for the other 49 events. The pace for the next decade was set, and the quest for speed and innovation brought about the creation of some of the most incredible "engines with wings" ever flown.

Drawing paying crowds in the midst of a poverty-stricken decade never seemed to be a problem.

Former-Army-pilot-turned-air-racer Jimmy Doolittle, left, grins from the cockpit of the Laird Super Solution, *in which he won the 1931 Bendix Trophy at an average speed of 223 miles per hour (359 kilometers per hour) over 2,043 miles (3,287 kilometers). Below, reporters surround master air showman and pilot Roscoe Turner at Floyd Bennett Field, New York, as he stands beside his Weddell-Williams Bendix-winning racer in September 1933.*

Two men—Jimmy Doolittle and Roscoe Turner—rose above the rest in fame and daring. After Doolittle won the 1925 Schneider Trophy and pioneered instrument flying with fellow Army Lieutenant Ben Kelsey, he left the service in 1930 for a position with Shell Petroleum. This gave him the opportunity to showcase the company's aviation gasoline through air racing. He won the first Bendix Trophy by flying Matty Laird's *Super Solution* from Burbank to Cleveland at an average speed of 223 miles per hour (359 kilometers per hour).

The Thompson Trophy of 1931 was a hairy-chested power meet marking the appearance of the first of the Granville Brothers Aircraft racers, the Gee Bee Model Z. With no formal aircraft-design training, head of the clan and self-taught auto mechanic Zantford D. "Granny" Granville and designer Robert Hall emulated what they considered to be the most naturally streamlined shape—the raindrop—and put an engine on it with as little wing and tail as possible. The resulting series of airplanes was, as Doolittle recalled, "the most unforgiving . . . I ever flew." Though Doolittle raced Gee

As E.J. Snow of Vacuum Oil wrote, "Curiosity and mass morbidity apparently grow with the square or the cube of possibility of danger or disaster. The more daring the flights become, the greater and more enthusiastic will become the crowd." Whether such flying hurt or helped aviation was the subject of countless debates, but the races went on regardless.

Manufacturer Vincent Bendix created the second classic speed race for the Nationals in 1931 by offering a trophy for long-distance flying. This not only attracted the raw-speed merchants, but even gave commercial aircraft a good shot at winning as there was no requirement to round pylons in steep, punishing turns.

Over the next nine years, the public adored pilots who were, according to historian Terry Gwynn-Jones, "aerial gladiators locked in mortal combat, duelling in twentieth-century aerial chariots, flirting with death for a pot of gold . . . . Lionized by the newspapers and radio stations, exalted by their cheering fans, the oil-stained, windswept fliers became heroes."

Above, Walter Beech's nearly 200-mile-per-hour (322-kilometer-per-hour) 1929 Mystery Ship. Top, Jimmy Doolittle wins the 1932 Thompson Trophy in the more than 250-mile-per-hour (402-kilometer-per-hour) Granville Gee Bee Sportster R-1.

Bees successfully, all seven crashed within four years, killing five pilots.

Another auto mechanic, Jimmy Wedell, built a series of barrel-chested racers with huge engines. Funded by wealthy Harry Williams, the Wedell-Williams Specials became the outstanding competition for the Gee Bees, and ended up being the "winningest" of the Thompson and Bendix trophy machines.

Pushing these homemade engineering marvels toward 300 miles per hour (483 kilometers per hour)

behind 800-horsepower engines took a special breed of pilots. With no detailed studies on what to expect, pilots of these machines had to rely on instinct and experience to survive. Generally, to achieve higher speeds, these racers had very little wing area. Careless movement of the stick could produce lethal results. High-speed stalls were not uncommon, and if a pilot didn't pay attention to the shudders and bumps he felt through the seat of his pants, he quickly became a fatality statistic. Landing speeds were very high for the day—over 100 miles per hour (161 kilometers per hour)—which made control finesse mandatory. In 1934, Granny Granville himself died at the controls of one of his own machines, stalling in from 75 feet (23 meters) while trying to avoid a blocked runway.

When Doolittle took the 1932 Gee Bee Super Sportster R-1 to altitude to practice pylon turns, it did two violent snap rolls as he simulated a high G bank. Drawing on his previous racing methodology, he avoided making steep turns, racing the airplane in a modified circle rather than roaring down straightaway and hauling around the pylons in near vertical banks. This not only won him the Thompson, but it saved his life—and he ended up with a world speed record of 296.287 miles per hour (477 kilometers per hour). The only trained aeronautical engineer with another degree from the racing circuit, Doolittle thought the aircraft too dangerous and the cost in lives too great regardless of the accolades. He quit the sport that year.

As Jimmy left the scene, Roscoe Turner's star was on the rise, and for the remainder of the decade he was the nation's most celebrated aviator. With a genius for promotion, Turner prospered during the Depression. Taking the honorary title of colonel from the Nevada National Guard, dressing in semi-military uniforms, sporting a long, waxed moustache, and taking his lion-cub mascot "Gilmore" everywhere, he flew some of the hottest machines in the world for an adoring public. Had he not been as good a pilot as he was a showman, he would have faded quickly. But there was no doubt among his peers that he was all business in the cockpit, with excellent judgment and consummate skill.

Flying the Wedell-Williams 57, Turner won the 1933 Bendix and the 1934 Thompson trophies, not

Women dominated the 1936 Bendix Trophy: Louise Thaden, right, in her Beechcraft C-17R, was the first woman to win this race, flying at speeds of over 165 miles per hour (265 kilometers per hour); above, Laura Ingalls boards her Lockheed Orion 9D, in which she placed second; above right, Amelia Earhart, who came in last, nevertheless was one of only five pilots who managed to finish the New York-to-Los Angeles race.

Jackie Cochran climbs out of her idling Seversky SEV-S2 in Cleveland, Ohio, after winning the 1938 Bendix Trophy. In May 1953, Cochran would become the first woman to break the sound barrier. At left, a sheet-music title page pays homage to Amelia Earhart's solo crossing of the Atlantic in 1932 in a Lockheed Vega that now resides in the collection of the National Air and Space Museum.

to mention the world land-plane record at Chicago in 1933 at 305.3 miles per hour (491 kilometers per hour). A crash in one of the Wedells and the competition of Ben Howard's excellent racers made 1935 and '36 rough years for Turner, but his promotional efforts never flagged and he stayed out of the bread lines.

The 1936 Bendix turned out to be a great one for America's most accomplished women pilots. Louise Thaden won in a Beechcraft C-17R Staggerwing, Laura Ingalls came in second with her Lockheed Orion, and Amelia Earhart was last in the futuristic, twin-engine Lockheed Electra. From this point on, the Bendix would be dominated by commercial aircraft. The all-metal Seversky SEV-S2, basically a civil version of the P-35 fighter, was the premier Bendix racer in the last three years before World War II. The Thompson was another matter.

Roscoe Turner came back on the scene with a vengeance in 1937, and the remaining three pre-

LADY LINDY
We're All for You

Dedicated to
Miss
AMELIA
EARHEART

lyrics by
HENRY M. NEELY
music by
HAROLD LEVEY

WITH
UKULELE ACC.

PHOTO
© G. P. PUTNAM

M. WITMARK & SONS
NEW YORK CITY
MADE IN U.S.A.

war Thompson Trophy races were his domain. To design a plane that would dominate racing for several years, he refined the basic Gee Bee shape, then had stress analysis and drawings done by Howard W. Barlow and John D. Akerman at the University of Minnesota.

Racing builder Lawrence Brown began construction after some extensive re-design, and Matty Laird finished it with, among other changes, new wings and a re-worked tail. The end result was not a technological breakthrough, but with its cantilever wing and Pratt & Whitney Twin Wasp 1,000-horsepower engine the airplane had the brute characteristics needed to win races.

The Laird-Turner Special, or LTR-14 (Laird-Turner Racer, 14-cylinder engine), was favored to win the 1937 Thompson. Nicknamed the MacMillan *Ring Free Meteor* after its sponsor, the aircraft had been disqualified for the Bendix after Turner suffered a burn during repairs to a leaking fuel tank, but plane and pilot were able to make the Thompson Trophy race.

After the usual thrilling horse-race start, Steve Wittman took the lead until a bird strike on the prop of his little *Bonzo* slowed him down. Roscoe then led the field, but one of his old problems—skipping pylons—came back to haunt him. Blind-

chute. Above, Gilmore, who died of old age, continues to fly with Turner's 1937 RT-14 Meteor *racer at the National Air and Space Museum. Designed by Turner himself, the 1,000-horsepower* Meteor *earned the veteran pilot his second and third Thompson Trophies, in 1938 and 1939. The aircraft was donated to the Smithsonian in 1972.*

Roscoe Turner, opposite (left), poses in the 1930s with his flight crew, including his pet lion, Gilmore, who sports his own flight suit and para-

Jimmy Doolittle, left, appears imperturbable as he awaits the start of the 1925 Schneider Cup race in Baltimore, Maryland. He won the event. Doolittle retired from racing soon after winning the Thompson Trophy, right, in 1932, believing that such flying stints were becoming too dangerous.

ed by the sun on the 20th and last lap, Turner thought he had cut a pylon, so he recircled it and came in third. Much to his chagrin, he learned from the judges that he had not missed the pylon after all. The unfortunate turn of events left him broke and owing the builders money for the racer's construction. Returning to his gift for self-promotion, Turner managed to float enough loans to make it through the winter.

After cleaning up the LTR-14 with streamlined wheel pants and landing-gear leg fairings, Turner, now deeper in debt than ever, put the aircraft, which was now named after its major sponsor, the *PESCO Special,* on the 1938 race circuit. At this juncture, Roscoe insisted that the aircraft be referred to as the Turner Racer, with no mention of either Brown or Laird; however, the official name never changed in the government registry.

Turner and the LTR won the 1938 Thompson with ease, finishing more than 10 miles (16 kilometers) in front of the competition at an average speed of 283.418 miles per hour (456 kilometers per hour). As the first two-time winner of the Thompson and with $22,000 in prize money, he started paying off his debts, though Brown and Laird never received full payment for building the racer.

The 1939 Thompson was held under the shadow of the two-day-old war in Europe. Roscoe, now the undisputed king of air racing, brought his usual flair to the event, along with the LTR, now named *Miss Champion* for its new sparkplug company sponsor. In spite of cutting a pylon on the second lap and having to recircle it, Turner won the race on brute Pratt & Whitney power at an average of 282.536 miles per hour (455 kilometers per hour). He was the first and only pilot to win the Thompson three times, and the only pilot to compete in seven on them. The trophy was given to him as a permanent possession,

and he retired from air racing that day at the ripe old age of 43.

With Roscoe Turner's departure from the scene, the golden age of aviation began to decline. No other single pilot embodied the thrill, challenge, and risk of the era more than he did, and America had followed his exploits throughout the '30s as if he were a living Buck Rogers. After all, he had survived 10 years of piston-busting flying, and had watched a third of his fellow Bendix and Thompson champions die in the sport. Although the races did not bring about much advance in design, they kept Americans air-minded enough to support a wartime aviation industry undreamed of even at the time of the last Thompson. Now, with World War II, came aviation's maturity.

Holder of three Thompson trophies and one Bendix, the flamboyant Roscoe Turner epitomized the age of air racing.

By the end of the summer of 1944, it was beginning to look like certain victory for the Allies in World War II. The Normandy invasion on June 6 and the subsequent advance across France had been a rough slog, hedgerow by hedgerow, but the Germans finally were falling back toward their own borders. From the east, Soviet forces, too, were pressing the Germans back into Germany. Axis air attacks against England were less frequent, and people dared to breathe a little easier.

Then, on September 8, 1944, with no warning, a huge explosion rocked London. There had been no aircraft overhead, no whistling of falling bombs, no air-raid sirens, no moaning pulse-jet sound of a V-1 "Doodlebug." At the bottom of the crater carved by the explosion, investigators discovered the remains of a large rocket; the world's first long-range ballistic missile had found its target from a launch site near the Hague in Holland. Hitler's Vergeltungswaffe, or Vengeance Weapon, Number 2, or the V-2, was now operational, climaxing an unofficial and largely unnoticed "rocket race" between Germany and the United States.

Even before the end of the First World War, visionaries on both sides of the Atlantic had dreamed of building large rockets and shooting them into space; transferring those visions into successful

ROCKET POWER

hardware proved to be excruciatingly difficult. Ridicule, lack of support, and a succession of failures were the common experience of all pre-World-War-II rocket experimenters.

The first to achieve even limited success was a 43-year-old Clark University physics professor named Robert H. Goddard. On March 16, 1926, when he launched the world's first liquid-propellant rocket from his Aunt Effie's Massachusetts farm, he realized a personal dream of 26 years' standing. Although the rocket's motor ran for only 2.5 seconds, boosting the rocket to an altitude of just 41 feet (12.5 meters) during a flight of 184 feet (56 meters), the spindly contraption repre-

At a blackboard in 1924, Clark University physics professor Robert Goddard, left, illustrates his theory of rocket flight between the Earth and the moon. By 1941, Goddard's 22-foot-tall (6.7-meter) P-series rockets, one of which appears at right with its plumbing exposed, featured most of the basic systems that made flight to the moon possible a generation later.

sented a giant stride along the path to the conquest of space.

As a teen, Robert Goddard had read H.G. Wells's novels with fascination, particularly *The War of the Worlds*. This tale of the Martian invasion of Earth affected him so deeply that one day in October 1899, while sitting in a backyard cherry tree, he experienced a vivid daydream in which he traveled to Mars in a centrifugally impelled craft. As Goddard recalled, "I was a different boy when I descended the tree from when I ascended. Existence at least seemed very purposive." For the rest of his life he quietly celebrated this date as "Anniversary Day."

When, a short time later, he fell ill with tuberculosis, he pulled back into this imaginary world as if on a mission, devouring science books, conducting experiments, and, through his daydreams, traveling in space. He missed a great deal of school, but he didn't let that stop him from educating himself. Although he continued to struggle with serious illness, by 1911 he had earned a doctorate in physics from Clark University, where he became a full professor in 1919.

During this time, Goddard narrowed his study of possible methods of achieving space travel to rocket propulsion. By 1908, he was conducting static tests of small, solid-propellant rockets at Worcester Polytechnic Institute. In 1912, he worked out the mathematical equations for using rocket power to reach extremely high altitudes and to achieve escape velocity from the Earth's gravitational pull. In 1914, he received U.S. patents for multi-stage rockets and a combustion chamber fed by liquid propellants. The next year, he proved experimentally that a rocket would provide thrust in a vacuum.

By 1916, Goddard was reaching so far ahead that he ran out of resources. He pleaded with a Worcester industrial laboratory to test gunpowder mixtures for him. Although the employees were fearful of his concoctions, "it was almost impossible to turn him down," recalled the laboratory's owner. "We ran off his test, not knowing what he was up to, but feeling sure he did."

In 1916, through a letter of appeal, he received a research grant from the Smithsonian Institution allowing him to continue his rocket research. The grant was approved on the basis of Goddard's 1913 paper, "A Method of Reaching Extreme Altitudes." When it was published in 1919, the paper brought reactions from both American and foreign sources. Newspapers latched onto Goddard's assertions that a rocket could reach the moon, dubbing him "the moon-rocket man."

The more he was belittled and questioned skeptically by reporters, the more he backed away from publicity. Shy and sensitive to begin with, devoted to his students, and unused to ignorant questioning, Goddard determined henceforth to keep his

research a closely guarded secret, and he no longer publicly mentioned methods for reaching the moon. His paper is now considered to be an original document in basic astronautics, one that has influenced almost every major step toward modern space travel.

With the entry of the United States into World War I in 1917, Goddard offered his services to the Army. He designed and built several types of tube-launched, solid-fuel rockets for anti-tank warfare. This work laid the foundations for American solid-propellant rocket development, and, particularly, for the famous Bazooka anti-armor weapon,

which emerged a generation later in World War II.

From 1920 to 1925, with continued Smithsonian funding and a grant from Clark University, Goddard experimented with liquid-propellant rockets in his small university lab. In March 1923, he solved one of the fundamental problems associated with liquid-propellant rocket engines: the cooling dilemma. Ingeniously, he designed an engine in which one of the propellants was circulated around the combustion chamber before being injected into it to be burned, thereby protecting the chamber from the fierce heat of ignition. Every liquid-propellant rocket built since has featured this process, which is called regenerative cooling.

Although he was singularly devoted to his work, Goddard was considered to be one of the most popular teachers at Worcester; his students often cheered him at the end of a class. He was warm and enjoyed his time off and vacations as well as his work, and, although he was shy, he did not shun contact with others. In the middle of this crucial period, when he was experimenting with regenerative cooling, he met and wooed young Esther Kisk. They were married in June 1924, and, until his death in 1945, she remained his most devoted assistant and confidant.

By March 1926, Goddard was ready to launch his prototype rocket, which looked more like a child's swing set than something that would make history. On Tuesday the 16th, Goddard and machinist Henry Sachs put the rocket on a trailer, placed two tanks of liquid oxygen on the seat between them, and drove out to Effie Ward's Auburn, Massachusetts, farm. It was cold, and snow still lay on the ground, but the two men, warmed by excitement and anticipation, set up the launch tower and rocket.

Esther, with movie camera in hand, was driven to the site by Percy Roope, assistant physics professor at Clark. After gasoline and liquid oxygen had been loaded, the 10.25-pound (4.6-kilogram) rocket was ready. The small group fortified themselves with some hot malted milk from Aunt Effie, and then gathered around the launch tower. From 30 feet (nine meters) away, Goddard turned a valve to let oxygen into the rocket through a hose that would pull away on liftoff. It was 2:30 P.M.

Henry Sachs then raised a blowtorch to the black-powder igniter. When the powder started to flame, Goddard opened the valves for the liquid oxygen and the gasoline. With a sharp bang and a white exhaust trail, the rocket ignited. "Even though the release was pulled," wrote Goddard the next day, "the rocket did not rise at first but the flame came out, and there was a steady roar. After a number of seconds it rose, slowly until it cleared the frame, and then at express train speed, curving over to the left, and striking the ice and snow, still going at a rapid rate. It looked almost magical as it rose, without any appreciably greater noise or flame."

Although Goddard informed a few relatives of the successful launch, he asked the Smithsonian not to make it public. The Institution's officials understood his compulsion for secrecy and agreed to his request, thinking that he was waiting until a spectacular public event could be staged. That was not in Goddard's mind. Not until 10 years later, on March 16, 1936, with the Smithsonian's publication of his *Liquid-Propellant Rocket Development,* did the world learn that Goddard had been the first to launch such a device.

After the second launch, on April 3, 1926, Goddard decided to build larger rockets with a number of improvements, including gyro stabilization, another development that became standard in rocketry. His fourth launch, on July 17, 1929, was spectacular, but not for reasons that pleased the inventor. The first rocket to carry instrumentation—a barometer, a thermometer, and a recording camera—the missile roared up to 90 feet (27.5 meters), and then plunged back to strike the earth with a tremendous explosion. Two ambulances, the police, a search aircraft, reporters, and spectators all rushed to the scene of the "airplane crash." As a result of this turmoil, the state fire marshal banned future tests.

Goddard hated the publicity that attended this launch, but the headlines attracted the attention of Charles A. Lindbergh, who soon visited the "moon-rocket man." Impressed by the man and his machines, the famed transatlantic flyer approached Daniel Guggenheim to seek support for Goddard's work from the wealthy philanthropist's aeronautical research foundation. A series of Guggenheim grants, running from 1930 to 1932 and from 1934 to 1941, enabled Goddard to move to the remote Mescalero Ranch, near Roswell, New Mexico, in 1930. There he not only was free from unwanted publicity, but he could launch his rockets without fear of destroying anything or starting any fires.

Meanwhile, other inventors who had no knowledge of Goddard and his work also dreamed of rocket-propelled space flight. In 1907, for example, when he was but 13 years old, the German Hermann Oberth, inspired by Jules Verne's *From the Earth to the Moon,* already was computing the force of gravity on the novelist's cannon-launched "spacemen." "They would be flattened into pancakes," he concluded with keen foresight, unless the cannon-launch method was abandoned in favor of rockets. Two years later he had designed a multi-stage rocket that burned solid fuel, but, like Goddard, he had abandoned it in favor of liquid propellants by 1912. In 1917, he proposed the concept of an 82-foot-high, gyroscopically stabilized, long-range, liquid-propellant rocket to the German military, but his idea was turned down.

A Goddard A-series rocket streaks skyward from its launch tower in Roswell, New Mexico, on August 26, 1937. The 15.5-foot-tall (4.7-meter), liquid-propellant rockets reached altitudes of up to 7,600 feet (2,316 meters). Left, Goddard (foreground) and his helpers carry large rocket components during tests in New Mexico.

After the war, in order to receive his doctorate, he wrote a thesis on space flight, but it, too, was rejected. These rebuffs did not deter him from developing his theories, however. In 1923, he published an expanded version of his thesis, *Die Rakete zu den Planetenraümen*, or *The Rocket into Planetary Space*. According to Smithsonian curator Frank Winter, the book "probably exerted more influence on the development of spaceflight than the work of either [Russian space-flight theorist Konstantin] Tsiolkovsky or Goddard. His book was, in fact, the cornerstone of the Space Age." Oberth's work covered every currently recognized aspect of manned and unmanned rocket flight— in hindsight, an astonishing achievement.

Die Rakete and its subsequent, enlarged editions gave birth to and fueled an international astronautical movement. Although some scoffed, Oberth's work inspired others to develop and apply scientific methods of study to space travel and rocketry.

In 1927, the Verein für Raumschiffahrt or VfR (in English, the Society for Space Travel, or, as it is popularly known, the German Rocket Society)

was formed in Germany under Oberth's inspiration. Although Oberth himself was primarily a theorist, there were many others who specialized in building and firing rockets, and they all shared the common goal of developing liquid-propellant motors.

Soon the VfR was attracting support and attention from many gifted individuals from various occupations, including Max Valier, Walter Hohmann, Rudolf Nebel, Guido von Pirquet, Klaus Reidel, Kurt Hainish, Willy Ley, and Wernher von Braun,

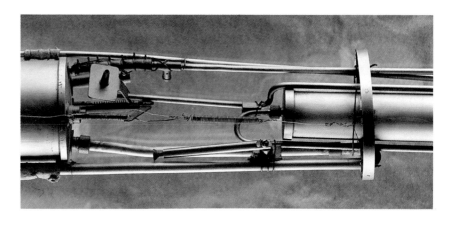

Liquid-oxygen and gasoline tanks, below, originally were installed in the world's first successful liquid-propellant rocket, which was

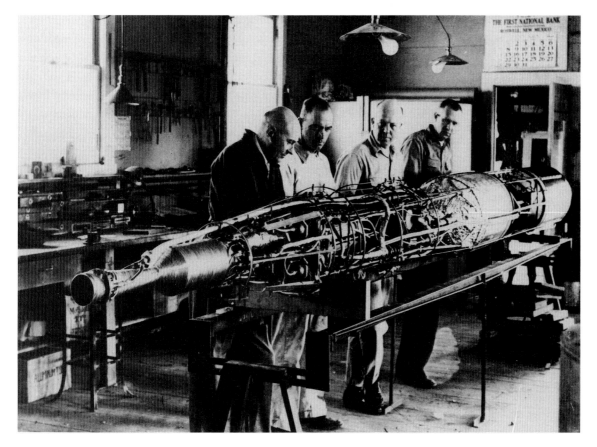

launched by Robert Goddard on March 16, 1926. Later, they were reused in a second, unsuccessful rocket. At left, Goddard and his team work on a P-series rocket in the Roswell shop in 1941. Plagued by pump failures, these rockets never flew as high as those of the A-series.

German physicist Hermann Oberth, left, designed a long-range, liquid-propellant rocket while serving in the Austro-Hungarian army during World War I. Oberth's Ph.D. dissertation, originally rejected, was expanded and published in 1923, far left, as, in translation, The Rocket into Planetary Space; *many feel it heralded the dawn of the space age. By 1930, the Verein für Raumschiffarht (VfR), or German Rocket Society, right, had a Raketenflugplatz, or "rocket-flight place," near Berlin, at which its members could design, build, and fly rockets.*

an 18-year-old student at the Berlin Institute of Technology who joined the society in 1930. That same year, Nebel signed a lease agreement for an old army ammunition depot near Berlin, which soon became the VfR's Raketenflugplatz, or Rocket Port. With access to their own experimental station, the members accelerated their research in spite of an increasingly ominous worldwide depression.

The society's Mirak and Repulsor series of rockets advanced in thrust and sophistication, in the end employing regenerative cooling, which was developed by the VfR entirely independently of Goddard. Before the VfR broke up in 1933, it had launched 100 flights, some to altitudes of over 3,000 feet (915 meters), and, for the Magdeburg rockets, as much as 550 pounds (2,447 newtons) of thrust. There were no earthshaking technical breakthroughs, but the mostly young experimenters gained invaluable experience—as well as the attention of the German Wehrmacht, the country's army.

In the spring of 1932, the Wehrmacht made an official visit to the Raketenflugplatz. That summer, Nebel and von Braun demonstrated their handiwork at Kümmersdorf, the government's rocket-

research station. By fall, von Braun had been hired to work on the Wehrmacht's new, secret rocket program as first technical assistant to its commander, Captain Walter R. Dornberger. By the time Hitler came to power in 1933, other VfR members also had been brought on to work on the project. Compared to the lean years they had known before, these budding scientists now had what must have seemed to them an almost unlimited amount of support. Because the Treaty of Versailles, which had formally ended World War I, did not mention rockets, there were no limits on what Germany might do to turn rockets into long-range weapons.

Across the Atlantic, meanwhile, Robert Goddard, thanks to the Guggenheim grants, was launching a succession of ever more sophisticated rockets at his ranch in New Mexico. Although the funding was cut off for two years early in the Depression, the Smithsonian and Clark University filled in with small amounts to keep the research being conducted in Massachusetts on track. When funding was fully restored and he was back in New Mexico, Goddard managed to advance his liquid-propellant rockets through a series of improve-

A young Wernher von Braun, seen below (right) carrying a Repulsor rocket, accompanies Rudolf Nebel at VfR's Raketenflugplatz in 1932.

ments that included remote-controlled, gyro-stabilized control vanes, a four-combustion-chamber cluster, gimbals steering, and centrifugal and turbine fuel pumps. Through 1942, he flight-tested 31 rockets in all, yielding several breakthroughs.

On March 8, 1935, one of his 15.5-foot-long (4.7-meter-long) rockets broke the sound barrier, a technological first, and two months later another topped 7,500 feet (2,300 meters). During a static test on July 17, 1941, Goddard pushed a motor to 825 pounds of thrust (3,670 newtons)—over 3,000 horsepower—for 34 seconds. Yet, despite these achievements, he remained secretive, a practice that doomed him to obscurity.

With the coming of World War II, Goddard again offered his services to the armed forces, but the military was unable to identify any real value in rockets as long-range missiles. Instead, it assigned him the task of developing liquid-propellant rockets for the rocket-assisted takeoff (RATO) of heavy aircraft. (The name of such rocket-assist systems was later changed, confusingly, to jet-assisted takeoff, or JATO.) Not only was this assignment largely a waste of Goddard's talents and experience, but

the results of his experiments were not very successful. The one exception to this was his work on a rocket engine that was capable of being throttled, research that eventually led to the Curtiss-Wright XLR-25 that accelerated the Bell X-2 research aircraft to Mach 3.

The German military machine suffered no such lack of foresight. By mid-1933, the little Aggregat-1 (A-1), a 4.5-foot-long (137-centimeter-long) rocket, was being tested, but its deficiencies spawned

An A-4 rocket roars off the launch pad, left, at Peenemünde on Usedom Island in the Baltic Sea during World War II. Below, Wernher von Braun briefs high-ranking German army, navy, and air-force officers on the potentially devastating new weapon.

ent of so many gifted scientists, combined with generous German government support, would form the basis for the postwar space-flight successes of the very nations against which Hitler would wage World War II.

In 1937, the German rocketry team built the 21.3-foot-long A-3 with a 3,300-pound-thrust (14,680-newton) motor, three-axis gyroscopic control, molybdenum exhaust vanes, radio-up-link fuel control, servos, and other advances. All three A-3s were launched in December 1937, but the stabilizing gyros were too weak and the exhaust vanes too slow to prevent the rockets, once airborne, from being pushed over by the prevailing wind.

development of the follow-on A-2, which featured a gyroscopic stabilizer. In late December, two versions of the A-2, *Max* and *Moritz,* named for the cartoon Katzenjammer Kids, were launched to an altitude of 6,500 feet (2,000 meters) above Borkum Island in the North Sea. Soon, motors of up to 3,300 pounds of thrust (14,680 newtons) were running in static tests.

When Luftwaffe (literally "air weapon"; the German air force) officials learned of Dornberger's team and its successes, they approached the Wehrmacht to explore the formation of a joint rocket-research facility. In April 1937, this singularly enlightened departure from bureaucratic infighting led to the establishment of just such a facility, under army control, at Peenemünde, on the island of Usedom, in the Baltic. Ironically, the focused tal-

Even as the A-3s were being built, Dornberger, Walter Riedel, and von Braun, who had obtained his Ph.D. in physics at the University of Berlin in 1934, already had designed the A-4. This huge rocket weapon was to carry a one-ton (900-kilogram) warhead for 170 miles (270 kilometers) on top of a 50,000-pound-thrust (222,420-newton) engine that would fire for 60 seconds. The A-5 recoverable rocket, about half the size of the A-4, was designed to test features that would be incorporated into the bigger rocket.

By mid-1938, the A-5 was reaching heights of 42,000 feet (13,000 meters), an astonishing achievement, but the Peenemünde team was more concerned with the design and building of the A-4's 50,000-pound-thrust (222,241-newton) engine. Everything about the A-4 was a major leap forward, technologically if not also in terms of the peaceful development of rocketry. To develop this giant engine, chemist Walter Thiel started small, with a 3,000-pound-thrust (13,345-newton) prototype, and then progressed to a double-walled-chamber, regeneratively cooled model of 9,000 pounds of thrust (40,035 newtons) that burned liquid oxygen and water-diluted alcohol.

With major contributions from Moritz Pohlmann, Walter Dornberger, and Wernher von Braun, the big engine slowly took shape. Von Braun's principal effort focused on how to pump the propellants into such a large engine. Not only did the pumps have to be reliable and light, but they had to force the liquids into the combustion chamber at the rate of 50 gallons (190 liters) or more per second. Thinking that this technology was close to impossible, he was surprised to learn from pump manufacturers that these requirements actually were similar to those of fire-engine water pumps. Von Braun studied these fire pumps, made the necessary changes, and transferred the design to the A-4.

When the first A-4 was rolled out, it represented a vision of the future of both terror weapons and space-launch vehicles: it was 46.9 feet (14.3 meters) long and 5.4 feet (165 centimeters) in diameter, and had a liftoff weight of 28,229 pounds (12,831 kilograms). The engine's final rating was 59,500 pounds of thrust (264,680 newtons) for 68 seconds.

The first flight test, which took place on June 13, 1942, was a disaster. The engine fired, but the A-4 failed to lift off. As the thrust gradually faded, the missile fell over and exploded in a blinding flash, destroying the launch pad and its facilities. The second launch, on August 16, went flawlessly—for 45 seconds. At that point, the rocket began to oscillate from side to side, until, finally, it broke apart in the air.

The third A-4 launch, on October 3, 1942, was a spectacular reward for so many years of hard work. The missile reached the astounding altitude of 60 miles (96 kilometers) above the Earth, the highest point by a great margin that any human-made object ever had attained. It traveled downrange for 125 miles (200 kilometers) at 3,300 miles (5,280 kilometers) per hour, and hit within 2.5 miles (four kilometers) of its target. That night, Dornberger hosted a very special gathering, and toasted this turning point in history by announcing "a new era in transportation, that of space travel." However, he reminded his staff that their present mission was to perfect the A-4 as a weapon.

The actual production of the missile took place in the underground factories of Mittelwerk in the Harz Mountains. Thousands of slave laborers were brought into the factories and driven under inhu-

A tunnel leads into the Mittlewerk factory in the Harz Mountains of central Germany, where more than 5,000 V-2 rockets—production versions of the A-4— were built between January 1944 and March 1945. An estimated 20,000 slave laborers died in the construction of the factory and its missiles.

man conditions to assemble and then push as many rockets out the doors as possible. It is a terrible but telling commentary on the politics both of the Third Reich and the officials who directed the A-4 program that more people died building the A-4 than eventually were killed by it as a weapon.

On July 7, 1943, Dornberger and von Braun met with Hitler, who viewed films of the missile's successful testing program. The Führer, who had been unmoved by previous rocket briefings, was electrified: the A-4 was to be given top priority as his second vengeance weapon against Britain, the V-2.

While the V-2s were being built, German engineers developed a highly mobile transportation-and-launch-trailer system to move the rockets to their launch sites. In the end, a small group of men with a minimum of training could pull the missile on its trailer to a launch site, raise the missile to a

A Meilerwagen lift trailer, above, raises a V-2 into launch position. Right, German and American rocket experts in Huntsville, Alabama, in 1956. Clockwise from front and center: Hermann Oberth (arms folded); Ernst Stuhlinger; U.S. Army Major General H. Toftoy; Robert Lusser, and Wernher von Braun. Opposite, Robert Goddard in 1925, the year before he launched the world's first liquid-propellant rocket.

vertical position, program it for a target, and then launch it. The simplicity of the scheme was deadly. Since it did not have to be fired from a fixed site, the V-2, like the Scud missiles of a later war, was difficult to spot before launch. Unlike the Scuds, however, once a V-2 was airborne, absolutely nothing could stop it—except, perhaps, its own mechanical failure. From September 1944 until the end of the war, 4,320 V-2s were launched, including some 1,120 against London, killing 2,511 people and injuring 6,000 more.

As the V-2s were raining down on England, the Peenemünde team continued to refine the missile. In order to extend its range, the A-4b was given swept-back wings with which to glide in the upper atmosphere. Drawings of a pressurized cockpit that would replace the warhead addressed the goal of putting the first man in space. With all its modifications, the A-9/A-10 was a far larger design than the A-4b, and, with either a warhead or a pilot on top of the 80-foot-tall (24.4-meter-tall) rocket, it was intended to reach Mach 4.4. The missile's first stage was to provide 440,000 pounds (1,957,295 newtons) of thrust from its engine; another rocket would provide the second stage. Its primary target was to be a bustling city some 3,000 miles (4,800 kilometers) away: New York. Yet another design, the A-11, was to be powered by a first stage of 3.5 million pounds of thrust (15,569,395 newtons) in order to achieve Earth orbit, while the A-12 would place a satellite in orbit, possibly by 1947. This would be the first step in building a space station.

All of these plans came to a halt, however, when World War II ended in May 1945. Dornberger, von Braun, and many of their colleagues went to great lengths to ensure their surrender to the Ameri-cans, while other, far less fortunate coworkers were captured by the Russians and treated nearly as badly as the Germans had treated their own slave laborers. Meanwhile, the seeds for the space race were sewn: interrogating von Braun, his captors sat wide-eyed as he described a future of artificial satellites, orbiting space platforms, and men on the moon. Little did they know that he would in large measure be responsible for making each of those predictions come true, even if that happened 10 years later than he originally thought it would.

When Robert Goddard and his staff dismantled a complete V-2 at the Navy's Annapolis Research Station in 1945, they were stunned. Although it was larger by far than any of Goddard's rockets, the layout was basically the same. Everyone but Goddard believed that the Germans had arrived at the same design on their own, since the American physicist's penchant for secrecy surely had kept almost all knowledge of his work from the rest of the world. Unable himself to accept that others could arrive independently at his hard-won secrets, however, Goddard was convinced that somehow the Germans had copied his designs. This idea shook him deeply, and he was never quite the same during the few months of his life that remained.

When Walter Dornberger was interrogated, he asked about Goddard, eager to know what his American counterpart might have been developing in parallel. Dornberger was stunned to find out that this pioneer's talents had largely gone unused. "We could not understand that a man of his genius did not get sufficient support of his government in time. We were interviewed by hundreds of incompetent representatives of the allies. They did not talk our rocket language and could simply not understand us. We wanted to talk to a man who was an expert and a fanatic rocketeer. We never received an answer about what happened to him."

Robert H. Goddard died on August 10, 1945, having received the highest praise for his pioneering work from the vanquished German rocketeers, who, ironically enough, would carry on with their own work to fulfill his dreams of space travel.

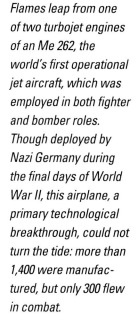

Flames leap from one of two turbojet engines of an Me 262, the world's first operational jet aircraft, which was employed in both fighter and bomber roles. Though deployed by Nazi Germany during the final days of World War II, this airplane, a primary technological breakthrough, could not turn the tide: more than 1,400 were manufactured, but only 300 flew in combat.

JET POWER

I n late 1942 and early 1943, fighter pilots flying the finest aircraft in Germany, England, and the United States began to think that they were hallucinating, both in training and in combat. A gunnery student at Muroc Army Air Base in the California desert watched with consternation as an airplane took off from the dry lake bed that surrounded this desolate bombing range facility. Not only was the airplane flying around on fire, trailing dark smoke, but its propeller was missing.

Some Lockheed P-38 pilots also experienced this hallucinogenic feeling while cruising near Muroc on a maximum-ceiling training flight. Confident that nothing could match their altitude, they watched a strange airplane pull up and fly formation with ease. There was nothing like it in the identification manuals. Not only was the propeller missing, but the pilot appeared to be a gorilla wearing a derby and smoking a cigar.

A Royal Air Force (RAF), high-altitude, Spitfire reconnaissance pilot, also confident that nothing could catch him in the stratosphere over England, was startled when a shadow darkened his cockpit. Looking up, he saw an obsolete Wellington bomber that he knew couldn't possibly have his altitude capability. Although no one would believe him, he was convinced that it was indeed a Wellington, and that both its propellers were stopped dead.

By 1944, Allied combat pilots deep over Germany swore they were being attacked by aircraft that not only went more than 100 miles per hour (161 kilometers per hour) faster than they did, but also had no propellers. The answer to these mysteries was that the jet age had arrived without warning, and aviation's gas-turbine engine—later called the turbojet—which had simmered in secret for many years, now was unveiled.

Gas turbines had been around since the early

1900s, but the idea of installing them in airplanes as an alternative to the piston engine had been viewed as a crackpot's dream. Quite simply, they did not produce enough power to haul much more than their own weight, never mind that of an entire airplane.

The turbine's possibilities for aeronautics lay dormant until two men, a young RAF flying instructor in England and a research engineer for the Heinkel aircraft company in Germany, started thinking about turbojets as primary aircraft-propulsion plants. Unbeknownst to each other, Frank Whittle and Hans von Ohain began to study future high-speed aircraft design and to read up on past work on gas turbines.

In 1928, flight at a speed over 500 miles per hour (805 kilometers per hour) and above an altitude of 20,000 feet (6,100 meters) generally was considered science fiction, but Frank Whittle thought that with rocket propulsion, or with a gas turbine driving a propeller (an arrangement later called the turboprop engine), it might be possible. By 1929, as he later recalled, "I was back to the gas turbine, but this time of a type which produced a propelling jet instead of driving a propeller." The British Air Ministry rejected Whittle's idea, but, in 1931, he was granted a patent for the world's first turbojet. The patent was not classified as secret, and, a year later, Whittle's findings were published for public use.

Without backing, Whittle continued with both his RAF career and his undergraduate studies at Cambridge University. His invention lay dormant until March 1936, when a small research firm, Power Jets, Limited, was created to develop the visionary pilot's idea. The first test engine, the W.U., or Whittle Unit, was fired up on April 12, 1937.

According to Whittle, "The experience was frightening." As the engine spooled up, it entered an uncontrolled acceleration, wailing like some impaled medieval monster, ready to explode at any moment. "Everyone around took to their heels except me," said Whittle. "I was paralyzed with fright and remained rooted to the spot." Fortunately, the engine started to wind down on its own, and the cause of the runaway malfunction was traced to fuel pooling in the combustion chamber.

Despite numerous successful engine runs, development at Power Jets suffered several setbacks: lack of money; apathetic government support; and extensive technical problems. Nevertheless, Whittle would not give up. After a nearly flawless engine run for a senior Air Ministry official on June 30, 1939, Power Jets was given a contract for the W.1 engine, which would be flown in a prototype test-bed aircraft built by the Gloster Aircraft Company.

After Great Britain declared war on Germany in September 1939, the new jet engine was looked upon as a potential advantage with increasing favor, but no one in England was aware that Ger-

many already had leaped ahead in the race.

While Whittle was at Cambridge in the mid-1930s, Hans von Ohain, obsessed with the idea of gas-turbine aircraft propulsion, was in the midst of doctoral studies at Goettingen University. By 1935, with the help of mechanic and machinist Max Hahn, von Ohain had a test engine running, although, according to its inventor, at first it "behaved more like a flame-thrower than an engine," producing barely enough power to turn faster than the starter motor. Rather than approach the German engine industry, which probably would have been uninterested, he asked aircraft manufacturer Ernst Heinkel for support.

Heinkel was interested in the project from the start, seeing in this young engineer's invention the means to build the fastest aircraft in the world. At the end of February 1937, the He S1 prototype turbojet was installed on a test bed and fired up a short

Hans von Ohain, standing at left, invented the power plant that boosted the first jet plane. Beside him sits Ernst Heinkel, the industrialist who gambled on this new venture. Below right, master mechanic Max Hahn inspects von Ohain's first experimental engine. Hahn fabricated it in an auto-repair shop in 1934. Three years later, an advanced prototype was run up on hydrogen gas, almost at the same moment that Frank Whittle, in England, bench-tested his liquid-fueled W.U., above right, ancestor of early Allied jet engines.

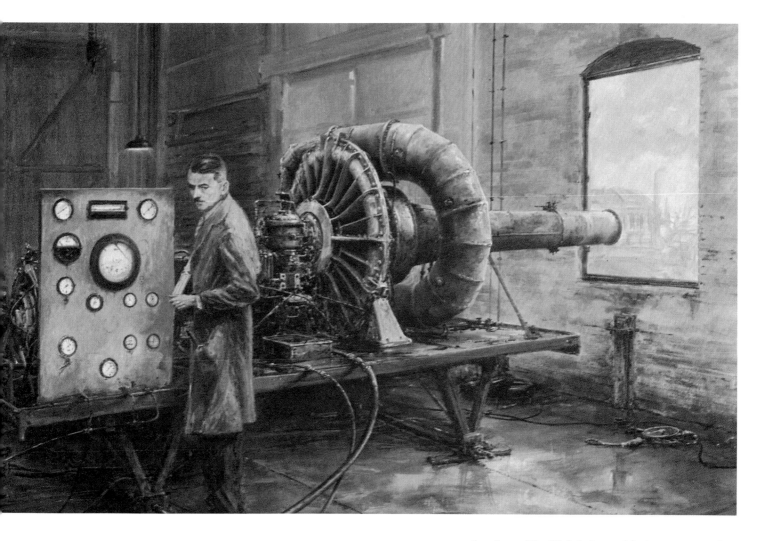

time later. The Heinkel-von Ohain team was electrified by the success, and Heinkel pressed for an immediate flight-test program in a company test aircraft, which would be built for this purpose.

By the late spring of 1939, the He S3 engine was test-flown under an He 118 bomber, then mated to an experimental airframe. On August 27, 1939, only a few days before the beginning of World War II, Heinkel test pilot Erich Warsitz made history by flying the world's first jet aircraft, the Heinkel He 178. As a result, the German Air Ministry decided to underwrite additional turbojet development at several other firms, a wise choice that would put Germany even further ahead.

Within a year, von Ohain had the 1,600-pound-thrust (7,117-newton) He S8 running for Heinkel's new jet fighter. On April 2, 1941, the twin-engine He 280 became the second turbojet-propelled aircraft—and the first jet fighter—to fly. Meanwhile,

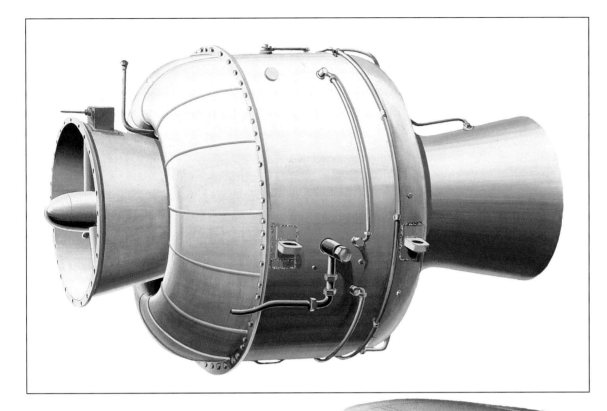

Below left, Hans von Ohain (right) presents a cut-away model of his He S3b jet engine to the Smithsonian Institution. The original engine powered the He 178, below. This stubby power plant, as seen in the schematic, left, belongs to the centrifugal-compressor class of turbojet. The other type, an axial-flow engine, is more complex to design and build; both von Ohain and Whittle started with centrifugal-compressor technology.

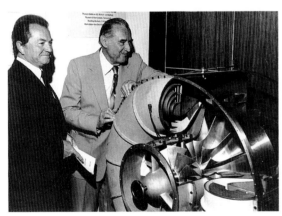

the Bavarian Motor Works (BMW) company was working on a more advanced, axial-flow engine, the 003, and Anselm Franz, at Junkers, was developing the axial-flow, 2,200-pound-thrust (9,786-newton) Jumo 004. Both of these were planned for trials with an experimental jet fighter being designed by Willy Messerschmitt.

When Italy's Caproni Campini N.1 flew for the first time on August 28, 1940, it was not equipped with a turbojet, but it did have a piston engine with a ducted-fan compressor similar to the one conceived and rejected by Frank Whittle more than 10 years before. Technically, then, the N.1 was jet propelled, but it was so slow and under-powered that it didn't even come close to matching the performance of the propeller-driven aircraft of the day.

By April 1941, the Whittle W.1X ground-test engine was being taxi-tested in the Gloster E.28/39 airframe. On May 15, 1941, after the airworthy W.1 engine was installed, test pilot Jerry Sayer made

Ernst Heinkel's He 178, at left, was designed around von Ohain's tame jet engine, opposite. The tiny aircraft had hardly more than a 23-foot wingspan, yet on August 27, 1939, it made history with the first jet flight. The engine itself, buried in the fuselage behind the wings, gulped air that was conveyed to it from the inlet in the plane's nose. Exhaust exited by the tail pipe.

Flight historian Paul E. Garber, at right in the photograph above, accepts the original British W.1 engine for the Smithsonian's permanent collection. On May 15, 1941, this centrifugal-compressor engine, illustrated in the schematic opposite, powered Great Britain's Gloster E.28/39 experimental aircraft, right, in its first flight.

Britain's first jet flight. So successful were the trials with the new engine and aircraft that Whittle and Gloster pressed on to create the nation's first jet fighter, the Gloster Meteor, which flew for the first time in March 1943. To increase the pace of testing, a Wellington bomber was fitted with a jet-engine mount where the tail-gun turret normally was located, allowing flight testing to be conducted with complete safety. Of course, when other pilots spotted the Wellington flying at high altitude with both engines shut down, and propellers feathered, they filed some interesting reports.

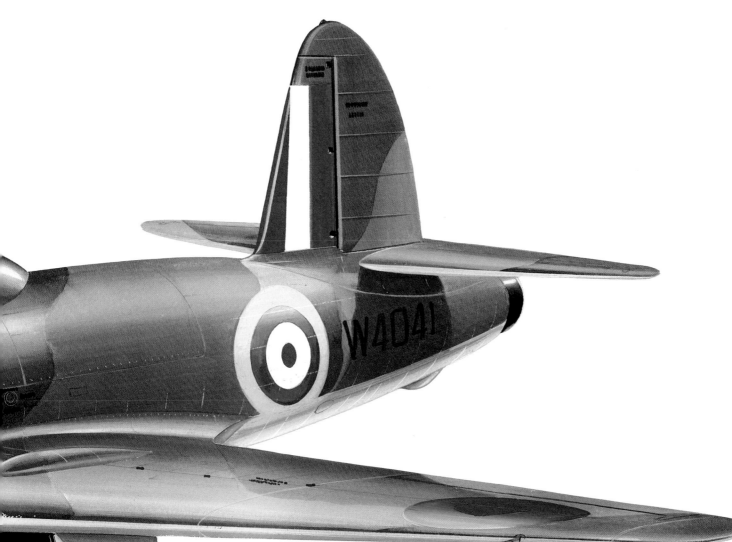

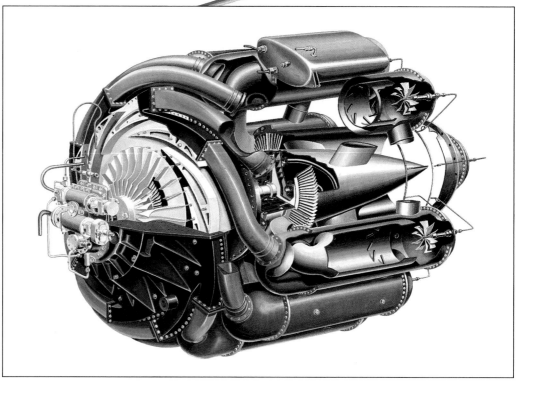

From left to right in the engine diagram, air enters and is compressed by vanes on a rotating disk. Spiral ducts carry the air to cylindrical combustion chambers where fuel burns fiercely. Hot gases escape, whirling a turbine connected to the compressor up front.

All of these early, relatively low-thrust jet aircraft provided some frightening experiences for pilots who were used to the almost instantaneous power and acceleration available from large, propeller-driven, piston engines. When the pilot pushed the throttle of a jet forward, there was almost no sense of acceleration—plenty of noise, but no action. The faster a jet engine moved, the more power it produced, so takeoffs were particularly hair-raising. Would the aircraft break ground before running off the end of the runway? Understandably, it took a while for pilots to trust an engine that at first appeared to have no power, and then "kicked in" about halfway down the field.

Landings also could produce their own moments of terror. Once a jet engine was throttled back for approach, it would not respond immediately when more power was needed. The lag between idle and full power could be well over 15 seconds, an eternity for a pilot who had come in too low and too slow and therefore was in need of immediate power to keep him from hitting the ground. If he throttled forward too fast, the engine often suffered a compressor stall that could lead to a flame out, at which point there was nothing to do but crash-land.

While the wartime flurry of innovation and experimentation was proceeding in Europe, virtually nothing involving the jet engine was taking place in the United States. In April 1941, U.S. Army Air Force chief Major General Henry H. "Hap" Arnold traveled to England, where he saw Whittle's work firsthand and watched the E.28/39 make its first hopping taxi tests. Throughout his career, Arnold had been known for his unorthodox, outside-the-rules methods of getting what he wanted for his under-funded branch of the service. When the first rumors of German and British jet experiments reached him, he helped form the government's National Advisory Committee for Aeronautics (NACA) Special Committee on Jet Propulsion under eminent propeller researcher William F. Durand. After seeing the Gloster jet Arnold knew that America had to obtain jet aircraft, and that it had no time for original research.

Arnold therefore struck an agreement with the British to have the W.2B engine built in the United States under license. Basic details were sent to the U.S. for study, and, three months after Arnold's visit, U.S. Army Air Force specialists were in England to receive firsthand information on Whittle's pioneering achievements.

Because General Electric (GE) had gained extensive experience with turbosuperchargers, it was chosen as the engine's U.S. manufacturer. In September, the Army Air Force ordered 15 copies of the Whittle engine, one E.28/39 airframe, and three prototype American aircraft for flight testing. The order later was reduced to a single engine, and the Gloster aircraft was canceled.

Bell Aircraft was chosen to design and build the new jet, a decision based on Larry Bell's enthusiasm for innovative experimentation, his company's proximity to GE, its talented engineering and design staff, and its lack of critical wartime production contracts. From the outset, the Army Air Force specified that the jet be struck from the fighter mold, so that if tests proved successful, full-scale production could begin and the aircraft could promptly go into combat. In order to create secrecy

German aeronautical engineers specified an axial-flow turbojet for their powerful bird of prey, the Me 262, right, itself the marriage of a Messerschmitt airframe to the Junkers Jumo 004 power plant, below.

The Me 262 demonstrated speeds more than 100 miles per hour faster than those of any Allied opponent. The efficient axial-flow engine, depicted above, kept air and hot gases moving in a straight line, rather than forcing them through two right-angle turns, as in the von Ohain and Whittle models.

Above, master crafts-men show off the newly restored Me 262A-1a Schwalbe ("Swallow") fighter. These experts work at the Smithsonian's Paul E. Garber Facility, the world-famous center for the care of historic aircraft. At left, two specialists fill and sand the Swallow's wing assembly after treating the metal to stop decay.

through confusion, the designation of a canceled Bell fighter, XP-59, was reassigned to the new project. The XP-59A, later named the Airacomet, was actually America's first jet. On October 1, 1941, the disassembled W.1X and a team from Power Jets were flown to the U.S., along with a set of W.2B drawings. Much to Whittle's amazement, the General Electric copy, Type I-A (GE production W.2B), was on the test bench by March 1942. Though the XP-59A airplane still was being built in an old automobile factory in downtown Buffalo, Bell received a contract that same month to build an additional 13 YP-59As with full armament. This certainly seemed like rapid progress at the time. Fortunately for the hopes of the enthusiastic Americans, they could not peer into Germany's secret jet-design bureaus.

The Messerschmitt P.1065, which, along with the He 280, had been ordered in 1940, had turned into the shark-shaped Me 262. As the Me 262 V1 prototype neared completion in early 1941, however, its intended Jumo 004A engine was producing only half of its projected thrust on the test stand. As a result, this most advanced of all jet aircraft then on the drawing boards made its first flight on April 18, 1941, with a Jumo 210 piston engine in the nose, instead of with two jets hung under the wings. By July, Messerschmitt had a contract for five test airframes and 20 preproduction Me 262s.

By November, two BMW 003 engines had been installed on the 262, but the piston engine was left in place for insurance. On November 25, the 262 was airborne again, but both jet engines failed, and it was brought back on piston power alone. In March 1942, after airborne tests under a Messerschmitt Me 110, the Jumo 004A was cleared for flight. The GE I-A engine reached the test bench in the same month.

On July 18, 1942, the Me 262 V3 was ready for its first flight on jet power alone. Shortly after eight A.M., at Leipheim, in southwestern Bavaria, test pilot Fritz Wendel started the engines and taxied to the extreme end of the runway. Holding the brakes, he slowly pushed the throttles forward until both engines were screaming.

As he hurtled down the runway, Wendel sensed

An engine specialist, right, matches main components of the Jumo 004B jet-turbine engine, and a colleague restores the fuselage, below. While the design of the Me 262 is legendary, and offered a clear glimpse into the future, German workmanship declined sharply during the downfall of the Nazi regime.

that the aircraft was not going to fly. The air-speed indicator showed that the jet already should have been airborne. At 800 yards (732 meters), he pulled the power to idle and slammed on the brakes.

After a long consultation with the engineers in attendance, Wendel agreed to give it another try. Guessing that the tail and its elevator controls had been blanked out aerodynamically by the wing, he was going to take a calculated risk: as the Me 262 reached flying speed—110 miles per hour (177 kilometers per hour)—Wendel hit the brakes briefly but solidly; the jet rocked forward and the tail popped off the ground. The unobstructed flow of air gripped the horizontal tail surfaces. He then eased back on the stick, and the roaring shark lifted into the air.

As the jet gained altitude and speed it went faster and faster. Wendel could not believe the air-speed indicator; he already had set the world's absolute speed record of 469.22 in April 1939, and now he was flying faster than 500 miles per hour (805 kilometers per hour). Negotiating a wide circle, he came

back in and landed after only 12 minutes in the air, and, upon opening the pilot's canopy, declared, "She's wonderful! I've never enjoyed a first flight more!" Later, in May 1943, when Luftwaffe fighter General Adolf Galland flew the Me 262 for the first time, he felt "as if the angels were pushing."

Unlike its other jet-pioneer contemporaries, the Me 262 was an advanced-airframe design, ideal for taking advantage of the jet engine's potential. Each Jumo engine was mounted in a sleek nacelle, one under each wing, a design that later would be copied and labeled the "stream-tube" style of engine mounting. In order to move the aircraft's center of gravity to the ideal position, the wings were swept back, a happy coincidence that increased the aircraft's speed significantly, although no one at the time knew about wing sweep and Mach numbers. The wing had leading-edge automatic slats and slotted flaps as well, while pitch trim was achieved with a variable-incidence, horizontal stabilizer actuated by an electric motor. All of these features later would become—and would remain—standard features on most jet aircraft.

Unfortunately for the Germans, the Me 262 program ground to a near halt as 1942 progressed. For one thing, Luftwaffe procurement chief Erhard Milch was pushing Messerschmitt to build the Me 210 bomber destroyer and devote less time to the

A close-up of the Smithsonian's restored Me 262A-1a Schwalbe, a fighter version of the World War II classic, reveals an open armament section where magazines held shells for four 30-millimeter cannons. Here, also, individual cartridges were automatically fed to firing chambers, locked in, and fired, with the spent brass finally ejected. This particular aircraft may have shot down as many as seven American and 42 Russian planes.

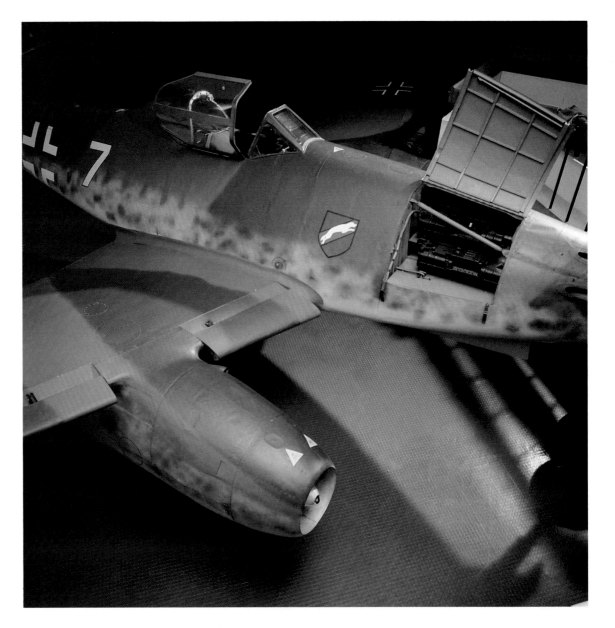

Proudly displayed at the Smithsonian's National Air and Space Museum, this Bell XP-59A Aira-comet was the first jet aircraft produced in the United States. Though only about 60 Aira-comets reached com-pletion, lessons learned from its design, produc-tion, testing, and deploy-ment led to such stellar performers as the Lock-heed P-80 Shooting Star.

jet fighter. A more technical reason for the slow-down was the tail-wheel landing gear on the first 262 prototypes. Pilots hated it; they had to stab the brakes on each takeoff to get the tail up and fly-ing. With the swept wing and the main wheels for-ward, there was not enough elevator force to raise the tail without this dangerous maneuver; the jet engines simply did not give enough initial acceler-ation to overcome the drag of an airplane with its nose up.

At first, Messerschmitt did not want to redesign the fighter for a nose wheel, since this would delay the program significantly. In the end, however, he had no choice, and, in November 1943, the rebuilt, tricycle-gear V3 flew for the first time.

The next month, Hitler decreed that the aircraft would be outfitted and deployed as a bomber in-stead of as a fighter, a decision that seemingly negat-ed almost all of the aircraft's attributes. In the end, however, that now notorious command only de-layed the program by a few weeks. The central prob-lem in the deployment of the aircraft was power. Because the metal within the engines was subject-ed to such intense heat that it broke down, the Jumo 004B production engines rarely lasted for more than five to ten hours' running time. Since Ger-many did not have ready access to such strategic metals as nickel, molybdenum, and cobalt, which were necessary in building high-temperature com-ponents, designers were forced to bring as much cooling air into the turbines as possible. Junkers, and eventually BMW, did a fine job, but the problems with the engine were not solved by the war's end. Although Germany built thousands of jet aircraft during the war, the airframes often would sit for long periods awaiting engines.

Nevertheless, when the Me 262, Arado Ar 234 jet bomber, and Me 163 Komet rocket fighter began combat operations in July and August of 1944, Allied pilots were stunned. They knew in an instant that they were flying antiquated airplanes that were powered by engines that might as well have been borrowed from steam trains.

By mid-1942, the first American Bell XP-59A was close to being finished. After a search for a flight-test location, Muroc Army Air Base, in the California desert, proved to be nearly perfect. One hundred miles (161 kilometers) northeast of Los Angeles, not only was it far from prying eyes, but its dry lake beds produced an ideal runway in all directions as far as the eye could see, and the weather was ideal most of the year. In August 1942, when the first two GE I-A engines arrived at Bell, they were matched carefully to the No.1 aircraft. The machine then was disassembled and shipped, along with the engines, to Muroc, arriving on September 19, 1942.

Compared to even standard wartime-security procedures, the project was accorded the most severe secret classification. Only those people directly involved with making the aircraft fly were told of the jet; probably no more than a dozen people at Wright Field, the Army Air Force's experimental test center, knew about it. A special hangar for Bell was built at the isolated north end of Rogers Dry Lake, and, as the XP-59A was reassembled inside, participants were forbidden to tell their families where they were working or what they were doing. Many of the Bell employees arrived from Buffalo without even knowing the type of airplane with which they would be involved.

Most of the Army officers assigned to the project were either out of the country or working in Washington, D.C., when the jet was moved from Buffalo to Muroc. Colonel Laurence C. "Bill" Craigie, chief of Experimental Aircraft Projects for the Air Technical Service Command at Wright,

was called in to see his boss, Brigadier General Frank Carroll, chief of the Engineering Division. Carroll suggested that Craigie spend a few days at Muroc as his representative to watch the aircraft's first test flights.

On October 1, 1942, Bell's Chief of Flight Test Robert Stanley made the first American jet flight, although many considered it just a "hop" since he flew at low altitude for 30 minutes on one engine (the other had failed to start) with the landing gear down. Nevertheless, the heavy smoke from the engine resulted in a call from the South Base tower offering help with whatever aircraft might be on fire up north. The tower operator was turned down with a polite "No, we can handle it alright." Before the puzzled observer hung up, he remarked

that he knew they must be a bunch of nuts up north, to take an airplane on fire so casually.

The next day, October 2, with military and civilian representatives present, Stanley made the first two official jet flights, taking the Airacomet up to 6,000 and then 10,000 feet (1,829 then 3,048 meters). General Electric had insisted that, after three hours' running time, including run-up, taxiing, and flight time, the engines be pulled and partially disassembled for inspection. That left very little initial flight time available.

When Stanley climbed out of the jet after his flight to 10,000 feet (3,048 meters), he turned to Craigie and said, almost offhandedly, "Bill, we only have about 20 minutes' time left before the engines

Bell's Airacomet XP-59 development program was wrapped in deepest secrecy, below, even to the point of mounting a dummy propeller on the ship between trial flights. During research, a full-size model was tested in the big National Advisory Committee for Aeronautics (NACA) wind tunnel, right, at Langley Research Center near Hampton, Virginia. First-line, propeller-driven fighters could outfly Airacomets, but jet propulsion's potential was sky high, and subsequent planes set many speed and performance records.

have to be pulled. Why don't you fly it?" As Craigie later recalled, "He didn't have to ask me twice. I didn't get very high or go very fast. My most vivid impression, after an extremely long takeoff run, occurred the instant the aircraft left the ground—it was so quiet! In an ordinary airplane with a piston engine the moment of takeoff is the moment of maximum vibration. With this rotary device it was very, very smooth. It was accentuated because we were only operating at half-power."

Craigie had had no idea he would be flying the XP-59A. He had come out to California for the tests as an observer. As a matter of fact, the Army pilots normally assigned to the project, Colonels Don Keirn, Ralph Swofford, and Ben Chidlaw, al-

ready had drawn straws to see who would be next after Stanley, but they had been detained by the press of assignments in England and Washington. "Although I had done a limited amount of test flying," said Craigie, "I was not really a test pilot. I had become America's first military jet pilot almost by accident. Things were certainly a lot less formal in those days."

After flying at half power, both Stanley and Craigie had some second thoughts about GE's reluctance to allow the pilots to use full power. "We were a little bit concerned," remembered Craigie, "they were being a little over conservative. We wanted to know just how much thrust we were getting, so Bob Stanley had them stick a metal fence post in the lake bed. We got a big spring scale and attached it between the fence post and the airplane. We revved the engines up as high as GE would let us go—we got a reading of 1,600 pounds on that spring scale, so we were getting 800-pounds' thrust per engine, which is not a hell of a lot!"

Despite the strict security restrictions, the new jet was spotted by people who happened to be in the right place at the wrong time. One Army Air Force lieutenant on a gunnery-practice flight saw the XP-59A take off in a cloud of smoke. Naturally curious, he flew close enough to notice that the aircraft had no propellers. When he excitedly told the other pilots in the group what he had seen, they laughed at him and told him that he must have an overactive imagination, since it was impossible for an airplane to fly without a propeller. It was only after the official American-British press release, in January 1944, that the lieutenant realized what he had seen.

By that time, Bill Craigie, in North Africa, "was receiving almost daily 'V-mail' letters from my wife, which were intended to keep me informed of the mysterious propellerless airplane. About the fifth day, I received a rather short letter in which she commented, a bit sarcastically, on my close-mouthed New England conservatism! She had just read in the paper that I had been the second pilot to fly the XP-59A—fifteen months earlier!"

In the 15 months during which the XP-59A prototypes were tested secretly over Muroc, Army pilots continued to report strange encounters with propellerless airplanes. On certain occasions, Bell test pilot Jack Woolams could not resist having some fun: he would put on a gorilla mask and a derby and stick a cigar in his mouth when pulling up to unsuspecting Army pilots flying across the desert.

In spite of its pioneering accomplishments, the P-59 was a major disappointment. As a result of

Lockheed's P-80 Shooting Star was designed by the legendary Clarence "Kelly" Johnson, and first flew on January 9, 1944. This ex-ample is the original XP-80, Lulu Belle, the prototype for a family of jet fighters and trainers.

the project's secret status, the only wind-tunnel experiments were done at Wright Field. The National Advisory Committee for Aeronautics, which had sophisticated wind tunnels, was not told about the project, so there was no opportunity to develop the aircraft into much more than a relatively unsophisticated carrier for the new engine. Top speed was barely over 400 miles (644 kilometers) per hour; the standard piston fighters of the day could easily outperform such a machine.

Furthermore, the engine installation created more aerodynamic interference than expected, and the airplane tended to "snake" during gunnery testing. This instability obviously made it a poor gun

platform. As a result, the initial Army Air Force order of 100 P-59As was halved, and the Airacomet became a trainer for future jet pilots.

Without a doubt, when the XP-59A lifted off the barren California dry lake near Muroc it ushered in a new era in test-flying. Informal, "seat-of-the-pants" testing would continue for several years, epitomized by the cavalier, almost off-handed way in which Bill Craigie achieved aviation history. Never-

theless, the specialized test pilot, with graduate degrees in engineering, had long since become the standard. Craigie, who graduated in the same Army Air Corps cadet class as Charles A. Lindbergh, was among the last of the maverick pilots. He had trained in Jennies and had earned his credentials flying open-cockpit biplanes at a time when about the only aids a pilot had were his skill and courage. With the coming of the jet engine, aviation changed forever.

At left, a historic photo shows Frank Whittle at work with a "slip stick," or slide rule, the analog counterpart of today's electronic digital computers. Through Whittle's genius, Great Britain was able to introduce the jet engine to Allied aviation.

THE SOUND BARRIER

W hen World War II pilots got their hands on such "hot ships" as the Lockheed P-38 Lightning and the Republic P-47 Thunderbolt, they reveled in the hitherto unthinkable availability of power. They could push past 400 miles per hour (644 kilometers per hour) without much effort and soar to altitudes near 40,000 feet (12,192 meters). That high above the Earth, pilots found their mounts could dive at even faster speeds, some approaching 600 miles per hour (965 kilometers per hour). The resulting, near vertical descents were adrenaline-producing, exhilarating, and horrifying: men died pushing their aircraft into an unknown regime that lay beyond the theoretical speeds a wind tunnel could generate.

With these advanced, propeller-driven fighters came a new phenomenon called compressibility, which had to do with the fact that the faster an airplane dived, the less control the pilot had over it. The controls would reverse and then become locked and immovable, while the nose "tucked" under. The fighter dived more steeply, in spite of all the muscle power the pilot could muster to pull back on the stick. When, in a steep dive, a North American P-51 pilot saw what appeared to be shock waves moving back across his wings, no one would believe him, so he tried such a perilous dive again, only this time he captured the phenomenon on film.

Such theorists as Austrian Ernst Mach, a 19th-century physicist and mathematician, had envi-

sioned such waves in trying to describe the theory of airflow. Mach worked out a ratio between the speed of a solid object through the air and the speed of sound: when these speeds were equal, the ratio was 1, or Mach 1, as, in honor of this brilliant thinker, it has come to be known. When pilots came near Mach 1 in their howling, screaming fighters, they seemed to reach an impenetrable barrier at around Mach .75 to .80 that no machine could breach without coming apart or going out of control. The only known objects that punctured this supersonic wall of compressibility—the "sound barrier," as it later was called—were bullets.

During the late 1930s theorists such as Theodore von Kármán of the California Institute of Tech-

California Institute of Technology aerodynamicist Theodore von Kármán, above, and others believed in the viability of supersonic flight as early as the 1930s. By the end of 1944, the Army Air Force and the National Advisory Committee for Aeronautics (NACA) had proposed the plane that would become the X-1.

nology's Guggenheim Aeronautical Laboratory and Wright Field Air Corps engineering instructor Ezra Kotcher came to believe in the possibility of supersonic flight. Kotcher's August 1939 report on the subject reached both the National Advisory Council on Aeronautics (NACA) and Air Corps chief Major General "Hap" Arnold, and included a proposal for a full-scale series of flight-test programs, with specially designed aircraft powered by gas-turbine or rocket engines.

More than 12 years before Kotcher's report, aerodynamicist John Stack had explored a series of supersonic-aircraft designs, so this technology was not a completely new idea. By 1943, the favorable conduct of World War II and the promising potential of technology freed up funds for serious research into level, transonic—Mach .7 to Mach 1.3—flight, which, with the advent of jet and rocket engines, was now possible. That such engines existed at all is a tribute to the tenacity of their designers.

Frank Whittle, for one, developed his turbojet engine without official government support. In New Jersey, a practical rocket engine created by Jimmy Wyld and his friends at Reaction Motors, Inc., emerged under similar conditions. Wyld and his team had been true believers from their first days, back in the early 1930s, as members of the amateur American Rocket Society. Lovell Lawrence, Jr., Hugh Franklin Pierce, John Shesta, and Wyld all loved putting their ideas into physical experiments for the society. They gave no thought to building prototype engines and running them on static tests with only surplus World War I helmets for protection. Cooling the rockets before they blew up was sometimes more of a goal than a reality.

The most practical solution for rocket-motor overheating was the use of cooler burning fuels, such as water-diluted alcohol, which also burned more evenly than gasoline. And when Wyld read of Austrian Eugen Sänger's use of regenerative cooling for rocket engines, he knew he had found a solution. This new system circulated liquid fuel around the combustion chamber before it was injected into the chamber and ignited, which had the two-fold effect of both cooling the motor and preheating the fuel for a more even burn.

By 1937, Wyld had his own regenerative engine on the workbench in a cramped space next to his New York apartment. John Shesta built the test stand, and they ran the 100-pound-thrust (445-newton), liquid-oxygen-and-alcohol engine for the first time in December 1938. It weighed an incredibly light two pounds (.9 kilograms), and it didn't blow up.

Wyld kept refining his engine as he took on a succession of jobs, some of which were respectable engineering positions, and struggled through periods of unemployment. In late 1941, Wyld and three friends formed Reaction Motors, Inc. (RMI), with $5,000 borrowed from relatives and friends, and started working out of a garage in New Jersey. When Lovell Lawrence, Jr., demonstrated Wyld's engine to the Navy, which had sent an observer to watch a test run, it sparked genuine interest.

Spurred by the attack on Pearl Harbor, the Navy signed a contract with RMI for a number of liquid-fueled JATO (Jet-Assisted-Take-Off) rockets, which shortened seaplane-takeoff runs considerably. RMI's 3,000-pound-thrust (13,345-newton) rockets were in operation by 1943, and the company moved into an old silverware factory at Pompton Plains, New Jersey. Practical, low-weight rock-

Nineteenth-century Austrian physicist and philosopher Ernst Mach first determined the ratio of the speed of an object traveling through the air at a particular altitude to the speed of sound. Mach numbers still are used today to measure the speed of an aircraft in relation to the speed of sound.

et engines that produced substantial thrust soon became a reality.

In December 1943, while attending a NACA conference, Bell Aircraft engineer Robert Wolf proposed that a transonic-research aircraft be developed by a joint Army/Navy/NACA team. The next month, Ezra Kotcher's 1939 study re-emerged within the Development Engineering Branch of the Army Air Force, resulting in a proposal for a Mach .999 high-speed research aircraft powered by rocket or jet engines. Kotcher and a number of other highly regarded engineers teamed up to persuade the Army bureaucracy to build such an airplane.

On March 15, 1944, upon the encouragement of the NACA's John Stack, representatives of the

NACA, the Army Air Technical Service Command, and the Navy Bureau of Aeronautics met at the Navy's Langley, Virginia, research facility. There, two transonic-aircraft proposals emerged: the Navy and the NACA would build a turbojet-powered machine with limited performance, while the Army would pursue its faster, rocket-engined aircraft. As a result, two projects, both of which involved the NACA's participation, were born.

The military services and the government at last were enthusiastically united; all they now had to do was find companies to build the aircraft. Ezra Kotcher made his way around the industry network, and, to his surprise and frustration, was met with an almost complete lack of interest. All the companies he approached were busy with wartime production, and, as Walter T. Bonney, a former Bell Aircraft employee, recalled, "the idea of sticking one's nameplate on the needle nose of a research airplane that, very possibly, would smash itself and its pilot to smithereens on the first flight, was, to put it mildly, not the sort of thing to be considered with great enthusiasm by any aircraft president

This Douglas D-558-2 research aircraft today hangs in the National Air and Space Museum. Originally equipped with both an XLR-8 rocket motor and a J-34 turbojet, the sleek machine subsequently was modified to feature all-rocket propulsion. In November 1953, NACA test pilot A. Scott Crossfield pushed it to 1,291 miles (2,077 kilometers) per hour, twice the speed of sound.

who was proud of the line of airplanes which he had already fathered."

It was not until the end of 1944 that Douglas Aircraft, under the leadership of Ed Heinemann, accepted a Navy order for the production of a turbojet-powered machine to be called the D-558. Bell Aircraft, under Robert J. Woods, then agreed to build the MX-653—later dubbed the Experimental Supersonic One, or XS-1, and, finally, by 1947, the X-1—for the Army. Bell signed the official contract for three airframes in March 1945.

Hedging its bets, the Navy had asked the Douglas team to design a second aircraft, the D-558-2, which was to be equipped with a rocket engine and swept-back wings. Because of its previous success in building the Navy's JATO power plants, RMI was the natural choice to produce the rocket components. Meanwhile, as the Bell design team wrestled with the aerodynamics of their new manned rocket, Kotcher was considering another young, rocket-engine company, Aerojet, for the job of building the power plant. The firm had built a 2,000-pound-thrust (8,897-newton) rocket for the

Seen here in service with the U.S. Navy, the National Air and Space Museum's D-558-2 drops away from its launch aircraft, a Boeing P2B-1S (a modified B-29), left. Below, Jimmy Wyld, one of the founders of Reaction Motors, Inc. (RMI), studies his first liquid-propellant-cooled rocket. Wyld's XLR motors would power a generation of X-planes, including the X-1 and the D-558-2.

stillborn XP-79 project, but the engine was hypergolic, that is, its liquid propellants ignited upon contact with each other—a sure means of obtaining ignition, but to some a rather hazardous plan, considering the pilot would be sitting just a few feet in front of the process. Furthermore, the propellants were highly caustic and difficult to handle. The Bell staff was not overly optimistic about the rocket's potential.

Through serendipity, Bell engineer Benson Hamlin discovered that RMI and Wyld's reliable, non-hypergolic, liquid-oxygen-and-water, diluted-ethyl-alcohol rocket was being upgraded for the Navy. This seemed almost too good to be true for both sides. Ezra Kotcher came to the Navy with hat in hand, but he needn't have worried: all the armed services had been on the same team since early 1944, and had been engaging in only friendly competition, so the Navy gave the engine to the Army for its rocket plane.

Wyld combined four of his 1,500-pound-thrust (6,673-newton) engines together in order to supply the needed total of 6,000 pounds (26,690 new-

tons) of thrust. When Kotcher came to New Jersey to see if the rocket would run, it had been painted black to hide all the rough modifications. The monstrous wail it made when it was running led to the nickname "belching black bastard," but later, for publicity reasons, this was changed to "Black Betsy."

Regarding the engine's production, RMI project engineer Jim Fitzgerald recalled: "Surprisingly, there were no major accidents in the development of the engine, yet testing means were very crude by today's standards. It was hellishly dangerous. The firing room, an unprotected quonset hut, was only 20 feet away from the test stand. Had the engine

blown up it would have come right through." But it didn't, and so the Army had its 10,000-horsepower XLR-11. Could Bell now produce a plane slick enough to go through the "barrier"?

Woods and his team had virtually no empirical data on supersonic flow. Wind tunnels of the time "choked" at high speed due to interference from shock waves reflected off of the side walls. Though small models of high-speed aircraft had been mounted on the wings of aircraft flown near compressibility speeds, and had been dropped from aircraft in flight, the only way to find out for sure about the sound barrier was to put a pilot in a rocket-powered machine and blast him through Mach 1.

Drawing on the knowledge that a bullet-shaped missile was the only object that was known to penetrate the sound barrier easily, Bell engineers Benson Hamlin and Paul Emmons decided to study the aerodynamics of the .50-caliber bullet in flight. Their data provided little information on how the projectile performed, but at least they verified that the bullet did remain stable. As a result, the rocket-plane's fuselage mimicked the shape of a bullet. Two sets of wings as thin as anyone had ever designed (a 10-percent and an 8-percent thickness-to-width ratio) were attached to the manned bullet, along with an "all-movable" horizontal stabilizer

that could be used for control in the event that the elevator surfaces were ineffective at supersonic speeds. Two sets of tail surfaces were built as well, each thinner even than the respective wing with which it would be matched. For instance, a six-percent-thick tail would be matched to an eight-percent wing, so that when the wing started to suffer the effects of supersonic shock waves, the tail would still be effective and would allow the pilot to retain control.

It was debated whether to fit the aircraft with landing gear for a conventional ground takeoff or to carry it aloft beneath a larger aircraft and drop it at altitude. In the end, these questions were settled by RMI's problems with the engine. Originally, propellants were to be pumped into the combustion chambers by a turbopump, which theoretically would provide the aircraft with a top speed of 1,700 miles per hour (2,735 kilometers per hour) with full tanks. But the young wizards could not come up with a pump that could work with liquid oxygen at -360 degrees F (-217.77 C). The only alternative was to increase weight and take up the room normally used for fuel with a pressurized-nitrogen delivery system.

Twelve super-strong, spherical, steel bottles that could hold enough nitrogen to force the fuel into

Douglas test pilot Bill Bridgeman, left, sits in the cockpit of one of the D-558-2 Skyrockets. In January 1951, Bridgeman and the D-558-2 accidentally were dropped from the launch aircraft after he had aborted and had shut down the plane's systems. Fortunately, he was able to ready the aircraft and fire the engine while falling, and landed successfully.

Bell test pilot Chalmers "Slick" Goodlin, below, a former Royal Air Force and U.S. Navy flier, was only 23 years old on December 9, 1946, when he flew the X-1 in its first powered test flight. Goodlin replaced Jack Woolams, Bell's original X-1 test pilot, who had been killed flying a Bell P-39 in preparation for the 1946 Thompson Trophy race.

the chambers had to be designed from scratch and installed in the fuselage. The resulting loss of fuel capacity limited engine-firing time to 2.5 minutes total, for a top speed of 1,000 miles per hour (1,609 kilometers per hour). This in turn dictated an air launching, lest too much fuel be burned in the climb to altitude. The nitrogen-pressure system also was modified to activate the landing gear, flaps, horizontal stabilizer, and cockpit pressurization as well.

On December 27, 1945, the first XS-1 was rolled out at Bell, attached to its B-29 Superfortress mother ship, and flown to Pinecastle Army Air Field near Orlando, Florida, on January 19, 1946, for glide tests. The first "Black Betsy" had yet to be delivered. On the 25th, Bell test pilot Jack Woolams flew the craft during its first drop from 27,000 feet (8,230 meters). It went like clockwork, and, after the 10-minute, gliding flight, Woolams concluded his written report with the words "due to the ruggedness, noiselessness, and smoothness of response of this airplane, it is the most delightful one to fly of them all." Bell, it seems, had designed a winner.

After 10 glide flights, the program moved to Muroc Army Air Base, the same barren stretch of California desert where the XP-59A had been tested. Woolams died while testing a Bell P-39 racer for the 1946 Thompson Trophy race, and Chalmers "Slick" Goodlin became Bell's chief test pilot on the XS-1. The second aircraft was delivered to Muroc on October 7, 1946.

Following another series of glide flights, the first

powered flight was made on December 9. A loose igniter nut allowed some fuel to leak and a fire broke out, but, much to everyone's relief, the engine shut itself down as it was designed to do. Goodlin found that the XS-1 flew just as smoothly under power as when gliding, and with all four chambers firing it went like greased lightning right up to the guaranteed contract speed of Mach .8, with only a slight shuddering. Of the 21 acceptance test flights, Goodlin made 20 and Alvin "Tex" Johnston of Bell one. By May 1947, the contractor's test flights had been completed. Both engine and airframe had proved to be exceptionally well manufactured, with only a few minor problems.

Before his death, Woolams had stated publicly that he was going be the first to fly at supersonic speed. When that mantle fell to Goodlin, he began planning for the initial exploratory flights to break the sound barrier. His role ended in June, however, when the Army Air Force and the NACA decided to use their own pilots for a two-phased attempt to break the sound barrier.

Under the Army Air Force's authority, aircraft No. 1, which featured the thinner wings, would press for Mach 1.1 in as short a time as was considered safe. Colonel Albert "Al" Boyd, chief of the Flight Test Division at Wright, picked three pilots: Captain Charles E. "Chuck" Yeager would be the primary pilot, with Lieutenant Robert A. "Bob" Hoover and Captain Jack Ridley as backups. The NACA, meanwhile, using XS-1 No. 2, would undertake a less rapid program with pilots

INSTRUMENT BATTERY

The cockpit of the Bell X-1 Glamorous Glennis, left, in which Chuck Yeager broke the sound barrier in October 1947, includes, to the left, the control column and yoke, which are used to move the elevators and ailerons. Once sealed, the cockpit was pressurized with nitrogen, and the pilot breathed oxygen through a mask. At right, the Bell X-1, now a graceful fixture at the National Air and Space Museum, exhibits its projectile ancestry: the fuselage was designed to resemble a .50-caliber machine-gun bullet.

Hydraulic lifts carefully lower a Boeing B-50 launch aircraft over Bell X-1 No. 3, above. Many of the X-planes were attached to bombers and carried to altitude for both gliding and powered flights. This X-1, *Queenie,* had a high-speed turbo-pump that fed fuel to its rocket engine. On a subsequent mission it exploded on the ground and injured its pilot. Right, a crewman fills the pilot's oxygen tanks on the second X-1.

Herbert Hoover and Howard Lilly; their goal would be the accumulation of more detailed information.

After instruction on the aircraft's systems and structure at the Bell plant in New York, the pilots flew out to Muroc, where, on July 27, 1947, the official flight-test program got underway. By this time, Yeager and his friends were no longer Army pilots; the U.S. Air Force had been created, and the Army Air Force was a thing of the past. The XS-1 was redesignated the X-1, the first in a string of "X" planes that would cross the frontiers of flight.

Chuck Yeager made his first glide flight in the X-1 on August 6. Although he did not have the advanced education of most of his colleagues, Yeager was recognized by Boyd to be an exceptionally fine, intuitive test pilot who knew just how far to push an airplane. Herb Hoover watched those first flights, and then wrote to fellow NACA test pilot Mel Gough that "this guy Yeager is pretty much of a wild one, but [I] believe he'll be good on the Army ship....On first drop, he did a couple of rolls right after leaving the B-29! On third flight, he did a two-turn spin!"

As with those before him, Yeager found the X-1 to be easy to fly, a pilot's airplane in every sense of the word—docile and without a mean bone in its body. He made his first powered flight on August 29. After making sure all four chambers would fire in turn, Yeager recalled,

I shut off the rocket engine, came down at 450 miles per hour in a steep dive across the field and pulled up and ignited all four chambers. The airplane really took off. I got up to .8 Mach number quite fast. In order to keep the aircraft below .82 which was our aim for mach number, I pulled the airplane almost into a vertical climb. I was doing sort of a modified barrel roll going straight up. But as I went through 38,000 to 40,000 feet, and dropped the nose a little bit, the first thing I knew I was up to .84 Mach number with no indication of any problems. So I shut off and jettisoned the remainder of my fuel and came on down and picked up my chase aircraft, and landed on the lake bed.

Al Boyd felt he had to step in and tame Yeager's tiger a bit, asking him specifically why he had gone faster than .82 when he had been ordered not to.

Yeager was on the carpet. "Jack Ridley and I sat

At Muroc Air Force Base in California, a Boeing bomber is towed into position over X-1 No. 1, which sits in a specially built pit. The X-1 then was hoisted into the Boeing's bomb bay and carried aloft for an air launch. In January 1949, at nearby Rogers Dry Lake, Chuck Yeager flew this aircraft in a conventional takeoff, the only ground launching of a piloted, rocket-powered X-plane. The craft soared to 23,000 feet (7,010 meters) in a minute and a half.

down practically all night trying to figure out a good answer. I told him...I was a little bit elated in flying the X-1 under power for the first time. He accepted it after a terse telephone call telling me to pay attention to what I was doing."

Although the X-1 was a plumber's nightmare on the inside, it was utter simplicity to fly. The XLR-11 engine had one ignition switch for each of the four chambers. There was no throttle; it was either full blast on each chamber or nothing. Speed was controlled by using a combination of the four chambers. With his extensive maintenance and mechanical background, Yeager appreciated the airplane more each time he flew it.

Here, in his own words, is how Yeager described a typical flight in the X-1:

After fueling the liquid-oxygen and water-alcohol tank and pressurizing the nitrogen system and loading it [the X-1] under the B-29, the X-1 pilot did not take off in the cockpit of the X-1...because the climbing speed of the B-29 was around 180 miles per hour. The X-1 Number 1 with the 8-percent wing and the 6-percent tail had a stalling speed fully loaded around 240 miles per hour. We figured that since I had no way of getting out of the cockpit of the X-1 once you were in, you were pretty well sealed in and that if we had an inadvertent shackle release or had to drop the X-1 anywhere under 12,000 feet you would end up in a spin at too low an altitude to recover from the spin. So I rode in the B-29 during take-off. When we got up to around 12,000 feet, I went back into the bomb bay of the B-29 where we had a ladder in the right side of the bomb bay opposite the entrance door on the right side of the X-1. I would get on the ladder and they would let me down into the slip stream just opposite the door on the X-1. I would slide into the X-1, feet first, wearing a seat type parachute, primarily to sit on, and get squared away in the cockpit. Then they would lower the door. Jack Ridley would normally come down on the ladder with the door and hold it against the right side of the X-1 and I would lock it from the inside. Once I got squared away with my oxygen mask and helmet, I got hooked up to the commu-

nications system and talked to the B-29 pilot and the two chase pilots, going through the check list during the climb to 25,000 feet. Prior to drop, I would load up the first stage, getting 1,500 pounds in my manifold for the [landing] gear, and then I would load up my second-stage regulators, pressurizing the liquid-oxygen tank and the water-alcohol tank. I would bleed off the liquid-oxygen manifold, getting the gas out of the manifold until I got liquid oxygen through the bleed valve, and then I would shut it down. I was ready for drop and ready to ignite the chambers of the rocket engine.

Usually the B-29 pilot would climb within gliding distance of Rogers Dry Lake until we got to about 25,000 feet; then he would back off to about Victorville, some 40 miles away, still within gliding distance of the lake bed, and pick up speed with the B-29. This meant dropping the nose and diving it somewhere around a 15-20 degree dive angle. Once they got up to 240 miles per hour indicated, he would give me a countdown of 10, 9, 8, 7, 6 on down to 0, and release the shackle that dropped me out of the B-29. After drop, once I knew I had fallen clear of the B-29, I would level the aircraft out and ignite one of the chambers of the rocket engine itself.

With roughly 588 gallons of propellants, I could burn up all of the propellants in 2 1/2 minutes, if I ran all four chambers. Five minutes with two running, and ten minutes with one single chamber running. On all of the flights that I made on the X-1, we never landed with any fuel aboard, because the gear was not designed to take that additional weight. The X-1 empty weighed somewhere around 6,800 pounds, with instrumentation and pilot aboard. Fully loaded with fuel it ran close to 13,000 pounds. So at the end of a run, if I had not used all of my fuel, I would jettison the remainder of the liquid oxygen and water alcohol and then come on down somewhere 5,000 or 6,000 feet above the lake bed at somewhere between 300 and 400 miles per hour.... break left or right, whichever the wind predicated, and roll the airplane out on downwind, put the gear down at around 250 miles per hour. The flaps would come down with

In Yeager's Quest, *artist Stan Stokes depicts the first X-1 just after its drop from a B-29. Pilot Chuck Yeager has fired the XLR-11 rocket engine to*

Chuck yeager

begin his climb through
40,000 feet (12,192 me-
ters), during which he
would become the first
person to attain speeds
greater than Mach 1.

the gear. The airplane, now empty, stalled around 190 miles per hour. So I held it around 220 on the base leg, flew a final at 220 and flared the aircraft and touched down at around 190 miles per hour on the lake bed. We had a roll out of about three miles on the lake bed, if I did not use brakes. With Rogers Dry Lake having a runway some eight miles long and five miles wide, I would normally pick a spot in the middle and aim for it so that if I undershot or overshot two or three miles it did not make much difference.

The X-1's first buffeting occurred when Yeager hit Mach .88. From that point on, in order to find out what would happen at higher Mach numbers, he would roll the X-1 over at the end of each run and pull 2 or 3 Gs. As the aircraft passed Mach .9, the buffeting increased, and as Yeager described it, "the airplane got a little squirrely, meaning that the stability began to break down laterally and directionally, a little bit as the shock waves were becoming more intense and moving back on the wing and the fuselage and the tail."

On September 12, his fifth flight, the speed was pushed to Mach .92. When he reached .94 at 40,000 feet (12,192 meters) and rolled over, he pulled back on the control column; nothing happened. The controls moved freely back and forth with no response whatsoever. Yeager cut all four chambers and decelerated until control returned, and then jettisoned the remaining fuel and glided in for a landing on the lake bed.

For the first time, Yeager, Ridley, the NACA pilots—just about everyone—began to worry about the outcome of the whole program. The predictions that had been based on compressibility problems with other aircraft and on designers' theories had implied that the X-1 would either pitch up or pitch down near the speed of sound, but not that it would simply cease to have control. Quickly pooling all of the recorded data, the engineers discovered that at .94 Mach the shock wave across the horizontal stabilizer was right at the hinge point of the elevator and thus was eliminating control effectiveness.

Since the X-1 had an adjustable horizontal sta-

bilizer that had not been used on any previous flights, the team decided to have Yeager make pitch changes with his trim switch alone and not with the elevator, beginning at Mach .8. Yeager was confident "we had the thing licked." He was more attached to the airplane than ever. As he had done in combat with his North American P-51s, Yeager had his wife's name painted on the nose of the bright orange X-1: *Glamorous Glennis.*

On October 10, during the eighth powered flight past Mach .94 and 45,000 feet (13,716 meters), Yeager proved he could use the pitch trim to fly through the shock-wave disturbance. As he started back down, however, frost covered the inside of the canopy so that he couldn't see. Unable to scrape it off, he had chase pilots Bob Hoover and Dick Frost in their Lockheed F-80s guide him through a blind landing on the lake bed. When the engineers correlated the data, they found that the X-1 actually had flown at Mach .997 right up to the sonic wall. The team decided that the next flight was going to be the real thing: right through and a little beyond, just to make sure.

Had the NACA and Air Force engineers known what Yeager did to himself that Friday night while they were hard at work, they would not have been thrilled. Chuck and Glennis had gone out to Pancho Barnes's watering hole, the Happy Bottom Riding Club, a favorite gathering place for pilots who lived in the Mojave Desert. After dinner they went riding, and, heading back at full gallop, Chuck did not see a locked corral gate. At the last minute, the horse dug in and threw its rider, who hit the ground with a thud, sending severe pain across his ribs.

Avoiding the Air Force flight surgeon, Yeager stopped in to see a civilian doctor in Rosamond on Saturday morning and discovered that he did indeed have two broken ribs. He had his chest taped as tightly as he could stand, nursed himself a bit over the weekend, and reported for duty Monday morning at Muroc, where he found that he was scheduled to fly the next day.

As the team prepared the X-1 for flight on the morning of October 14, 1947, Yeager confided in Jack Ridley. Chuck was confident he could make the flight without any problem, but he didn't think he could reach over and pull the lever to close the hatch once inside the X-1. They'd have to figure some way to increase the leverage.

The B-29 launch crew also knew about Yeager's having been thrown, but they were not aware of his injuries. Jokingly, they presented him with glasses, a rope, and a carrot. After coffee at the base club, Yeager did a preflight check of the X-1, and then met with Walt Williams and the other NACA engineers. The word was that he was not to go past Mach .96 unless everything was up to par.

This time the inside of the canopy was coated with Drene shampoo, the only substance anyone knew of that could prevent frost from forming. Around 10:00 A.M., the B-29 lifted off and started to climb for altitude in a wide spiral, followed by Hoover and Frost in their F-80s. When Yeager, assisted by Ridley, eased himself sideways into the cockpit of the X-1, sharp pain shot through his side. Opening his jacket, Jack removed a section of broom handle he had sawed off, and attached it to the hatch lever. With a great deal of pain, Chuck then managed to get the hatch locked shut, and to ready the airplane for flight.

Ridley got on the intercom. "You all set?" he asked. Hunched over, and with each breath bringing pain, Yeager shot back, "Hell, yes, let's get it over with." *Glamorous Glennis* dropped from the B-29's bomb bay at 10:26 A.M. Yeager lit the chambers and took the bright-orange rocket ship "out to .96 Mach number and sat there in relatively heavy buffeting and the Mach meter was fluctuating at around .96. As I accelerated up, the Mach meter jumped from .96 to 1.05. I would like to say that they really did have a lot of confidence in our program because the Mach meter only went to 1.0. It sat there and fluctuated and then jumped off the scale . . . it worked out to about 1.05 Mach number," or 700 miles (1,126 kilometers) per hour. Eight miles (13 kilometers) below, the

ground team heard the first double-crack sonic boom ever produced by a manned aircraft.

The buffeting quit, I got back a little bit of elevator effectiveness, and the airplane flew quite nicely. I shut off the rocket motor after about 20 seconds beyond Mach 1 and came back through the speed of sound, got into the same buffet, the same instability, and the loss of elevator effectiveness. I jettisoned the remainder of my fuel and liquid oxygen and came on down and landed. . . . I was kind of disappointed that it wasn't more of a big charge than it was.

In the words of General Hoyt Vandenberg, the flight "marked the end of the first great period of the air age and the beginning of the second. In a few moments, the subsonic period became history and the supersonic period was born."

Colonel Chuck Yeager holds a model of Bell's famous rocket plane in 1963. Yeager made the 59th and last flight in X-1 No. 1 on May 12, 1950; it was then refurbished and presented to the Smithsonian.

THE JET AIRLINER

Boeing test pilot Tex Johnston picked up the phone. Company president Bill Allen was on the other end. "Tex, can you conduct a test flight on Gold Cup day and conclude with a pass over the Gold Cup racecourse?"

The Gold Cup hydroplane races on Seattle's Lake Washington were an annual event, attended by several hundred thousand spectators. That year, 1955, the International Air Transport Association and the Society of Aeronautical Engineers had decided to hold their annual meetings in Seattle during the week-long festival surrounding the races. These were the world's most influential airline-industry executives and designers. Understandably, Allen wanted to show off his prototype four-engine passenger jet, the 367-80, to these important potential customers—and rivals.

Sunday, August 7, Gold Cup day, was, in the pilot's jargon of the day, CAVU—ceiling and visibility unlimited. After performing a series of tests over the Olympic Peninsula, Johnston turned the "Dash 80" east for the lake. On the way down, he leaned over to his copilot, Jim Gannett, and said, "I'm going to roll this bird over the Gold Cup course." Jim's jaw dropped. "They're liable to fire you," he replied.

Coming down low over the racecourse, Tex performed a steep, left, climbing turn to 1,500 feet (458 meters). Then, "proceeding on a southwest heading," Johnston recalled, "in a shallow dive across

Wearing his trademark cowboy boots and hat, jet-age test pilot A.M. "Tex" Johnston, above, sits in the cockpit of the original Boeing 367-80, which he and Richard "Dix" Loesch piloted through a flawless maiden flight on July 15, 1954. This four-engine jet, called the Dash 80 after the final digits in its model number, was the prototype for America's first

passenger-jet airplane, the legendary Boeing 707. Opposite, the 367-80 under construction at Boeing's plant outside Seattle on January 21, 1954. The Dash 80 is now part of the National Air and Space Museum's collection of historic aircraft.

179

the racecourse to 300 feet (92 meters) altitude, speed 490 miles per hour (785 kilometers per hour), I established a 35-degree climb and released the back pressure. The airplane was climbing at one G, the same as level flight. I applied full left roll control and, as the airplane approached the inverted position, applied slight back pressure, bringing the nose down slightly to maintain one G, continually holding full left roll control. The roll was completed in level flight at 1,500 feet (458 meters) altitude."

Johnston pulled the big transport around in a 180-degree turn, dropped back down over the course, and then made a second climbing roll. Over 250,000 people witnessed an airliner being put

through a maneuver it was not supposed to be capable of doing. "The airplane never knew it was inverted," Johnston later said. "The entire roll maneuver was executed at one G, the same gravity force as at level flight."

Watching from his boat was Bill Allen, with Bell Aircraft Company president Larry Bell as his guest. Bell had taken a heart pill earlier in the day. When Allen's one-of-a-kind prototype, built as a gamble with company money alone and no outside backing, rolled overhead, he turned to Bell and said, "Larry, give me one of those pills. I need it more than you." Bell, Tex Johnston's former employer, laughed. "Bill," he said, "you don't know Tex very

The Boeing B-47 bomber first flew on December 17, 1947, the 44th anniversary of the Wright brothers' first flight. The jet's slender wings sweep back from the fuselage, and support six General Electric J47 turbojet engines, which, along with flames from takeoff-assist rockets, are visible in the photograph below.

well. He just sold your airplane."

On Monday morning, Johnston was called into Allen's office, where Boeing's top management awaited him in silence. Allen wasted no time. "What did you think you were doing yesterday?" Tex carefully explained that the airplane did not know up from down, and that his smoothly executed, constant-one-G maneuver had not put any undue stress on the airframe. Allen looked at the men around him, then at his skilled test pilot. "You know that. Now we know that. Don't do it anymore." He didn't, but Larry Bell was right: Tex's famous barrel roll certainly helped to sell the airplane. "I knew we had to do something to impress them," Johnston said, years later.

In fact, the birth of the world's first successful jet airliner, the Boeing 707, production successor to the Dash 80, represented a much greater gamble than Tex Johnston's barrel roll. Known for its innovation and willingness to take risks, Boeing had pioneered the era of large jet aircraft with the B-47 and B-52 bombers. Now it was about to go head to head with Douglas, the company that had dominated the airliner industry. However, this move from military to civilian design was not an unusual step for Boeing; the company had applied its military-aircraft technology and manufacturing experience to civilian-airliner design in the past. The firm's military products of the 1930s and 1940s had led to such commercial aircraft as the 307 Stratoliner, the first pressurized-cabin airliner, although not a great commercial success; the 314 flying boat, which had become famous as part of Pan Am's Clipper fleet; and the 377 Stratocruiser, which had been based on the B-29 and B-50 bombers and sold to the U. S. Air Force as the C-97 transport and KC-97 aerial-refueling tanker.

Large jet aircraft in themselves were no longer revolutionary. By 1950, the U.S. Air Force was creating the world's most powerful fleet of high-speed, high-altitude, multi-jet-engine strategic bombers. Boeing's XB-47 bomber flew in December 1947 with a number of design innovations. The sharply swept wing carried its six jet engines in external pods hung under the wings, and the fuselage was as sleek as a rocket.

The larger, next-generation XB-52 originally was designed for turboprop engines, but Air Force officials at Wright Field asked if turbojets could be fitted. After an intense weekend design session at Dayton's Van Cleve Hotel, Boeing engineers presented an eight-jet, swept-wing design that eventually became the B-52 Stratofortress. The aircraft made its first flight in April 1952; B-52s are still

A frontal view of the trim Boeing B-47 bomber in flight. With its engines enclosed in nacelles suspended beneath the wings by pylons, the B-47 set the style for large jet aircraft for a quarter-century. The pilots sit in tandem in the Plexiglas canopy atop the fuselage.

flying missions for the U.S. Air Force today.

The development of Boeing's bombers and the efficient Pratt & Whitney J57 axial-flow turbojet engine convinced Boeing to offer a jet-transport to the world's airlines. This 1950 jet-transport design, the Model 473, had a scaled-down B-52 wing and four J-57 engines. After visiting every large airline in the United States and Europe, however, the Boeing sales team came home without a single serious order. No one seemed interested, even though the British already had flown a jet-airliner prototype, the de Havilland Comet.

Turning to the Air Force, its trusted, steady customer, Boeing tried to sell the concept of the large, four-jet airliner as a tanker/transport, a successor to the KC-97, but, as company executive John E. Steiner recalled, Boeing representatives were successful only in "wearing our shoes out treading the halls of Dayton [since] Wright Field did not look kindly upon a 35-degree, swept-wing jet for the tanker mission."

Two years later, in April 1952, Boeing chief Bill Allen and several others were on hand to watch the first flight of the B-52 from the factory outside Seattle to Moses Lake, Washington. As the huge aircraft lifted off, Allen's faith in his design staff convinced him to gamble $16 million, or about a quarter of the company's net worth, on the future. As he watched the Stratofortress climb out, Allen later remembered, he was "determined that we would build a prototype and enter the jet transport age. I laid the proper groundwork with certain members of the board, brought it to a vote [on May 20, 1952] and we were on our way. We used 100 percent Boeing money and built the Dash 80."

The British de Havilland company already had taken the same gamble, and they were far ahead. Their stunningly sleek and beautiful prototype Comet had flown in July 1949. The Comet I entered service with the British Overseas Airways Corporation (BOAC), and made airline history by flying 36 passengers from London to Johannesburg, South Africa, on May 2, 1952, less than three weeks before Boeing voted to build its jet airliner. Within a few months, airlines began to realize that the time saved by 500-mile-per-hour jet aircraft would offset high jet operational costs. Pan American World Airways was impressed enough to order three long-range Series 3 Comets for its transatlantic routes. If this newer Comet could meet its performance guarantees, Pan Am made clear, the company would buy more of the aircraft.

De Havilland was in fact well on its way to dominating the new era of jet transport when a series of disasters nearly destroyed the Comet program and the company as well. On January 10, 1954, a Comet took off from Rome and was climbing to its cruising altitude when it came apart in midair. On March 23, after a thorough investigation that blamed sabotage, operations resumed. Only a short time later, however, on April 8, another Comet disintegrated near the Italian island of Stromboli in much the same manner as the first.

The British government launched a full-scale inquiry. Carefully reassembling the first Comet's fuselage, the investigators found that repeated pressurization cycles had caused metal fatigue and cracks in the skin, which, in turn, had allowed the fuselage to burst open in flight. Neither the military nor the airlines had had much experience with pressurized aircraft flying at altitudes of up to 40,000 feet (12,200 meters). The lesson of the Comet I was costly in lives and in the accumulation of data as well. Henceforth, all new types of pressurized aircraft would be tested in giant water tanks, repeatedly pressurized and de-pressurized until they failed. And, although later Comet models were successful airliners and were employed effectively in military roles as well, de Havilland struggled under the weight of apparent failure and near bankruptcy for some time.

Just over a month after the last Comet I crash, Boeing rolled out the Dash 80, and, on May 14, 1954, Mrs. William E. Boeing christened it the new "Airplane of Tomorrow." The company's gamble

Veteran test pilot Tex Johnston, below right, prepares to take the giant YB-52 jet bomber through its stability tests at Boeing Field, Seattle in 1952. In 1948, Boeing engineers emerged from a weekend brainstorming session with the design for the long-range, eight-jet B-52 Stratofortress, right. The largest all-jet bomber ever built, with a wingspan of 185 feet (56 meters), the B-52 also lays claim to more throttles, above, than any other aircraft in the U.S. Air Force.

looked more like a crap shoot at this point, but Boeing's engineers were confident that they had avoided the Comet's problems. The Dash 80's fuselage was similar in cross section to the reliable "double-bubble" fuselage of the Boeing 377 Stratocruiser, and featured a large, upper, circular-arc passenger section and a smaller, circular-arc lower lobe for baggage, systems, and nose landing gear. Redundant load paths and a number of structural innovations, such as chemically milled window panels, gave the fuselage great strength.

The prototype originally was to be numbered 707, but at the last minute Bill Allen changed it to 367-80. The number 367 was actually the company's designation for the propeller-driven KC-97 tanker. To keep his new project under tight security, Allen simply assigned the number for the KC-97's 80th version, or "80," to the entirely new and different jet airliner.

Although Boeing's experience with the B-47 and B-52 contributed a great deal to the design of the new jet airliner, its engineering team made every effort to give airline pilots an airplane that, compared to the two bombers, would be familiar, and even easy, to fly. As John Steiner said, "We felt it had to fly more or less like the airplanes the airline pilots were used to, so it had to have tricycle landing gear allowing the pilot to lift the nose at takeoff and to depress the nose at landing. It was no easy task to fit a tricycle gear on a swept-wing airplane." Both the Stratojet and the Stratofortress had a "bicycle" type of landing gear that made them very demanding to land; both the front and rear sets of wheels had to touch down at the same time, at just the right air speed, or the aircraft tended to bounce violently. The Dash 80 team solved this problem by incorporating the airliner's main landing gear into wings that, unlike the bombers', were mounted low on the fuselage. There were some worries that the airliner's 35-degree wing sweep and its low mounted wings would cause the engines, cantilevered in pods below the wings, to drag on the ground in a hard landing. Fortunately, these fears proved to be unfounded.

The Dash 80's flight-control system was, to some degree, a reversion to piston technology, but it paid off. Only the rudder and spoilers were hydraulically powered; the rest of the controls were boosted aerodynamically through tabs and mechanical linkages. Not only were these controls surprisingly effective, but their simplicity also saved airlines

The Dash 80's cockpit and flight-control system, below. Above, workmen add finishing touches to the Dash 80's interior on May 11, 1954.

untold amounts of money in maintenance. And pilots making the transition from piston-engine aircraft to the new jet felt right at home with its controls, so similar were they in feel to those of the older generation of aircraft.

By May 21, 1954, pilots Tex Johnston and Dix Loesch had completed almost all of the ground-maneuvering brake and taxi tests. All that was left before signing the aircraft off for its first flight was a high-speed taxi test. After pushing the Dash 80 to 110 miles per hour (176 kilometers per hour) on the ground, Johnston pulled all four throttles to idle, popped the spoilers to reduce lift, and applied light braking to slow down. As the aircraft turned off the runway, it lurched to the left, and the number-one, or left-outboard, engine hit the ground.

The left main landing gear had failed, dropping the left side of the airplane onto the ground and driving two wheels up through the rear of the wing. Fortunately, the fault was traced to flaws in the metal, not in the design, and six weeks later Johnston and his flight-test team were hammering the big jet around on the runway again. They wanted to ensure that if anything were to go wrong, it would go wrong before they actually flew.

By July 15, two months after the taxiing accident, the Dash 80 again was ready to fly. After

greeting Bill Allen, who, along with many other Boeing employees, was on hand to watch the take-off of the first test flight, Tex and his crew boarded the bright-yellow-and-brown aircraft. After engine start, they taxied out, ran through their pre-takeoff checks, and lined up on the runway. Moving the throttles up to full power, Johnston held the brakes, checked the instruments, and then let her go.

"The airplane leaped forward and accelerated rapidly," recalled Johnston. "We obviously would be airborne by midfield. As airspeed passed the calculated V1 speed, I applied back elevator. The nose gear lifted off. Dix called 130 mph, and we were airborne.

"Eyeballing the airspeed, I continued to increase the climb angle to avoid exceeding the flap-down placard limit of 225 mph (360 kilometers per hour). We were at 1,200 feet (366 meters) as we climbed past the end of the runway. Dix commented, 'Is this thing going to climb straight up?'"

Johnston knew that the steep climb performance by the Dash 80, a very large aircraft for the time, was bound to have given those on the ground a real fright. Later, Allen and a few of his colleagues admitted that they thought the prototype was encountering control problems when they saw it rear up and climb so steeply. In fact, though, the airplane simply was exhibiting excellent performance.

Throngs of Seattle-area residents turn out to witness the debut and maiden flight of Boeing's 367-80, or Dash 80, on May 15, 1954, at the Renton, Washington, plant. With this sleekly designed, successful aircraft, Boeing took the lead in the commercial-jet industry.

185

The initial flight went without a hitch, although Johnston noted that the aircraft experienced some instability at low speeds—the so-called Dutch-roll instability that is especially characteristic of swept-wing airplanes. Flight testing now began in earnest, with flights almost every day. On August 4, 1954, after conducting maximum braking tests, Johnston landed the Dash 80 again, and applied the brakes, only to discover that nothing whatsoever happened: his foot pressure on the brake pedals had no effect. The brakes were completely gone, and the emergency-back-up system was out as well. In seconds, Tex ran through a number of options: Ground loop and risk tearing the airplane up? Apply power and get airborne again, then make a belly landing? Steer off the runway into the turf?

Johnston headed for the turf, hoping that the grass would bleed enough speed from the aircraft to enable him to make a U-turn at the end of the runway and avoid the other aircraft parked on the field. Instead, the nose landing gear hit some chunks of discarded concrete hidden in the weeds by the side of the runway. The entire nose landing-gear assembly was ripped off, the nose fell into the dirt,

and the jet slid to a stop. The incident was a setback, but Tex had made the right decision; the damage that might have resulted from either of the other options would have been much worse. The brake failure was traced to the hydraulic-brake fluid, which had overheated and foamed and ultimately had triggered a safety valve that deactivated the whole system. The braking system subsequently was modified.

During the tests that followed, the pilots pushed the brakes to their limits. After two landings with maximum braking from 110 miles per hour (176 kilometers per hour), Johnston worried that the hard braking had superheated the tires. The brake manufacturer's engineers checked the temperatures and passed word to the pilot that they were within safety limits. But Johnston's concern remained as he took off again and climbed through 20,000

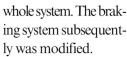

On May 15, 1954, as Boeing president William Allen looks on, Mrs. William E. Boeing christens the Dash 80 prior to its roll out from the Renton hangar. The 367-80 also served as the prototype for the U.S. Air Force's KC-135 jet tanker, above. Boeing developed a system of telescoping pipes and pumps called a "flying boom" that could transfer as much as 1,000 gallons (3,800 liters) of fuel per minute. Above, a McDonnell Douglas F-4 Phantom II jet fighter hooks up to a Boeing KC-135E for refueling.

feet (6,100 meters) with the wheels still down to cool the tires as much as possible. After retracting the gear, he heard "a terrific explosion—a sound similar to someone shooting off both barrels of a twelve-gauge shotgun in the cockpit." Two more explosions followed. Johnston looked over at his copilot, Jim Gannett, and commented laconically, "Those damn tires are on fire and exploding." As Tex lowered the gear, they heard another explosion. He held the Dash 80 at its maximum geardown speed of 305 miles per hour (488 kilometers per hour) to try to blow the fires out. As the Dash 80 landed, the remaining tires blew out. As Johnston remembered, "the bare wheel rims were noisy and the ride a bit rough," but the big jet slowed down without a problem, and he turned off onto the taxiway. He never flew it again with superheated brakes.

On another flight, the Dash 80 experienced severe rudder flutter when the aircraft inadvertently was allowed to exceed its test-speed limit of Mach 0.72 (72 percent of the speed of sound) for the first time. With Air Force Colonel Guy Townsend in the pilot's seat, Tex, flying copilot, noticed that the noise of the airflow outside the aircraft was increasing. As he jerked the throttles to idle and pulled the nose up, "the airplane began shaking violently—so violently that the flight engineer's [instrument] panel partially ripped from its moorings. With the speed reduction, the shaking ceased, having lasted only two or three seconds. I suspected rudder flutter and Guy [Townsend] reported an unusual feel in the rudder pedals." A change in the rudder's mass balance and control tab eliminated any further flutter problems, even at much higher Mach numbers. Other improvements in the Dash 80's rudder-control system tamed the airplane's Dutch-roll tendencies.

The Dash 80's test program proved to be one of the most successful in Boeing's history. Not only had the aircraft made its first flight three weeks ahead of schedule, but Phase I tests were completed in the latter part of 1954, two months ahead of schedule.

A photographer on board the big Dash 80 airliner prototype captured this upside-down view during one of Tex Johnston's famous barrel rolls on the August 7, 1955, demonstration flight over Seattle's Lake Washington, where hundreds of thousands of spectators had gathered for the Gold Cup hydroplane race. "I'd heard Douglas was telling people our prototype was an unstable airplane," Tex later explained, "and I believe that...you sell the product by demonstrating what it can do." Boeing chief Bill Allen, whose company had invested $16 million to develop the Dash 80, was so unnerved by the display that he asked fellow observer Larry Bell for a heart pill.

Competition between Boeing and Douglas in the commercial-jet-airliner market intensified in the late 1950s and early '60s. Douglas's DC-8 Series 32, left, here carrying the colors and logo of Northwest Airlines, entered service in 1959, at which time Boeing's 367-80 prototype, right, had been flying for more than a year. In the end, Douglas sold 556 DC-8s to the commercial airlines, while Boeing sold more than 900 of its 707s.

During that period, General Curtis E. LeMay, the commander of the U.S. Air Force's Strategic Air Command, decided to pay a visit and fly the new jet himself. Although the Air Force once had responded coolly to Boeing's proposal for a jet tanker, no other aircraft company had anything that might be modified as an aerial tanker that was close to flying. LeMay wanted to find out if the Dash 80 would indeed make a good tanker. After simulating a series of mission conditions to match B-47 and B-52 in-flight refueling speeds and altitudes, the general went away happy. Johnston remained impressed with LeMay's piloting skill, which had been amply demonstrated during previous flights in the B-52.

In late 1954, a contract was awarded to Boeing for the first batch of KC-135 Stratotankers, which entered service in 1957. The new airplane differed substantially from the prototype. "It gave the engineers a second chance," recalled John Steiner. "We saw this as an opportunity to obtain tooling commonality with a commercial derivative." The fuselage for the KC-135 was enlarged from 132 inches (3.35 meters) across to 144 inches (3.66 meters), which would allow four-, five-, and six-abreast seating. Boeing now was ready to hit the airline market with a working, off-the-shelf airplane. The

big gamble was starting to pay off, save one obstacle: Douglas wasn't going to let Boeing win the jet-airliner contest without a fight.

Eleven months after the Boeing Dash 80's first flight, Douglas announced that it was offering its planned DC-8 jetliner for sale. Although the DC-8 was only a "paper" airplane that had yet to fly, its design followed the same basic layout as the that of the fast, reliable Boeing. The DC-8's biggest selling points were its larger fuselage diameter, which translated into more paying passengers per flight, and the Douglas reputation: the company had dominated the passenger-airliner market for more than 20 years.

The corporate head-butting began in 1955 when United Airlines, which wanted to be among the first in the United States to offer jet service, weighed the Boeing Dash 80 against Douglas's DC-8. Boeing was confident it would win the decision as it was already flying its airplane, the production version of which would be called the 707. But, in the end, Douglas got the contract, which called for the production of 30 DC-8s. United had based its final decision on the Douglas aircraft's larger fuselage cross section, which meant a higher passenger payload, and thus more profit for the airline. Boeing had gambled on the KC-135/707's fuselage's being big enough, but, in fact, when compared to that of the DC-8, it wasn't.

Boeing scrapped the idea of trying to achieve commonality between its Air Force KC-135 version and the 707 airliner model, and widened the 707's cabin four more inches (10 centimeters) to 148 inches (3.76 meters). This meant that the company could not use the KC-135 tooling, which would greatly increase production costs. Despite their advantage in possessing an already proven flying aircraft, Boeing now struggled to meet the challenge of a savvy competitor with a great deal more experience in the civil-aircraft marketplace.

When Pan American Airlines put out its feelers for the purchase of jet airliners, Boeing once again made its pitch, and once again lost. In late September 1955, Pan Am ordered 25 DC-8s, fitted with JT-4 engines (a civil version of the military J 75). The smaller 707 with less powerful JT-3s did not meet Pan Am's requirements for nonstop transatlantic and intercontinental flights. Nevertheless, three weeks later, the airline put in an option for 20 707s.

John Steiner and his engineering colleagues at

189

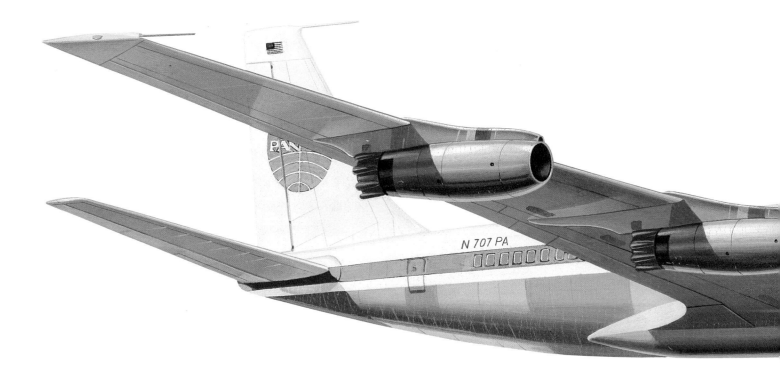

In October 1957, three years after Tex Johnston, opposite, performed his immortal barrel rolls in the 367-80 prototype, the first of Boeing's 707-120 production series rolled out of the company's factory. Pan American airlines, above, put the first 707-120 into service on its New York-to-Paris route on October 26, 1958.

Boeing knew that the order was not a great victory. "Pan Am told us they were buying the 707s because of their earlier delivery date and they considered them to be interim equipment. The scene this time was the Ritz Tower Hotel in New York, instead of the Van Cleve Hotel in Dayton, but the results were similarly traumatic. Over a weekend, we decided we had to meet the competition or face failure. We laid out a new wing and made aerodynamic estimates in the hotel room. Ed Wells then went back to Seattle to re-orient the program while some of us stayed in New York to tell Pan American what we were doing. The result was a two-model program, with two different wing areas, two different engines, and two different body lengths."

The new wing meant that there was even less commonality between the KC-135 and the 707, which translated into even more retooling costs, but Boeing was now back in the running with a fully competitive airplane. On November 8, 1955, American Airlines ordered 30 of the smaller 707s with the larger fuselage diameter. In October 1958, Pan American initiated passenger-jet service on its transatlantic route with a 707-120, the first 707 to enter airline service. National Airlines followed suit

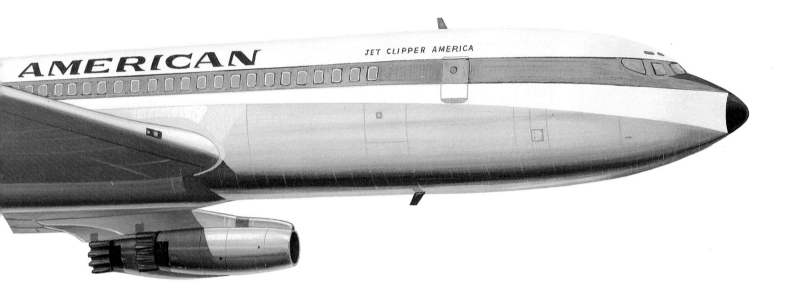

on domestic routes with the inauguration of New York-Miami service in December 1958.

The numerous design and model changes to the 707 line forced Boeing to risk greater and greater sums in the battle to control the jet-airliner market. The company offered the 707 for $300,000 less than Douglas was asking for its DC-8s, driving it ever deeper into debt. Douglas, in turn, although ahead financially for a time, ended up spending a tremendous amount of money once production of the DC-8 began. To make up time, it entered into production of the DC-8 without flying a prototype first to work out all the bugs. When performance figures then did not match predictions, necessary changes had to be made to existing aircraft. The vigorous competition between Boeing and Douglas yielded numerous improvements to both types of aircraft, and, in the end, both

companies lost money on sales all the way up to the last quarter of 1960.

The Boeing 707 left an indelible stamp on history. From the time it was rolled out until today, the 707, with its moderately swept wings and podded engines, served as the model for the basic shape of the modern jet airliner. And in one stroke, the 707 cut the size of the world in half by doubling the speed of airline travel. Passengers found themselves in a much quieter environment, with less vibration and more comfort, than had been offered in any previous aircraft. The airlines, for their part, discovered that their expensive new jets in fact were more economical and much safer than propeller-driven aircraft. The amazing Dash 80 made the age of air travel envisioned by the early pioneers a reality.

THE THRESHOLD OF SPACE

Frost coats the liquid-oxygen tank of the National Aeronautics and Space Administration's (NASA) X-15 rocket plane prior to its launch from its B-52 mother ship. Built by North American in 1958, the craft used anhydrous ammonia and liquid oxygen at a temperature of less than -212 degrees F (-100 degrees C) as propellants for its 57,000-pound-thrust (253,559-newton) XLR-99 motor.

When Wernher von Braun and his fellow colleagues from Peenemünde, on the island of Usedom, in the Baltic Sea, arrived in America in 1945, literally as spoils of war, they were ready to resume their reach toward space flight. Vaguely aware of the outlines of Robert Goddard's work, the German scientists assumed that an American rocket program was well along in development. They talked of orbiting satellites and manned rocket ships that could be ready for launch before 1950.

They were astonished to learn that Goddard had been largely ignored during the war, and that there was no American space-rocket program. They were probably further dismayed to discover that their tasks were to be those of launching surplus V-2 military rockets and developing ballistic missiles for the U.S. Army, just as they had for the German army. From the outset, von Braun began to seek a way to transfer his research and that of his cohorts to civilian-government control. But that would take a while. In the meantime, at least through the late 1940s, it seemed that America's rocket-research efforts would be directed toward the development of piloted supersonic-research aircraft that operated within the atmosphere, rather than toward true, rocket-propelled spacecraft.

The success of the Bell X-1 and X-2 and the Douglas D-558-2 Skyrocket rocket-research aircraft programs had catapulted aircraft speeds just beyond Mach 2, but knowledge of the factors affecting aircraft control at twice the speed of sound was limited; often the aircraft were dangerously uncontrollable at those speeds. During World War II, Germans researchers—principally von Braun, Eugen Sänger, and Irene Bredt—had made studies of rocket-powered aircraft that could fly beyond Mach 4 in the upper reaches of the Earth's at-mosphere. These scientists continued to discuss the feasibility of such fantastic flying machines. By 1950, senior National Advisory Committee for Aeronautics (NACA) researchers, including John V. Becker and John Stack, who in large measure had been responsible for the creation of the sound-barrier-breaking Bell X-1, were listening to them.

In contemplating such Mach-4-and-beyond ma-chines as the Germans had conceived, designers and engineers once again were reaching far beyond the state of the art, this time toward the ragged edge. There were no wind tunnels in which to test aerodynamic shapes at these blistering Mach numbers; it was back to flight-testing as the Wright brothers had done it: design it, build it, fly it. The aircraft would have to be built of new alloys to with-stand the extreme temperatures of high-speed at-mospheric flight. It would have to be reasonably stable both at hypersonic and landing speeds, and controllable both when leaving and re-entering the atmosphere.

The NACA's first formal proposal for a hyper-sonic-research aircraft came from X-1 designer Robert J. Woods. At an aerodynamics committee meeting on October 4, 1951, he challenged the or-ganization to come up with an airplane that would match the performance of the German V-2 ballis-tic missile. That same year, NACA engineer Wal-ter C. Williams was coming home late one night after a fishing trip with test pilot A. Scott Cross-field when he heard a radio-news broadcast that a 75,000-pound-thrust (333,630-newton) Viking research rocket had been launched. He turned to "Scotty" and asked, "What could we do with a manned-aircraft with a 75,000-pound-thrust engine?" To answer his own question right then and there, he worked through the basic calcula-tions on the back of an envelope that he took from his glove compartment. As it happened, several other talented engineers were working on the same problem.

Six and a half months later, the NACA aerodynamics committee and Robert J. Woods called for the design of an aircraft to investigate the "problems of unmanned and manned flight in the upper atmosphere at altitudes between 12 and 50 miles (19 and 80 kilometers), and at Mach numbers between 4 and 10, and that the NACA devote a modest effort to problems associated with unmanned and manned flights at altitudes from Mach number 10 to the velocity of escape from the Earth's

gravity." Von Braun, still working on Army ballistic missiles, and Dornberger, now at Bell Aircraft, feeding hypersonic-boost-glide airframe concepts to Woods and his associates, began to envision their dreams of space flight becoming reality.

By 1953, the Office of Naval Research had contracted with Douglas for the D-558-3, a 22,000-pound (10,000-kilogram) aircraft powered by a 51,000-pound-thrust (226,868-newton) Reaction Motors, Inc., (RMI) engine that ran on liquid oxygen and ammonia. The airplane also would feature thick magnesium skin to absorb heat, wings with an 18-foot (5.5-meter) span and solid-copper

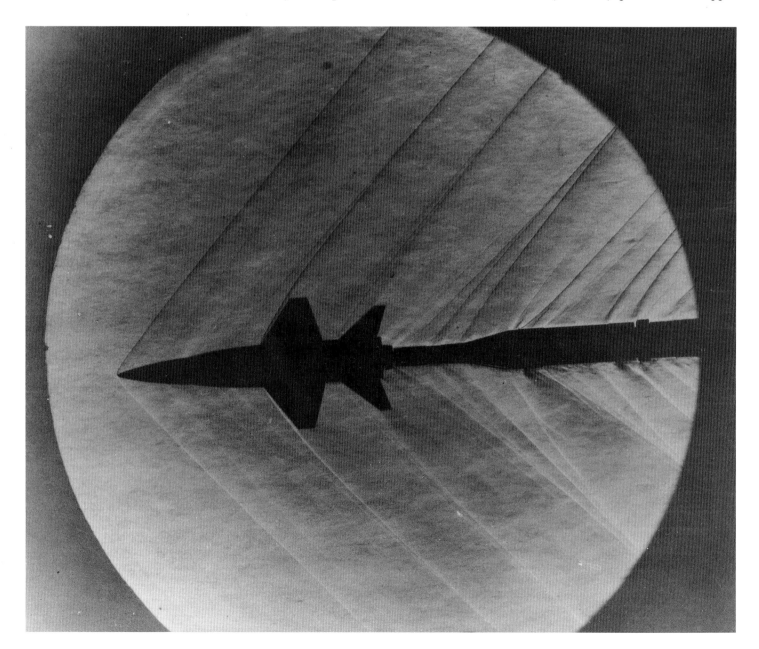

leading edges, and small, hydrogen-peroxide thruster rockets for reaction control when the aircraft was flown beyond the atmosphere. In October 1953, the Air Force Scientific Advisory Board called for the creation of a hypersonic-research aircraft. The individual NACA laboratories were beginning to cross pollinate one another.

All of these plans and concepts came together in 1954. John Becker, head of an informal hypersonic-research group at the NACA's Langley, Virginia, laboratory, submitted a design to the NACA headquarters for an aircraft with a cruciform tail, an Inconel-X chrome-nickel-alloy skin that could withstand high temperatures, and a wedge-shaped vertical fin for increased stability at Mach numbers. In June, Hugh Dryden, the NACA's research director, decided to call for a pooling of effort; a project of such advanced technology and complexity would take plenty of both money and talent. The Air Force and the Navy thus were invited to join the NACA, a formal agreement was signed in October 1954, and Dryden, Brigadier General Benjamin S. Kelsey, USAF, and Rear Admiral R.S. Hatcher, USN, became the charter members of the Research Airplane Committee.

The proposed aircraft would be air-launched. It would be capable of flying at 6,600 feet per second (2,000 meters per second), or more than 4,100 miles per hour (6,560 kilometers per hour); of tolerating temperatures as high as 1,200 degrees F (635 degrees C); and of climbing to an altitude of 250,000 feet (76,000 meters). In early 1955, this machine was designated the X-15. Four companies entered its design competition: Bell, Douglas, North American, and Republic. In September, a contract to build three examples of the X-15 was awarded to North American.

Although the design process went relatively smoothly, largely because of input from the NACA and from John Becker's original work, everything else about this airplane presented a challenge. The aircraft would fly so fast that a special test corridor, labeled the "High Range" and measuring some 485 miles (775 kilometers) long and 50 miles (80 kilometers) wide, had to be created along a series of dry lakes that stretched from Utah to Edwards Air Force Base, California, at the site formerly called Muroc. All the flight-monitoring equipment, from radar to telemetry to real-time-data link, was new, and later would become standard technology for the space program. The aircraft's pilot would be fully wired for physiological monitoring.

Placing a human being in something that traveled so fast posed a number of significant problems. Some form of space suit would have to be designed and tested to keep a person alive should cabin pressurization fail. Should something go drastically wrong, getting the pilot out of the airplane looked nearly impossible. An ejection seat that would function at speeds up to Mach 4 and at altitudes up to 120,000 feet (36,600 meters) was designed, but, as NACA test pilot Scott Crossfield commented, such an escape system basically offered the pilot "a way to commit suicide to keep from getting killed." Crossfield was released by the NACA to work directly with North American on the human-factors aspects of the aircraft, which he then would test-fly for the contractor. He was an outstanding choice for the projected new aircraft's pilot, having flown both the X-1 and the Skyrocket, the latter of which won him the distinction of being the first human to fly at Mach 2. The NACA assigned Joe Walker as its project test pilot, while the Air Force awarded the position to Bob White and the Navy sent Forrest "Pete" Petersen.

The 57,000-pound-thrust (253,559-newton) en-

A Schlieren photograph, opposite, of an X-15 model in the supersonic-pressure tunnel at NASA's Langley Research Center reveals the shock waves that would be generated at a speed of Mach 1.4. Langley engineer John Becker, left, conceived the design for the 4,100-mile-per-hour (6,560-kilometer-per-hour) X-15.

gine, a derivative of the Reaction Motors Viking rocket XLR-30 engine, proved to be the most difficult aspect of the program, even though RMI had had a head start with the stillborn D-558-3. The liquid-oxygen/anhydrous-ammonia XLR-99 was to be capable of being throttled from 40- to 100-percent thrust—a major design headache, since up to this point missile engines simply had run at full thrust until the propellants were gone. Understandably, program planners wanted to give the pi-

lot some control over the one-million-horsepower, fire-breathing monster behind him. In earlier rocket planes, increasing or decreasing thrust was a matter of lighting off or shutting down separate combustion chambers, each of which always ran at full thrust when in operation.

When North American pushed out X-15 No. 1 in October 1958, there was no airworthy XLR-99 engine to go with it. To prevent the flight-test program from falling behind, two XLR-11s, one of which had powered the X-1 through the sound barrier, were modified to produce 8,000 pounds (35,587 newtons) of thrust each and then fitted to the airframe for the so-called "slow-speed" tests that were to reach speeds "only" up to Mach 3.

The sleek X-15 was impressive even on the ground, a 50-foot, 9-inch (15.48-meter) needle with stubby wings that spanned only 22 feet, 4 inches (6.8 meters) and a wedge-shaped vertical tail. It had to look good: the Soviets had launched Sputnik I in October 1957, and the U.S. was in second place in the technology race, trying feverishly to catch up. The incredibly tough, heat-resistant Inconel-X alloy that was used to make turbine blades for jet en-

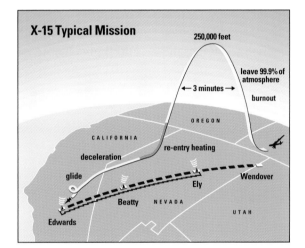

A rocket-boosted version of the Lockheed F-104 (NF-104), left, enabled pilots to simulate X-15 descents from altitudes of more than 100,000 feet (30,480 meters). The NF-104s were temperamental, however, killing one pilot and seriously injuring Colonel Chuck Yeager. A diagram, above right, plots an X-15's mission sequence—including departure from the Earth's atmosphere—in flight over Nevada and California. In Maxine McCaffery's watercolor, Securing X-15 to B-52 mother ship, *right, hydraulic lifts raise the hypersonic aircraft to its launch cradle.*

gines formed the fuselage, which was basically a 2,500-gallon (9,500-liter) propellant tank painted a menacing black. Even before Sputnik had been launched, North American had had the X-15B orbital version on the drawing boards, so confidence ran high that the new ship could win back quite a bit of prestige for America.

The first two X-15s were trucked to Edwards and fitted with two XLR-11s each, while No. 3 remained at the factory to await the XLR-99. A B-52 bomber was modified to carry the aircraft aloft for airborne release. Although the X-15s had a nose wheel, the main landing gear consisted of two skids that were short enough to require the lower half of the ventral vertical fin to be jettisoned before landing.

By early 1959, X-15 No. 1 was ready for so-called captive-flight-testing, maneuvers that would pave the way for free-fall gliding flights. North American project pilot Scott Crossfield began a series of flights in a North American F-100 Super Sabre jet fighter to simulate the X-15's descent for landing. To match the X-15's high sink rate, Crossfield would pull the F-100's power to idle, extend the air brake, lower full flaps, put down the landing gear, and deploy an eight-foot-in-diameter drag chute behind the fighter. Such actions were "suicidal" in Crossfield's opinion, since the F-100 didn't handle well this "dirty," but he managed to conduct several flights before moving on to the Lockheed F-104 Starfighter.

With air brakes out, full flaps, gear down, and

The first of three X-15s lands in the California desert: the rear skids and forward wheels are deployed, frost caused by the liquid-oxygen tank clings to the plane's belly, and the pilot's helmet is clearly visible in the canopy window.

idle power, the F-104 provided a more realistic simulation of X-15 flight, although it was even "sportier" to handle than the F-100. "I went through all this nonsense," said Crossfield, "but I don't think it contributed to anything."

Meanwhile, newspaper headlines proclaimed Russian space successes, and everyone was anxious to get the flight-testing started. The first captive flight under the B-52 was made on March 10, 1959. Even from the outset of these captive flights, during which the rocket plane remained suspended under the bomber's wing, the X-15's auxiliary power units (APUs) would burn out, filling the cockpit with smoke. "Smoke in the cockpit" came over the interphone from Crossfield on almost every flight. On the final captive flight, when he happened to remark "Holy smoke!" about something else, North American engineer Charles Feltz jumped up, yelling, "Wha'd he say? Wha'd he say?"

By June 8, everything was ready for an unpowered, free-fall flight. From the moment the X-15 was dropped at 38,000 feet 11.600 meters), Crossfield had 3 minutes and 58 seconds to learn all he could about flying and landing the aircraft for the first time. As he approached the lake bed for landing, he jettisoned the ventral fin's lower half. The X-15 began to porpoise, pitching up and down in movements that were out of phase with Crossfield's control inputs.

"Now the nose was rising and falling like the bow of a skiff in a heavy sea. Although I was putting in maximum control I could not subdue the motions. The X-15 was porpoising wildly, sinking toward the desert at 200 miles an hour (320 kilometers per hour). I would have to land at the bottom of an oscillation, timed perfectly; otherwise, I knew, I would break the bird."

Crossfield had the overwhelmingly uncomfortable feeling that somehow "we had pulled a tremendous goof. The X-15, in spite of all our sweat and study, our attempt at perfection, had become completely unstable." In a nearly miraculous moment, however, as the aircraft was about to impact on the desert, the nose pitched up, the skids slammed into the lake bed, the nose gear hit, and the aircraft slid safely to a halt.

Much to everyone's relief, the porpoising problem was not one of design. A valve in the boosted-control system was modified to prevent the pilot's inputs from becoming out of phase with the control surfaces, and, from that point on, the X-15 displayed excellent handling characteristics. A short time after that first harrowing drop to Earth, the Southern California Soaring Society awarded Crossfield a trophy for the shortest powerless-descent time from 38,000 feet.

Crossfield made the first powered X-15 flight on September 17, 1959, in airframe No. 2. This, as historian Richard P. Hallion wrote in *Test Pilots* (Smithsonian Institution Press), would be "a sim-

ple check flight to Mach 2.11—pretty tame stuff by 1959." And, indeed, it was routine, as was the second. The third powered flight, however, was anything but. Just after launch on November 5, a failure in the engine's fuel-sequencing system resulted in an explosion. Having lost power and still heavy with a full fuel load, the X-15 fell like a stone, leaving Crossfield unable to jettison most of the fuel before the emergency touchdown on Rosamond Dry Lake. As the nose gear slammed down, the heavy load broke the X-15's back.

When the rescue pilot arrived, he noticed that the canopy wasn't open and assumed that Crossfield's back had been broken, too. Grabbing a rescue backboard to immobilize what he thought would be a severely injured X-15 pilot, "the rescuer wanted to throw the canopy wide open to get the backboard in," remembered Crossfield. "I didn't want it open because if it goes past the T-pin, it arms the ejection seat. I can't say anything because I am sealed in my pressure suit, so I'm hanging on to the canopy for dear life while this big football player is trying to lift it. Here I am strapped in and pulling the canopy down, fighting until the other guy decides I didn't have a broken back after all." Scott finally got his face plate off and told the anxious, confused good samaritan not to pull the canopy off. "I had visions of the ejection seat cre-

mating my rescuer and finding myself at 400 feet [120 meters] with no airspeed and the parachute in my lap."

It took three months to repair No. 2. In the meantime, in early 1960, the National Aeronautics and Space Administration (NASA), the new name of the NACA, accepted X-15 No. 1, which was flown by Joe Walker and Bob White in March and April of that year. And then, finally, the third X-15 was ready for static-engine test runs with the XLR-99. On the last ground run of a series of these tests with Crossfield in the cockpit, a pressure regulator stuck; "the world came unglued," he recalled, as the propulsion system, not the engine, blew the airplane in two. The front section of the aircraft shot forward 40 to 50 feet (12 to 15 meters) after "the biggest bang I'd ever heard." After experiencing a 50 G acceleration, Scott climbed out of the battered front section with a sore neck. He subsequently developed a series of eye problems that forced him to wear dark glasses at certain times, but he didn't tell anyone, fearing that the condition would cost him his place in the program.

In November 1960, Crossfield made the first XLR-99-powered flight in the re-engined No. 2 airframe. With the throttle almost at idle, he hit Mach 2.97, making it clear to everyone that the machine was ready for its prime purpose: aerody-

Unable to keep pace with the X-15, a chase-plane pilot snapped this shot of the rocket aircraft's contrail. At right, as Brigadier General Irving Branch (right) looks on, Colonel Chuck Yeager (left) congratulates Major Bob White after his November 9, 1961, X-15 mission, during which he flew 4,093 miles per hour (6,586 kilometers per hour) and the aircraft's right windshield cracked.

namic research at Mach 6. From that point on, the X-15 program went like gangbusters. Within a year, Bob White had hit Mach 6.04—an incredible 4,093 miles per hour (6,550 kilometers per hour)—at 101,600 feet (31,000 meters), driving the aircraft's skin temperature even beyond its design limits to 1,300 degrees F (690 degrees C). By August 1963, Joe Walker had taken the X-15 up to 354,200 feet (108,030 meters) or more than 67 miles (107 kilometers) above the Earth, more than 100,000 feet (30,000 meters) above its planned maximum altitude and a world altitude record for winged aircraft that still stands today. Since space was considered to begin at an altitude of 50 miles (80 kilometers), the X-15 pilots who flew this high or higher later were awarded astronaut's wings.

Although the wind-tunnel estimates of the X-15's performance matched actual flight tests quite closely, there were unforeseen discrepancies and problems with the aircraft and its performance. The rocket's blunt rear end, for example, caused about 15 percent more drag than predicted, and greater than predicted heat at Mach 6 buckled the wing skin and fractured some of the windshield's outer glass. Modifications were made to correct these problems, and engineers also beefed up the landing gear and strengthened the fuselage to reduce supersonic flutter.

A roll-control problem made it impossible to fly the X-15 at angles of attack greater than 20 degrees during re-entry. When engineers removed the lower portion of the ventral fin that was able to be jettisoned, however, pilots found they gained back full control. This discovery led to the use of flight profiles for atmospheric re-entry at a 26-degree angle of attack and a descending flight-path angle of -38 degrees at speeds up to Mach 6. Needless to say, pilots had to use all their skills during such flights.

A number of pilots from the Air Force, including Joe Engle and Mike Adams, now were assigned to the program. After completing the F-104 simulation program, Engle felt so comfortable during his X-15 flight that he rolled it, just as Chuck Yeager had done with the X-1 on his first flight.

Pushing the X-15 up into space provided pilots with a thrilling ride and a spectacular view of the

Earth, but, on the way back down, maintaining stability until the airplane re-entered the atmosphere and the wing surfaces again began to generate lift was extremely critical. And aircraft No. 1 and No. 2 proved difficult to fly, in part because three separate flight-control sticks had been designed into their cockpits: a conventional stick in the center for slow-speed flight during landing; a smaller side stick on the right for moving the aerodynamic control surfaces, such as ailerons, elevators, and rudder, during launch, acceleration, climb out, and re-entry; and a reaction-thrust side stick on the left to maneuver in the near vacuum of the upper atmosphere, where the lack of air precluded the normal aerodynamic controls from having any affect. Using both hands to make the transition from one control to another took an extraordinary amount of coordination. In the No. 3 model of the X-15, all three systems were linked to a single control stick, thus reducing the pilot's workload significantly.

Air Force pilot Joe Engle discovered that the X-15 had a number of quirks, including the "spectacular symptom at Mach 5.7 of heat build up, which caused the steel to expand. The rear of the airplane had expansion joints but there were none up front. At that point in the flight the steel on the side of the canopy would pop and get my attention at a very critical time."

NASA now contributed several pilots to the pro-

In this view of the cockpit in one of the first two X-15s, above, the center stick and rudder pedals control the flight surfaces while the left side stick fires the thrusters for maneuvering outside the atmosphere. Above right, Neil Armstrong occupies the cramped quarters of the X-15. Right, a hangar at Edwards Air Force Base accommodates all three X-15s, three NASA lifting bodies, and a C-47 support aircraft.

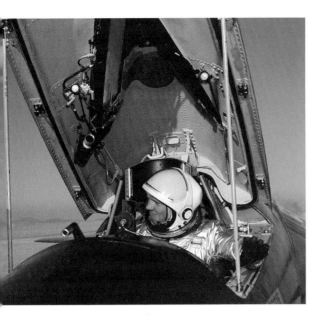

gram as well, including Neil Armstrong, who would later become the first person to set foot on the moon, and Milt Thompson. Both found the X-15 to be just as challenging as Engle, Crossfield, and the other pilots had. As Thompson remembered his first flight, it "was pretty impressive. I had a problem adapting to the X-15 since I was thrown in the middle of the program without the benefit of early centrifuge [high G-force] training." The air launch for his first X-15 flight kicked off a rapid succession of events. Thompson was "shot off the hooks and falling in free flight. I finally got the engine lit, straightened up and started uphill." The thrust was more than that of any plane Thompson had flown. "The longitudinal acceleration approached 2 Gs and built up to 4 Gs and though I

throttled back, I was pressed back into my seat. The instrument panel looked strange. I was behind the airplane all the way up to burn out. It was the first airplane I'd flown that I was happy to shut the engine off. The acceleration was very uncomfortable."

For the first time ever, a manned, winged rocket was leaving the atmosphere, shifting from conventional flight to space flight, and then returning to Earth. Although the aircraft was built for hypersonic research within the Earth's atmosphere, it in fact was paving the way toward future manned space flight. John Becker, who had pushed the X-15 program from the beginning, later looked back on all that was accomplished. "If you take a broad look at all of the contributions of the X-15 program and consider relative values based on the actual use that has been made of the results, it becomes quite clear that the space-oriented results have been of greater value and importance than the hypersonic aeronautics contributions. This is the reverse of what was expected in the beginning." Except for the old V-2 hands, who immediately recognized the importance of the X-15 program to space flight, the United States had made its first investment in manned space flight without really realizing it.

"The result of the focusing and stimulating effects of the program," recalled Becker, "was to generate aerospace vehicle technology at a highly accelerated rate compared to the leisurely paced rate that existed prior to the X-15. Thus when it became clear in 1958 that the Space Age was upon us and the need to put a man in orbit became a matter of national urgency, a massive backlog of aerospace technology was already at hand in the X-15 program." Although the first manned space missions of 1961 and 1962 overshadowed the X-15's accomplishments, those people who had toiled on the aircraft behind the scenes knew the extent to which the rocket plane was paving the way toward the future. By 1964, 65 percent of all data gleaned from the X-15 was being applied to other programs, including the Apollo-Saturn launch vehicle that was designed to place humans on the moon.

However, it was the November 2, 1962, emer-

gency-landing crash of X-15 No. 2, with pilot John B. McKay aboard, that finally splintered the X-15 program into two different directions. At the terrible cost of McKay's serious injuries, No. 2 was rebuilt to press on toward Mach 8. The aircraft's modifications included the installation of external fuel tanks that could be dropped after the airplane reached Mach 2; the application of heat-resistant "ablative" coatings to the external surfaces; and a mount for a prototype hypersonic "scramjet" engine, a type of ramjet engine designed for very-high-speed atmospheric flight. The X-15A-2, as No. 2 was re-designated, now had an increased engine burn time of 145 seconds, as compared to the original airplane's 86-second burn, but increased drag caused by the modifications meant that its realistic top speed would be somewhere around Mach 7.5, instead of Mach 8, as had been planned. When rebuilt, the aircraft was 29 inches (73.6 centimeters) longer in order to accommodate a liquid-hydrogen tank for the scramjet. Air Force test pilot Bob Rushworth made the first flight on June 25, 1964. At Mach 4, during a subsequent A-2 flight, Rushworth heard and felt "an awful bang": the nose gear had dropped out of its well, rendering the X-15 nearly uncontrollable. The overloaded

A head-on view of X-15 No. 2, below, rebuilt after a serious crash in November 1962, reveals longer landing gear and two large saddle tanks that nearly doubled the fuel capacity. The new X-15A-2, seen here in flight, received a white thermal coating that protected the aircraft from atmospheric friction.

nose-gear tires blew out on landing, and the rocket coasted to a stop on its magnesium wheel rims.

By early 1967, NASA started to prepare the aircraft for its initial high-Mach trials. It received an ablative coating that consisted of a resin base, a catalyst, and glass-bead powder; if this protection worked, it would prevent the aircraft from reaching temperatures above 2,000 degrees F (1,080 degrees C) as it rushed through the atmosphere. The ablative coating then was intended to burn off as a sticky residue, with the unfortunate side effect of hitting the windshield and rendering it opaque. To circumvent this problem, North Americans added an "eyelid" on the left windshield that could be controlled by the pilot. After launch, the pilot would use the right windshield until it became opaque, which usually occurred at about Mach 3. From that point up through speeds of about Mach 6 and then back down to Mach 3, the pilot was totally blind until he opened the eyelid on the left.

The Air Force had re-assigned William J. "Pete" Knight, who had been a pilot with the now defunct X-20 *Dyna-Soar* space-plane program, to the Mach-8 X-15 effort. When he first saw the X-15A-2, with its coating of pink ablative material, he was astounded. "I said I wouldn't fly a pink airplane! They painted over it with white paint."

During one of his initial flights in X-15 No. 1, Knight was passing through 107,000 feet (32,600 meters) and Mach 4.17 when the engine quit. "Six or seven lights came on in the cockpit, then everything went out—total silence." Both auxiliary power units (APUs) and the generator had failed as the aircraft continued to climb: the aircraft had experienced a total electrical failure, and the pilot was left with no computed flight information or guidance.

"The aircraft began to roll a bit and I had 15 to 20 seconds to assess the situation. Going over the top I got the emergency battery on, then used the reaction-control system to right the aircraft. Looking down at [the dry] lake below I said to myself, 'You'd better enjoy the view because its probably going to be the last one you see.' Coasting to 180,000 feet [55,000 meters] at Mach 4, I was well above safe ejection limits."

Knight finally got an APU running, which provided hydraulic power for the aerodynamic controls. "I was afraid to reset the generator because I knew the problem was probably caused by some electrical malfunction. . . . I didn't want to repeat it." With nothing in the cockpit to rely on—no lights, no instruments—he decided on a manual, visual re-entry. Peering out, he lined up on what looked to be a straight flight path, and then pulled the nose up until the X-15 began to slide off one way or the other. This enabled him to maintain the maximum angle of attack.

Holding 6 Gs, Knight brought the crippled rocket back into the atmosphere, leveled out, spotted Mud Lake and entered a base-leg turn, and then rolled out on the final landing approach, falling like a rock the whole time. The no-flaps landing was heavy, but nothing broke. Knight was "pleased and satisfied and excited to be on the ground," but

a gurgling noise in the nose quickly got his attention. "I said, 'I'm getting out of this thing—I got it on the ground, it's up to someone else to take care of it.'"

Wasting no time, he started to unstrap, and got everything off except the oxygen and nitrogen leads to his helmet and mask. Increasingly flustered, at first he couldn't get them undone, but then he relaxed and removed his helmet. At that point he could really hear the gurgling. He pulled the emergency release—which then proceeded to blow the headrest off the seat. It hit the canopy, ricocheted forward, and struck Pete's bare head. Climbing out of the aircraft, Pete waved to Chase 1 as it flew by, and was picked up by the next aircraft. Back at Edwards there was great concern over Knight's head wound, which took six stitches to close up. Meanwhile, Pete was mad at himself: he hadn't been able to get the leads undone because he had forgotten to turn off the oxygen and nitrogen controls in the cockpit. It was the pressure in the lines that had prevented them from disconnecting. Certainly no one else was mad at him, and he soon received a Distinguished Flying Cross for pulling several rabbits out of what should have been an empty hat.

On August 21, 1967, Pete Knight took the X-15A-2 up for its first flight with the new ablative coating, and pushed the aircraft up to Mach 4.94 with no problems. Now the pilot and the plane

Above, three perspectives of the rugged X-15 rocket plane. Made of highly heat-resistant Inconel X nickel-steel alloy, this most successful of all research aircraft reached an altitude of more than 67 miles (108 kilometers) and speeds of nearly Mach 7. The only other aircraft that came close to such performance was the Mach 3 Lockheed SR-71 reconnaissance jet, right.

would go for "all the marbles." On October 3, Knight separated from the B-52 over Nevada, lit the engine, and pointed the aircraft toward Edwards as he climbed. When the large external tanks had spent all their fuel, he ejected them, leveling off at 102,000 feet (31,000 meters) and keeping the throttle up. When the engine exhausted its fuel, he was traveling at Mach 6.73: 4,520 miles per hour (7,232 kilometers per hour).

After making a landing, Knight was accustomed to seeing the recovery crew gather around the front of the aircraft to offer congratulations. "This time they all went to the back of the aircraft . . . something must be wrong. I got out and looked. The scramjet had burned off the lower ventral, which had severe damage due to high temperatures. It was like a blow torch had melted through into the engine bay and cut the stainless steel lines."

The 3,000-degree-F (1,635-degree-C) temperature created by the airplane's friction with the atmosphere not only had burned off the model ramjet, but had opened up a seven-inch-by-three-inch (17.8-centimeter-by-7.6-centimeter) hole in the leading edge of the ventral fin that allowed the searing heat to enter and to weaken the internal structure. According to historian Richard Hallion, "the blackened and charred research airplane . . . resembled burnt firewood." So much for a spray-on ablative coating that could be re-applied after each flight: the X-15 had come within a few seconds of disintegrating from aerodynamic heating. Plans for flights to Mach 7 were abandoned, and, although the aircraft was rebuilt, it never flew again. Pete Knight and the X-15A-2 still hold the world's speed

record for a winged flying machine.

Just over a month later, on November 17, Mike Adams was flying No. 3 with Pete Knight stationed below as the ground controller. As the X-15 climbed out of the atmosphere, it began to drift in heading, slowly turning away from the direction of the flight path. By the time it reached the flight's peak altitude of 266,000 feet (81,100 meters), the aircraft had yawed 15 degrees in heading off its flight path. No one ever was able to determine just what happened next, but, as Adams descended through 230,000 feet (70,000 meters) at Mach 5, he radioed that he was in a spin, an extremely dangerous situation for the X-15. Although Knight tried to help Adams, he had no duplicate attitude indicator on the ground, and thus had no way to tell what was happening. At around 120,000 feet (36,600 meters), Adams recovered into a steep dive at Mach 4.7, but it didn't last.

The No. 3 aircraft featured the combined variable-gain, rate-command, self-adaptive control system that had only one control stick, which should have made it easier for the pilot to recover control of the X-15. Unfortunately, as Adams re-entered the atmosphere, the control system caused the control surfaces to oscillate, and the rocket plane started to pitch wildly, going through one and a half to two cycles above 18 Gs, and then pulling 8 to 9 Gs laterally. At 62,000 feet (19,000 meters) and Mach 3.93, the forces became too severe for the missile, and it broke up, taking Adams to his death. The recovered cockpit recorder and telemetry data revealed that the X-15 had re-entered the atmosphere backwards before going into the spin. Over the top, Adams had become distracted by the machine's malfunctions, and increasingly disoriented, and in the end was so affected by vertigo that he was unable to determine the attitude of the aircraft until it was too late.

With only X-15 No. 1 still airworthy, the sun now set on one of the most valuable and daring flight-research programs in history. On October 24, 1968, NASA pilot Bill Dana made the 199th and last flight in the X-15 series,

and, although technicians tried desperately to pull off a 200th, it was not to be. The next year, X-15 No. 1 was shipped to the Smithsonian Institution's National Air and Space Museum as an artifact of history.

Yet breakthroughs that had been achieved by the X-15 program were pivotal in proving that a spaceworthy winged vehicle not only could work, but could be flown by human beings out of and then back into the Earth's atmosphere. Without the massive amount of practical data generated by the X-15 and its 12 talented pilots, the space shuttle would have taken much longer to lift off the launch pad. Astronaut John Young, the commander of the first shuttle mission, paid homage to the X-15 black bullet after it had been all but forgotten. "The lift-to-drag ratio of the Space Shuttle is almost identical to that of the X-15," he reminded us. "They were very similar programs and there was a great deal of feedback from the X-15 to the Shuttle. It really paid off."

A Boeing B-52, opposite, carries X-15 No. 3 to altitude. At right, from left to right, pilots Pete Knight, Bob Rushworth, Joe Engle, Milt Thompson, Bill Dana, and Jack McKay stand with X-15 No. 3.

In the early 1930s, the German Rocket Society (Verein für Raumfahrt, or VfR) was the scene of many heated debates regarding the future of rocketry and space flight. Hermann Oberth, for example, thought that fellow member Max Valier's concept of reusable spacecraft was all wrong; such craft would never replace expendable rockets in putting payloads in space. Although outsiders considered the VfR a lunatic-fringe group, filled with science-fiction fanatics, those visionaries with a sol-

TO SPACE AND BACK

id background in physics knew better.

Austrian Eugen Sänger was one of those educated visionaries. Inspired by Oberth's *Die Rakete,* he studied aeronautical engineering and earned his doctorate. Combining the principles of space flight with those of aeronautics, he designed a rocket-propelled craft he called *Silverbird* that could reach Earth orbit like a rocket, carrying the materials needed to build a space station, and then glide like an airplane back through the atmosphere to Earth. In 1933, he published his theories in the book *Raketenflugtechnik (Rocket Flight Technology),* which now is recognized as one of the seminal works in astronautics.

Focusing his efforts on regeneratively cooled rocket engines as well as on the design of his space plane, Sänger received a number of patents before transferring his work to the Deutsche Versuch-sanstalt für Luftfahrt (German Aviation Research Institute) in 1937. His wind-tunnel tests and plans for a 220,560-pound-thrust (981,140-newton) rocket engine were progressing well when World War II began. Since a civil space plane had no place in wartime plans, the craft was renamed the Antipodal Bomber and funded as a weapon.

Sänger and his assistant, the brilliant mathematician Irene Bredt, whom Sänger eventually would marry, laid out a proposal for a 100-ton (90,900-kilogram), supersonic, Earth-orbiting transport with a range of 14,000 miles (22,400 kilome-

Former National Aeronautics and Space Administration (NASA) X-15 pilot Milt Thompson, above, stands beside the steel-and-plywood M2-F1 lifting-body glider he flew in the early 1960s to test wingless aircraft shapes. At right is artist Pierre Mion's depiction of Austrian Eugen Sänger's hypersonic, sub-orbital bomber, which, fortunately, remained on the drawing boards during World War II. Sänger's design for the rocket-propelled ship inspired such subsequent aircraft as the space shuttle.

ters). The craft would be launched at 1,000 miles per hour (1,600 kilometers per hour) by a giant, track-mounted sled. Then, boosted by rockets, it would zoom to an altitude of 155 miles (250 kilometers), essentially above the atmosphere. It would coast back down to an altitude of about 25 miles (40 kilometers), where it would re-enter the denser air of the upper atmosphere and bounce off it, skipping back up to 80 miles (130 kilometers) or so, much as a flat rock skips across the surface of a pond. It could skip like this across the Earth's upper atmosphere, with shorter and shorter bounces, until its energy was drained by drag and friction, at which point it would glide back to Earth for a landing.

By 1942, German military planners were pushing the development of expendable V-2s, which were far less expensive and technologically far less challenging than any kind of piloted spacecraft. The boost glider lay dormant until the early 1950s, when V-2 project director Walter Dornberger, who had been brought to the United States as a kind of war booty in 1950 and by then was working at the Bell Aircraft Company, tried to generate interest in applying the "boost-glide" theory to the U.S. Air Force's MX-2145 bomber study.

In 1958, the Air Force issued a request for proposals for a rocket-boosted, hypersonic-research glider that could fly strike, reconnaissance, and anti-satellite missions. The Sänger-Bredt studies were dusted off and re-read with great interest: the basic idea was intriguing. The space plane could be built and flown not only as a suborbital aircraft but as an orbiting spacecraft as well. Seven companies, including Boeing and the team of Bell and Martin, responded to the Air Force's challenge.

Although the Air Force had to devise a rocket powerful enough to get the boost glider into space, the space plane's real problems centered around

heat. Re-entering the Earth's atmosphere at Mach 25, the craft would generate a 20,000-degree-F (12,000-degree-C) plasma layer around the nose. Bell and Martin proposed the installation of cooling tubes on the nose and leading edges of the craft's fuselage and wings, while Boeing focused on refractory materials and high-strength steel alloys combined with liquid hydrogen to cool the skin.

In early 1960, Boeing won the competition to build the "dynamic soaring" vehicle, which now was officially designated the X-20A, although it was commonly called by its nickname, *Dyna-Soar*. Martin was given the contract to develop its Titan III intercontinental ballistic missile (ICBM) as a booster. Boeing designed a black, single-seat, blunt-nosed, delta-wing craft with wing-tip-mounted vertical fins, a configuration offering many advantages for a test aircraft, including desirable aerodynamic characteristics at both very high and very low speeds.

The *Dyna-Soar*'s testing included three stages: suborbital flights; a boost into orbital flight; and, finally, operation as a military space plane. Although the first suborbital flight was slated for 1963, the Soviet Union's triumphant manned orbital flights of 1961 spurred the United States to increase spending and speed up its space-flight programs. In late 1962, X-20 program managers omitted the first suborbital-flight-test stage. For the orbital flight, a Titan III launch rocket was fitted with large solid-fuel rocket boosters to push the X-20 into orbit.

The X-20 itself brought major advances to flight technology. Wind-tunnel experiments at laboratories around the country provided a large data base of practical information for a space plane. A side-stick controller allowed the pilot to manage both aerodynamic controls for atmospheric flight and small rocket-thruster controls for space flight. An advanced "fly-by-wire" computer helped eliminate the cables and push-pull rods associated with the control systems of more conventional aircraft.

The first X-20 mission was scheduled for 1965. Then, in December 1963, the X-20 *Dyna-Soar* lived up to its nickname, becoming extinct as the program suddenly was canceled. So passed a dream—almost a reality—that could have flown almost 20 years before the first launch of the space shuttle.

Very likely, a combination of factors did in the *Dyna-Soar*. Secretary of Defense Robert S. McNamara thought the program was far too expensive. Then, too, in 1963, President John F. Kennedy had called for the United States to direct its efforts toward achieving a moon landing by the end of the decade. The fastest way to reach this ambitious goal was to use the "spam in the can" combination of space "capsules" boosted by expendable rockets. The acme of this approach was the Apollo program. It certainly worked, but at the expense of $24 billion in non-recoverable, high-tech junk that was allowed to splash back into the ocean or was left in Earth orbit, in lunar orbit, or on the lunar surface, and the Apollo mission's ultimate cost also included the pioneering and preparatory Mercury and Gemini programs. Further working against the *Dyna-Soar* in 1963 was the member nations' of the United Nations signing of a treaty that called for severe limitations on the military use of space.

Fortunately, alternative methods for space flight and re-entry were under investigation. Researchers already had learned that intuition and conventional rules would not work in a spacecraft; high-speed wings, with their sharp, heat-concentrating leading edges, were out. A blunt, curved shape would work very well for re-entry into the atmosphere, creating a "detached" shock wave that would bleed off heat generated by atmospheric friction, as was being proved during re-entry of the Mercury space capsules. In the early 1950s, NASA and Air Force scientists had designed and tested "lifting bodies"

Opposite top, Boeing's mockup for the X-20 Dyna-Soar, a proposed space plane that never made it beyond the design stage. Opposite bottom, Eugen Sänger discusses his Silverbird space plane, which has yet to be realized. Sänger began the theoretical groundwork for a trans-atmospheric aircraft in the early 1930s. His design schematic for the ship's liquid-fuel rocket motor appears below.

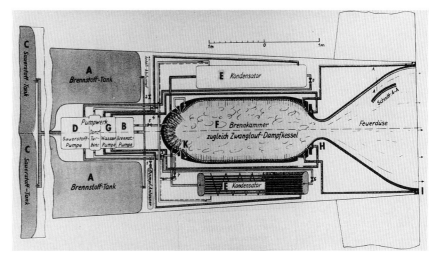

that could produce lift with their shapes alone—without wings. Only one problem stood in the way of further research of such advanced aircraft: lack of funds.

Paul Bikle, director of NASA's Dryden Flight Research Center, charged ahead independently. Since the NASA Dryden flight-test complex, along with the USAF Flight Test Center, was located away from prying eyes at Edwards Air Force Base in the California desert, Bikle seized an ideal opportunity. He and engineers from the Ames Research Center designed a craft based on a 13-degree cone with a flattened upper surface. Flights with small radio-controlled models proved the con-

Paul Bikle, right, director of NASA's Dryden Flight Research Center in California, oversaw the frugal program for the development of lifting bodies. Below, an M2 model undergoes flight testing in the wind tunnel at NASA's Langley Research Center in Virginia.

A NASA C-47 tows the wood-and-steel-tube M2-F1 to 10,000 feet (3,048 meters) over Rogers Dry Lake, California. Released, the craft will glide swiftly and steeply down to the lake bed.

cept. In 1962, without telling NASA headquarters in Washington, Bikle had the Sailplane Corporation of America build what would be designated the M2-F1. Constructed of welded-steel tube with a smooth skin of plywood, the M2-F1 was one of the ugliest homemade airplanes ever conceived, but the construction made it possible to build a flyable airplane in just two months. Two vertical fins and rudders controlled yaw, while two trailing-edge flaps controlled pitch, and elevons—combined ailerons and elevators—were fitted for pitch and roll control. For simplicity, the landing gear was not retractable.

Bikle had the "tub," as the M2-F1 was called, tested in Ames Research Center's full-scale wind tunnel—and it flew! Out of the laboratory and into flight testing, first it was towed at low altitude behind an automobile. Bikle's cohorts in crime headed for Rogers Dry Lake near Edwards Air Force Base, obtaining a Pontiac convertible souped up by famed speed-mechanic and racer Mickey Thompson. The words "National Aeronautics and Space Administration," painted on each side, made it all look official. Hooking the M2-F1 to a towline, the researchers raced up and down the dry lake bed, the Pontiac's big V-8 engine roaring for all it was worth to get the car and its tow up to speed. At 125 miles per hour (200 kilometers per hour), the plywood marvel hopped off the white surface and flew. So far so good. A few flights later, Bikle let NASA's

senior management in on what was happening. Much to their credit, the bureaucrats were impressed, and a program to develop the lifting body—as such flying shapes are called—was funded.

NASA provided a Douglas C-47 (the military version of the classic DC-3 airliner) to tow the M2-F1 aloft for gliding trials. X-15 veteran Milt Thompson made the first flight on August 16, 1963, gliding to the dry lake bed from 10,000 feet (3,048 meters) in about two minutes. Milt found it had X-15-like, "streamlined-brick" landing-approach characteristics, which he was used to, but it also exhibited an inherent problem with such shapes, resulting in poor lateral stability. In the hands of experienced test pilots, the M2-F1 generated a significant amount of excellent data in over 100 successful flights, but it was, at times, a dangerous aircraft to fly.

Pleased, NASA put out contracts for two "real airplanes," which, with power provided by rocket engines, would be capable of supersonic speed. One, the M2-F2, was based on the Ames design, while

A veteran B-52, above, carries a rocket-powered Northrop M2 to 45,000 feet (13,700 meters) for an air launch. Tick marks on the bomber record launches of another aircraft, the X-15. At right, a diagram of the flight profile of an M2 lifting body. An unpowered descent from 45,000 feet lasted 3 minutes, 37 seconds.

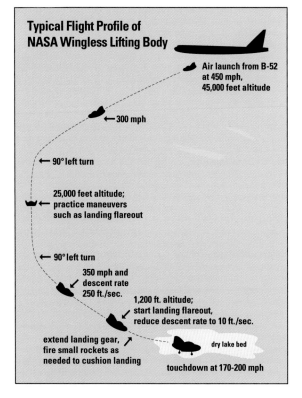

Typical Flight Profile of NASA Wingless Lifting Body

Air launch from B-52 at 450 mph, 45,000 feet altitude

← 300 mph

← 90° left turn

25,000 feet altitude; practice maneuvers such as landing flareout

← 90° left turn

350 mph and descent rate 250 ft./sec.

1,200 ft. altitude; start landing flareout, reduce descent rate to 10 ft./sec.

extend landing gear, fire small rockets as needed to cushion landing

dry lake bed

touchdown at 170-200 mph

the other was the HL-10, a NASA Langley Research Center "fattened-delta" design; both machines would be built by Northrop. Once again, Reaction Motors, Inc., now a division of Thiokol, supplied the 8,000-pound-thrust (35,587-newton) version of its X-1 engine, the XLR-11. Dropped from a B-52 at 45,000 feet (13,725 meters) on July 10, 1966, Milt Thompson piloted a flight that ended three and a half minutes later. The M2-F2 exhibited lateral and directional instability from the outset, much as the F1 had. Pilots found they had

to stay far "ahead" of the aircraft, trying to predict what it might do next in order to keep it under control.

On December 22, 1966, Bruce Peterson made the first HL-10 flight. From the moment of release from the B-52, the aircraft was nearly uncontrollable due to aerodynamic flow problems. However, Peterson was able to save the craft, and a later modification, a vertical fin, made it docile and pleasant to fly.

During the M2-F2's 16th flight, on May 10, 1967, Peterson encountered severe oscillations on his final approach to the lake bed. Altering the approach path to regain control, Peterson dodged an errant chase helicopter and crashed into the desert. With the landing gear only partially deployed, the M2-F2 impacted at 217 miles per hour (347 kilometers per hour) and rolled six times, tearing itself apart, yet, incredibly, Peterson survived and recovered to fly again. The crash became famous as the opening sequence for the television series, "The Six Million Dollar Man." Also astonishingly, the smashed M2-F2 lived to fly again. The lifting body was rebuilt as the M2-F3, with an improved vertical fin and a reaction-control thruster system. Before being retired in December 1972, it reached an altitude of 71,504 feet (21,810 meters) and achieved Mach 1.613.

Rocket-powered flights began on October 23,

Appearing front to back in a hangar at Edwards Air Force Base, California, in 1967, are the Northrop HL-10, the M2-F2, and the M2-F1 glider. Former X-15 pilot Bill Dana, right, flew the rocket-powered HL-10 to 92,303 feet (28,134 meters) in the 1970s.

A rear view of the M2-F3 lifting body, above, exhibits the central vertical fin that distinguishes it from the M2-F2. On May 10, 1967, NASA pilot Bruce Peterson, right, survived a crash of the M2-F2. Dramatic footage of the accident provided the opening sequence of the popular television series "The Six Million Dollar Man."

Martin Aircraft Company built a low-speed manned vehicle, the SV-5B, or X-24A. Jerry Gentry and NASA's John Manke made 10 glides before the first powered flight in March 1970. The powered flight demonstrated that the X-24A had an alarming tendency to nose up when the XLR-11 engine was fired. Not only that, but the vehicle was ugly: a "finned potato," wrote historian Dick Hallion.

In 1971, the "potato" was grounded so that it could be rebuilt as the sleek and maneuverable X-24B, which embodied the shape of the future. Called a "blended body" for its blend of wing and body shape, this flying delta wing was a pilot's dream. Impressed with the X-24B's excellent handling qualities, John Manke and Air Force test pilot Mike Love asked the program managers if they could make precision landings on Edwards Air Force Base's concrete runways, which were much more convenient than the distant, vast dry lake beds.

On August 5, 1975, after several weeks of simulated approaches in T-38 and F-104 aircraft, Manke dropped away from the B-52 launch aircraft in the X-24B, fired the rocket engine, and climbed to 60,000 feet (18,300 meters), and then headed down. Seven minutes after launch, he touched down on the runway with the same precision as a regular aircraft. These X-24B tests had proved that a space

1968, when Air Force pilot Jerauld "Jerry" Gentry lit the liquid-propellant, rocket-motor XLR-11 in the HL-10 vehicle. By May 1969, the HL-10 was sliding through Mach 1 with no problem, representing a major milestone in the lifting-body, proof-of-concept tests, and in 1970 Peter Hoag took it to Mach 1.86, or 1,288 miles per hour (2,060 kilometers per hour). Although the HL-10 was fitted with small rockets to aid in landing, pilots found that powered landings were more difficult than unpowered, gliding approaches, which served as an important piece of information for future space-plane operations.

A third lifting-body program, the Air Force's SV-5 project, went through the hypersonic-model-testing phase before the

The M2-F3, left, hangs today in the National Air and Space Museum. Rebuilt after Bruce Peterson's crash, also left, the aircraft received a central vertical fin to improve its yaw and roll characteristics.

The helium wind tunnel at NASA's Langley Research Center subjects a model of the space-shuttle orbiter to conditions of atmospheric re-entry at 20 times the speed of sound. Construction of the first of these 122-foot-long (37-meter) space trucks began in 1974.

plane could be flown back from a space mission to a pinpoint location on the Earth, and even landed on a conventional runway. A real space plane was taking shape by the time the X-24B was retired with honor in November 1975.

In the late 1960s, as the Apollo program neared its lunar-landing phase, NASA began to consider options for the next step into space. The most popular concept among both military and civilian experts was the assembly of an Earth-orbiting space station, the dream of visionaries since Robert

Goddard and Hermann Oberth. Unfortunately, putting into orbit the materials necessary for a space station would demand a prohibitively expensive number of expendable rocket boosters. Such an extravagant delivery system would make the money that already had been spent on Apollo look like a child's piggy-bank savings.

Throughout 1968, NASA studied an array of concepts for reusable spacecraft. Although both

Above, over Edwards Air Force Base, the U.S. Air Force X-24B is air-launched from a B-52 in August 1973. Below, pilot Dick Scobee stands by the sleek X-24, a test bed for space-shuttle concepts.

the *Dyna-Soar* and Sänger's boost glider had had less ambitious objectives than the new spacecraft, the projected model would be a derivative of both that employed the same principles for aerodynamic braking in the atmosphere and gliding down to land like an airplane. By mid-1969, the concept became known as the space shuttle, and four companies submitted designs for an Integrated Launch and Reentry Vehicle (ILRV). The orbiter, a piloted space plane, would be mounted on a gigantic winged booster with its own pilots. The combined weight of the orbiter and the booster would total 3.2 million pounds (1,454,545 kilograms) at launch. The maximum payload that the system would be able to deliver to Earth orbit was estimated to be 40,000 pounds (18,182 kilograms), none too much for the task of building and supplying a space station.

By 1971, Department of Defense requirements had increased the system's payload to 65,000 pounds (29,545 kilograms). However, the cost as well as the weight of the system itself continued to climb, until the project was going to cost at least $10 billion in 1970 dollars. Sam Beddingfield, NASA's project-assessment chief at Kennedy Space Center, Cape Canaveral, Florida, called a halt to further development of the spacecraft even before Congress had voted on the allocation of funds. The concept of a manned, winged booster was eliminated; the orbiter would be fitted with boosters that could be jettisoned.

In July 1972, Congress set aside a total of five billion dollars in the federal budget to enable the winning contractor, Rockwell International, to

build five examples of a four-part Space Transportation System (STS). The STS included the piloted, winged orbiter and a giant external fuel tank that would hold liquid hydrogen and liquid oxygen for the orbiter's three main engines. The fuel tank would also serve as the mount upon which the orbiter would ride during the launch phase of the flight. Two solid-propellant rocket boosters provided extra thrust for liftoff and for the flight up through the atmosphere. When used up, both the tank and the boosters would fall away. The STS combination as a whole was named the space shuttle.

Imposing design problems remained, but many pioneers, who had enjoyed far fewer resources and little government support, had already paved the way to space. For the first time in history, these visionaries' old dream would be realized: a nation would put humans into a spacecraft, launch them into space, bring them back—and then send the same spacecraft up again with a new crew for another mission.

The orbiter's three liquid-propellant rocket engines would have to generate 375,000 pounds of thrust (1,668,149 newtons) apiece, while each of the two solid-propellant rocket boosters would add 2.9 million

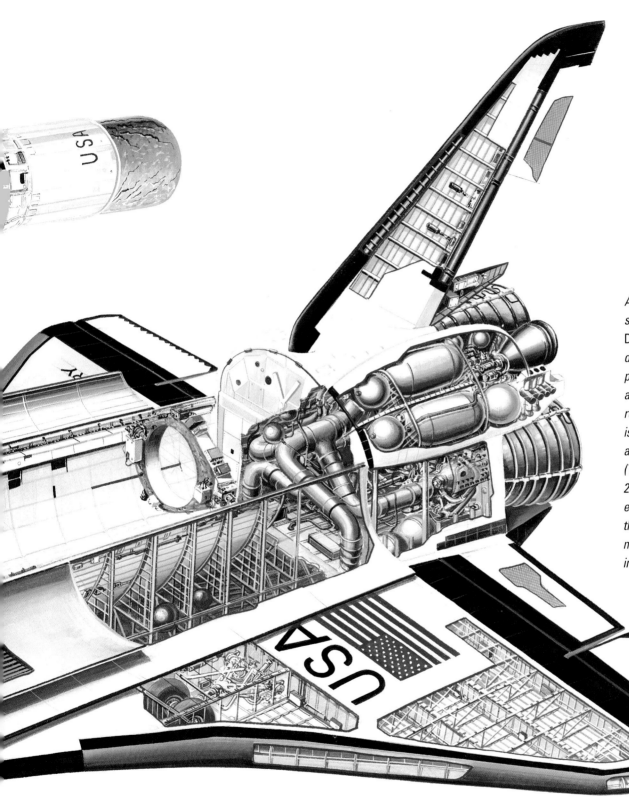

A cutaway illustration of space shuttle OV-103 Discovery reveals details of its crew compartment, payload bay, and engines. Here, the remote-manipulator arm is deploying a Tracking and Data Relay Satellite (TDRS). More than 20,000 borosilicate-coated ceramic tiles cover the conventional aluminum structure, providing a crucial heat shield.

pounds of thrust (12,900,355 newtons). Although these thrust figures were much larger than those of any previous rocket-plane engines, once again pioneers had designed and even built hardware for such large engines years before.

The orbiter itself was designed as a conventional, delta-winged aircraft, rather than as a wingless lifting body. Although the lifting-body flight-test program had not been completed when the orbiter's design was frozen, researchers had gathered enough data from the program's early flights and from other flight-test programs to convince them to select the more conventional, delta-wing-aircraft design for the shuttle. The final shuttle design yielded a 150,000-pound (68,182-kilogram) craft with a wingspan of around 78 feet (23.8 meters), a length of 122 feet (37.2 meters), and a cargo bay that measured 60 feet (18.3 meters) in length and 15 feet (4.57 meters) in diameter. Convinced that it would be best not to build the shuttle out of an exotic alloy, despite such an alloy's ability to withstand excessive heat, NASA asked Rockwell to fashion a "normal" aluminum-alloy aircraft structure that could be covered with Lockheed's heat-resistant ceramic tiles. When it was finished, the orbiter appeared fat and stubby, but its hypersonic aerodynamics were more efficient than those of the much sleeker-looking X-15. A fly-by-wire, digital-computer-generated control system that drew on the X-20's pioneering control-system research and testing was installed. Today such computer-managed, fly-by-wire control systems that do away with the mechanical links between controls and control

Opposite left: Joe Engle (left) and Richard Truly hold a model of the space shuttle they glide-tested on September 13, 1977. Opposite right, the most recent orbiter, Endeavor, *is mated to the Boeing 747 Shuttle Carrier Aircraft (SCA). The shuttle will ride piggy-back to Kennedy Space Center, Cape Canaveral, Florida. At left, a technician installs tiles on* Columbia *at Kennedy Space Center. Below,* Challenger, *with Vance Brand and Robert Gibson at the controls, returns to Kennedy from space in 1984.*

surfaces are common in both military and civil aircraft. When installed in the shuttle, they were revolutionary.

Construction on Orbiter OV-101 began in June 1974, and it rolled out of Rockwell's Palmdale, California, plant on September 17, 1976. A Boeing 747, which had been purchased from American Airlines in 1974, was modified to carry the orbiter aloft over Edwards for low-speed glide tests that would prove its aerodynamic efficiency and handling. Since this particular orbiter would never fly in space, it made its glide tests without engines and without a full set of thermal-protective tiles. NASA chose veteran test pilot and astronaut Donald K. "Deke" Slayton to oversee the initial phase of testing.

In January 1977, the first orbiter, named *Enterprise* after the famous fictitious starship of the "Star Trek" television series, was trucked to NASA's Dryden Flight Research Center at Edwards Air Force Base, there to be mated to its Boeing 747 transport aircraft. On February 18, the NASA 747, piloted

by Fitz Fulton and Tom McMurtry, with engineers Vic Horton and Skip Guidry also along, carried *Enterprise* aloft, reaching 288 miles per hour (460 kilometers per hour) and 16,200 feet (4,940 meters) in its first "inert," or unpiloted, captive flight. For such an unsightly, ungainly combination, the two craft handled beautifully. After landing, Fulton commented, "I couldn't even tell the orbiter was aboard!" The next few flights went so well that Slayton canceled the sixth in order to press on with the next phases of the program.

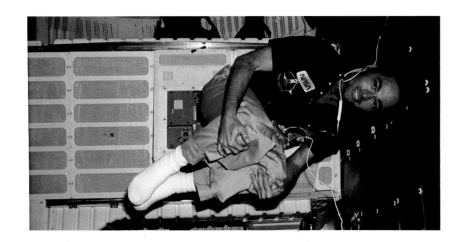

For the "captive-active" flights, in which the orbiter was carried with a crew aboard, NASA assigned two teams of pilots: Fred Haise and Gordon Fullerton, and Joe Engle and Dick Truly. These men would also make the slow-speed Approach and Landing Test (ALT) flights, during which the orbiter would be released from the mother 747 to glide to Earth on its own. The captive flights went smoothly, and the planned four flights were reduced to three.

In preparation for free flight, the crews spent many hours flying steep approaches from 35,000 feet (10,675 meters) in the orbiter simulators, which were two reconfigured Grumman Gulfstream II corporate jets. The computers aboard the two Gulfstream IIs could duplicate the feel and performance of the orbiter, even its X-15-like, 15,000-foot-per-minute sink rate. Former X-15 pilot Joe Engle found himself right at home pointing straight down at the desert with no power.

At 8:00 A.M., on August 12, 1977, the piggy-back combination of orbiter and 747 left the Edwards runway, with a gaggle of T-38 chase planes following. At 8:48 A.M., 747 pilots Fulton and Mc-

Murtry eased their big transport into a shallow dive from 28,000 feet (8,540 meters), and then or-biter pilot Fred Haise radioed, "The *Enterprise* is set. Thanks for the lift." With a punch of the sep-aration button and the bang of explosive bolts, Haise and copilot Fullerton pulled the orbiter up and away from the 747 in a right turn while Ful-ton rolled the 747 to the left—a necessary precau-tion, since no one was sure that the orbiter would

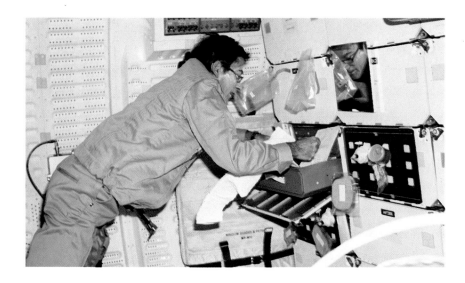

clear the Boeing's tall tail.

Haise continued his turn to the west and start-ed down for the lake bed at a tame 12-degree an-gle of descent; later operational shuttle flights would descend at 24 degrees. To their delight, the pilots discovered that the orbiter handled just fine as an aircraft; five and a half minutes after launch, *En-terprise* touched down on Rogers Dry Lake.

After several free flights—with a tail-cone fair-ing covering the orbiter's dummy rocket-engine nozzles and with the fairing removed and the dum-my-engine nozzles exposed—the tests proceeded so smoothly that Slayton reduced the number of remaining flights. At the orbiter's controls, Joe En-gle found that he was "very busy getting data all the way to the ground." Because the exposed dum-my-rocket nozzles created such high drag, the flights without the tail cone lasted only about two and a half minutes. Engle related that the aerodynamic characteristics of the *Enterprise* were straightfor-ward. "It was a good aircraft with the personality of an electric airplane. The computer responses

were noticeable...it was apparent this was a fly-by-wire" machine.

The orbiter's last unpowered free flight was made to Edwards's 15,000-foot (4,575-meter) concrete runway on October 26, 1977. As the craft touched down, it rolled to the left. Haise corrected the roll and the shuttle bounced back into the air. Although Haise relaxed his grip on the stick, the machine bounced back into the air one last time. A poten-tially serious handling problem had arisen. Engi-neers modified the orbiter's control system, but, from that point on, at various times pilots noted that the orbiter required considerable skill to fly. It was, after all, the first of its kind, and test pilots would have to work out the bugs for the benefit of future space flight.

Next in the shuttle's test program came simu-lated launch-vibration and dynamic-flight-load testing of all four mated STS components. The tests were conducted in the old Apollo program's Sat-urn V launch-vehicle test building at Marshall Space Flight Center in Huntsville, Alabama. By the end of 1978, *Enterprise* had served its purpose; although it would never fly in space, it had cleared the way for the launch of the next orbiter.

In March 1979, Orbiter OV-102, named *Co-lumbia*, arrived at Kennedy Space Center, where hopes ran high that the craft soon would be in or-bit. More than two years passed, however, before that goal was reached, as the shuttle's engines and its heat-protection system suffered one problem af-ter another. The complex arrangement of over 30,000 thermal-protection tiles proved difficult to perfect, leading to cost overruns and delays in the program's schedule. The price of the shuttle pro-gram had risen to nine billion dollars. Predictions of a disaster in space and calls for budget restraints grew louder as delays grew longer. But the STS program hung on, and, by 1981, *Columbia* was cleared for flight.

NASA's chief astronaut, John Young, at 50 a vet-eran of the Apollo program and of a lunar land-ing, and Robert Crippen had been selected as the crew of the first shuttle flight, which was designat-ed STS-1. Young in fact had flown in space four times during the Gemini and Apollo programs, but "Crip" had been waiting in the wings for 15 years.

As Young put it, "We're 130 percent trained and ready to go." Both were ready to fly *Columbia*.

On April 12, 1981, at 7:00 A.M., *Columbia*'s three main engines and then its huge solid-fuel boosters roared into life, shaking the earth with 7.5 million pounds of thrust (33,362,989 newtons) and lifting the space shuttle off Kennedy Space Center's Pad 39A. As the orbiter arced and rolled out over the Atlantic, monitors on the ground recorded launch-veteran Young's heart rate at a calm 85 beats per minute, while Crippen's hummed along at 135. At just over two minutes after launch and 31 miles (49.6 kilometers) up, the solid-rocket boosters ran out of propellant and were jettisoned. (They would later be recovered from the sea and reused.) At six and a half minutes after launch, the orbiter had reached a speed of Mach 15. Just over two minutes later, in low-earth orbit at 73 miles high (117 kilometers), *Columbia* jettisoned its empty propellant tank. By then its speed was Mach 25, or more than 17,400 miles per hour (27,840 kilometers per hour). Using the craft's rocket engines, the crew maneuvered the shuttle up to a 150-mile-high (240-kilometer-high) orbit.

Settling into a 36-orbit, two-day mission, Young

and Crippen opened the cargo-bay doors to discover that several of the thermal-protection tiles had popped off. Although these were non-critical portions of the spacecraft, the astronauts—and everyone else—wondered if any tiles had come off the bottom. There was no way to tell whether tiles in heat-critical areas of the orbiter had all stayed on, and during re-entry it would be too late to do anything about it if they hadn't.

The mission went very well. On Tuesday morning, April 14, the crew started back home. After turning *Columbia*'s tail forward, Young and Crippen fired the orbital-maneuvering engines. Braked by the thrust against the direction of flight, *Columbia*'s orbit began to decay out over the Indian Ocean. Touchdown at Edwards was 45 minutes away. For the first time, a pilot would maneuver a spacecraft back into the Earth's atmosphere, and then fly it all the way down.

Young put the Shuttle's nose down 18 degrees, with the ship's flat underside side facing the Earth. As it descended, the orbiter slowly pitched nose-up until it was pointing 40 degrees above the horizon, giving the belly full exposure to the atmosphere. At about 400,000 feet (122,000 meters), hurtling at Mach 25, the shuttle brushed the upper atmosphere. Within seconds, the ionized bubble of gas around the craft became so dense that radio contact would be lost. Mission Control, in Houston, radioed, "Easy does it, John, we're all riding with you." All Young could say before losing touch with the ground was a brief "Bye, bye."

On-board computers initiated a series of S-turns to slow-down *Columbia*. The dynamic pressure created by the passage of the shuttle through the upper atmosphere already allowed *Columbia*'s aerodynamic controls to work, reducing speed and increasing the descent rate. About 1,000 miles (1,600 kilometers) from the landing site at Edwards Air Force Base, *Columbia* was at 213,000 feet (65,000 meters), traveling at Mach 18 with a skin temperature of 3,000 degrees F (1,635 degrees C). Good news: if *Columbia*'s belly tiles had been damaged at launch, the craft would have vaporized by now. Houston was elated when *Columbia* emerged from the black-out zone of ionization, and Young radioed in. The ship was fine, sailing in toward California's Big Sur region at Mach 10.3 and at 188,000 feet (57,340 meters).

After another roll reversal to bleed the speed down to Mach 6.6 at 139,000 feet (43,400 meters), the computer had done its job. Young took control, rolled the Shuttle back and forth to quench more momentum, and headed for Edwards. As the orbiter came through 54,000 feet (16,470 meters) and Mach 1.3, over a half million people, waiting below for the landing, heard the double crack of a sonic boom.

Young found the orbiter to be a real handful to fly, particularly because of fatigue from the mission's heavy workload and from dehydration caused by breathing an oxygen-rich atmosphere. Both pilots exerted maximum skill and determination to bring the shuttle home. And although all those who flew later shuttle missions had to face the same challenges, the public never really appreciated how much old-fashioned, seat-of-the-pants flying skill was required to get the shuttles back safe.

Eugen Sänger's *Silverbird* had flown at last, but he was not there to share the triumph; he had died in 1964. Yet, without a doubt, Young, Crippen, and the entire space-shuttle team were standing on his shoulders. Despite all its high-tech glamor, in the end the space shuttle was just another brand-new, temperamental, developmental airplane requiring test pilots and their skills to get the most out of it.

With an arcing left turn, *Columbia*'s pilots lined the craft up on the lake bed's runway 23, and now all was familiar. *Enterprise* had done this part before. With four T-38 chase planes zooming close by, their pilots inspecting the orbiter for damage, Young lined up the shuttle right on the money, lowered the landing gear 11 seconds before touchdown, and flared onto this historic piece of desolation beautifully, as had so many experimental aircraft before.

THE LAST GREAT WORLD RECORD

"Holy bananas! Look at that shadow! What have we done?" exclaimed pilot Dick Rutan on June 22, 1984, during the Voyager's first takeoff. The aircraft's special mission—to fly around the world without refueling—dictated its unusual shape. Fuel tanks built into almost all parts of the Voyager's structure gave it a fuel capacity of 1,489 gallons (5,636 liters) of gasoline, almost three-fourths of the airplane's total takeoff weight. Voyager was equipped with a forward elevator, called a canard, and a rudder on the right vertical stabilizer.

Dick Rutan had asked his younger brother, Burt, out to dinner. Mojave, California, wasn't known for its sophisticated cuisine, but there were few better places in the world for aircraft construction and flight testing. It was 1981, and the Rutan Aircraft Factory was now a standard fixture at Mojave Airport, which was fast becoming the civilian flight-test center of the United States. Company president Burt Rutan already was famous as the world's most unconventional aircraft designer. A lot of people had built his VariEze and Long-EZ composite, canard-equipped, two-place airplanes in their garages and living rooms. The aircraft industry had also taken notice: Burt had designed a two-thirds-scale T-46 jet-trainer demonstrator, and he was working on a corporate turboprop design that later would become the futuristic Beech Starship.

A retired U.S. Air Force lieutenant colonel, Dick was a man in need of a challenge. He had worked for Burt for a while after retiring from the Air Force, but older-brother fighter pilots don't listen well to younger-brother slip-stick jockeys, and, by mutual consent, he had left the company. Now, Dick wanted Burt to design a competition aerobatics aircraft that Dick could sell to enthusiasts and serious "akro" (slang for the older term "acrobatics") pilots alike. Dinner was a good way to grease the skids. Dick and his girl friend of one year, pilot and draftswoman Jeana Yeager, looked across the table at Burt with genuine eagerness.

But Burt didn't want to design an airplane that would compete for sales with his own products. Burt tried to divert Dick and Jeana with another plan. Why not design an airplane, he proposed, with which they could conquer the last remaining unaccomplished goal of aviation record setters: a nonstop flight around the world with no refueling? Such a feat would require an airplane capable of

doubling the existing nonstop-flight distance record, which had been set by an Air Force B-52 bomber. But the Rutan brothers weren't known for letting the impossible, let alone the merely difficult, stand in their way. Burt sketched his ideas for a record-flight airplane on a restaurant napkin. The drawing depicted a large flying-wing design with a 15-degree swept wing. Both Dick and Jeana had set aviation records flying Burt's designs, but a flight around the world without landing was another story. The more they talked it over, however, the more enthusiastic they became. They decided to try it, but all three agreed that it would be Dick and Jeana's project. After Burt had designed the airplane, Dick and Jeana would have to raise the money and build it themselves, with Burt's spare-time help. Without even asking Burt to prove he could make it work, Dick and Jeana went out with a sketch and started looking for sponsors to donate a million dol-

Designed by Dick Rutan's younger brother, Burt, Voyager *dwarfs the other aircraft in Hangar 77 at Mojave Airport in Southern California; in the foreground, a Long-EZ (left) and a VariEze (right), also designed by Burt Rutan. Burt's company, the Rutan Aircraft Factory, is still based at Mojave; by the mid-1970s, it had revolutionized the home-built airplane market with its plans for unique, canard-equipped aircraft.*

lars to the project. At some point, Jeana named the aircraft *Voyager*.

Using the old Louis Breguet formula for aircraft range, Burt realized that his quickly sketched, flying-wing design would not be capable of making the flight. The aircraft would require a long wing, but a flying-wing design, with no fuselage, did not have room to carry the necessary fuel, which would comprise three-fourths of the total takeoff weight of the airplane. Such an immense fuel load would have to be distributed between wing tanks and tanks in large fuel booms to maintain structural integrity.

The first detailed calculations produced a design that still had a 110.33-foot-long (33.65-meter-long), span-loaded wing with built-in fuel tanks, but, to provide for greater fuel capacity, Rutan now combined the wing with a twin-tail-boom, central-fuselage structure. Forward of the main wing, a smaller canard wing ran from the front of each boom to the central fuselage, which resembled an elongated pod with an engine at each end—one pushing and the other pulling—and the crew compartment in the middle. A vertical fin rose from the after end of each boom. An ultralight graphite-composite structure would give maximum strength, yet would comprise only eight to nine percent of

the total takeoff weight. Under load, the wings would flex as much as a full 10 feet (three meters) per G (force of gravity); imposing a load of more than 1.5 Gs could cause catastrophic failure of the wing structure. Rutan reached a very sobering conclusion: the margin of safety between safe flight and over-stressing the airframe came to a slim 10 percent. The only way to widen that margin would be to install more efficient engines, thereby reducing the fuel load, and that would cost a whole lot of money.

Burt Rutan's basic concept called for the front tractor engine to be used only at the start of the flight. The rest of the time it would be shut down, with the propeller feathered, its blades turned into the wind for low drag, while the rear pusher engine provided the power for cruising. Less power would be required as the fuel was consumed and total weight decreased.

While Burt was refining the design, Dick and Jeana hit the lecture circuit and haunted corporate offices to find sponsors and raise funds. To their surprise, even well-funded companies were not anxious to climb onto the *Voyager* bandwagon. As the months went by, depression set in for the fliers. Apparently no major American sponsor was willing to underwrite the flight. Privately, Rutan and Yeager were told that no company wanted to risk having its name on an experimental airplane that was likely to end up on the evening news, exploding in a fireball at the end of a runway.

Rutan and Yeager decided to change tactics: they would shift their fund-raising focus from the large-scale to the small. From that time on, no group, gathering, or person was too insignificant to be considered a prime donor. And, in the end, most of the money for *Voyager* came from individuals in the aviation community who shared the Rutans' and Yeager's daring vision of a non-government, non-corporate group of Americans doing the impossible. Volunteers started lining up to help.

In the end, a few corporations were willing to share the risks. Hercules, Inc., became the first corporate sponsor, donating quantities of its Magnamite graphite composite materials, which, in the end, comprised 90 percent of the airplane. A solid Magnamite spar ran the length of the wing, and

A preflight Voyager *briefing in Hangar 77 includes, from left to right: engineer Glenn Maben, Burt Rutan, engineer Doug Shane, and* Voyager *pilots Dick Rutan and Jeana Yeager. In the end, the success of* Voyager's *record-setting, around-the-world flight depended heavily on volunteers, who, from 1982 to 1986, worked long hours to build the aircraft, test it, make repairs, and plan the route.*

Magnamite-covered cores of Hexcel honeycomb provided ultralight, ultrastiff panels for all of the aircraft's surfaces. In an equally important gesture, Teledyne Continental agreed to provide both engines: the conventional, air-cooled front engine, and an experimental, maximum-efficiency, liquid-cooled engine for the rear pusher power plant. This critical engine would have to run at full throttle for most of the flight. King Radio offered the avionics, and Mobil provided fuel and oil.

Burt Rutan forced himself to keep the structure simple and very light. There would be no money for major changes after it was completed. As the components went together he would test samples, but there would be no way to test the fragile aircraft, as a whole, before it flew. Even a one-G, static-load test on the ground was out of the question: the slightest bang on the skin would do severe damage. And, as for Burt, it was still a spare-time project. He wasn't getting paid, and no one was checking his work behind him. It was a back-burner job for him, while Dick and Jeana searched for funds and actually built *Voyager*.

When construction of the aircraft finally began, Bruce Evans was there to help, and Mike and Sally Melvill jumped in, followed by Chuck and Joan Richey, who designed the landing gear. Lee Herron and Diane Dempsey, owners of a pilots' flying-gear store at Mojave, put their hands in, while Ferg Fay and Glenn Maben handled installation of the front and rear engines, respectively. Soon the ranks grew to include, among others, the Rutans' and Jeana's parents, who wanted to see their offspring achieve success.

In Mojave Airport's Hangar 77, *Voyager* slowly began to take shape. Everything was makeshift, including the oven made from a house furnace that the builders used to "cure" the composites. The shortage of funds put increasing stress on the entire team, which already was pushed hard by long hours and very little reward. Debts piled up, but the work went on. As Amelia Earhart had remarked, aviation records don't fall until someone is willing to mortgage the present for the future.

By 1984, the outlook began to improve; *Voyager* was rolled out on June 2 to begin a two-year test program. Dick Rutan and Jeana Yeager would fly

The glider-like design of Voyager*'s wings, left, reflects the need for maximum efficiency. Because the wing spars overlap, the left wing is positioned two inches farther forward than the right. During takeoff for the epic flight, the vertical winglets (foreground) dragged on the runway and eventually broke off, reducing the aircraft's wingspan by about two feet. Weight was such a critical concern for this venture that only the top of* Voyager

was painted. Above (at left), pilot Dick Rutan confers with crew chief Bruce Evans (right). Team members spent some 22,000 hours building Voyager *.*

the craft, but a mission-support group on the ground would have to plan and monitor the flight. The complex team required to manage the flight finally came together in 1986. While Peter Riva handled the office and media relations, the mission-control team assembled under director Larry Caskey. Len Snellman would handle weather, Don Rietzke communications, and Jack Norris performance and technical direction.

That *Voyager* differed outwardly from more conventional aircraft was apparent to even the most ignorant observer. Even experienced pilots shook their heads after one peek in the cockpit. Two people were going to have to stay in this claustrophobic tube, about the size of a telephone booth lying on its side, for almost a week and a half. Spelling each other, one pilot would fly *Voyager* from the seat under the tiny canopy, the only place in the cabin with enough overhead space for a person to sit up, while the other pilot would lie down and try to rest. Comfort had not been given much consideration in the design. Clearly, the cramped space, the constant engine noise, and the lack of sleep would make the flight a severe physical trial for the pilots. Although the idea that the pilots would relieve each other periodically to provide for rest had sounded good in planning sessions, in reality the cockpit environment would prove to be a roaring, smelly cylinder from which, furthermore, there was no way to escape quickly in an emergency.

From the outset, the team knew that the aircraft would be unstable longitudinally until a considerable quantity of fuel had been burned off. Because no pilot would have the stamina to fly the unstable machine manually for several days, an autopilot was mandatory equipment. The first flight showed just how bad it was going to be.

With Dick Rutan, much the more experienced pilot of the two, at the controls, *Voyager* flew for the first time on the afternoon of June 22, 1984. Once airborne, he found things worse than bad. *Voyager*'s lateral and directional handling were not good, but they were adequate for the gentle climbs and shallow turns the aircraft would have to make during the flight. Adverse yaw, the tendency of the aircraft to reverse direction during turns, was severe, forcing Rutan to use a great deal of rudder and aileron. The aircraft developed oscillations that would cause the wings to flap to destruction in three to five cycles (about 15 seconds) unless the pilot immediately applied the controls to counter the motion. If the *Voyager* was ultrasensitive to changes in pitch, just the opposite was true of the ailerons, which control rolling movements. The pilot had to use both hands to move the stick to either side, and even when the stick was moved, the airplane responded with only slight changes in attitude. In short, the airplane was dangerous to fly. Constantly alert and skillful handling would be mandatory if they were to make it around the world. Burt and Dick had some serious discussions. Both knew the chances of a fatality were high. The margin of safety was so narrow that they decided not to test *Voyager* at full gross weight, almost 9,700 pounds (4,410 kilograms), until the actual world attempt. They wouldn't know how much more unstable it might be until then. If it couldn't be flown at maximum weight, then so be it, but if the mission were successful, the brothers knew that *Voyager* would never have to fly again.

Since the aircraft handled much more poorly when it was heavy than when it was light, Dick Rutan made the decision to stay at the controls himself during the first portion of the attempt. Jeana would fly *Voyager* after enough fuel had been burned to reduce the aircraft's instability. As flight testing proceeded, the pressure of flying a dangerous airplane, together with the constant struggle to find enough money to continue and disagreements among team members caused tension to soar. Eventually, the stress drove a wedge between Dick and Jeana. Their romance soured, and they broke up. Still, though the change in their relationship worried brother Burt, the two pilots were determined to go ahead with the flight.

Testing continued, with the pilots pushing the

airplane a little harder on each flight. In July 1986, Dick and Jeana broke a closed-course distance record. Flying 20 laps in a racetrack pattern from north of San Francisco to just south of Vandenburg Air Force Base, near Lompoc, California, they stayed aloft for more than four and a half days, flying 11,600 miles (18,560 kilometers). They managed to adapt to the cramped cockpit, but the constant 110-decibel noise level drove them to distraction. And, although they did not feel unusually thirsty during the flight, dehydration hit them hard. Just after landing at Mojave, the two attended a press conference, and Jeana fainted. In response, mission flight surgeon Dr. George Jutila decreed that, in the future, the pilots would have to pay stricter attention to their physical well-being.

After the record closed-course flight and its attendant noise problems, the Bose Corporation, known for its innovations in audio electronics, adapted an earphone headset for the *Voyager* pilots that countered and canceled the engine noise with precisely tuned sound waves. The Bose headsets reduced the noise to a tolerable level.

In the meantime, after exhaustively analyzing world weather patterns, Snellman and his four fellow meteorologists predicted that the best weather window for the flight would appear in September. Everything, in fact, was looking good for a September attempt when, during a test flight, the

Voyager's front engine, above, an air-cooled, 130-horsepower Teledyne Continental O-240, ran for a total of 70 hours, 8 minutes during the flight. It was used for takeoff, for climbing above bad weather, and for extra power when Voyager was still heavy with fuel. The airplane had almost lost its front engine during a test flight after its propeller lost a blade and the whole machine began to shake violently.

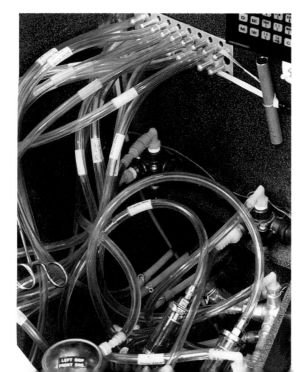

Teledyne Continental's liquid-cooled, IOL-200, above, Voyager's rear engine, ran continuously for 216 hours—the duration of the flight—except for a brief but disconcerting shutdown after a problem involving the fuel system. Below, a seeming tangle of plastic tubes constitutes Voyager's fuel-supply system. Managing the flow of fuel from Voyager's 17 tanks to its front and rear engines occupied more than half the pilots' flight time.

front engine threw a propeller blade. The sudden imbalance caused a nearly catastrophic vibration. The front engine's mounts failed, but the engine somehow stayed on the aircraft as Rutan made an emergency landing. Examination showed that the aircraft could be repaired, but not in time to make the September weather window.

The *Voyager* team decided to replace the wooden propellers with new Hartzell metal props. Although the new propellers were heavier than the originals, their thinner airfoils yielded an increase in fuel efficiency, a tremendous boost toward the success of the flight.

By December, the plane was airworthy again, but weather on the round-the-world flight path was going to be much worse than it would have been in September. Flying more than 25,000 miles (40,000 kilometers) around the Equator, primarily in the tropics, in December meant facing thunderstorms and turbulence that could tear the aircraft apart. Still, they didn't have any choice over the flight route. Without the consistent, nine-or-ten-mile-per-hour (14.5-to-16-kilometer-per-hour) tail winds that the airplane would find on the tropical route, *Voyager* would run out of fuel short of the goal. Burt, Dick, and Jeana huddled, although each already knew what they would decide. Dick and Jeana wanted to go, ideal weather or not. They would have to depart on December 14 so as to have a full moon for visibility at night. Although Jeana had lost a great deal of training time during the engine-mount and propeller repairs, she thought she could handle the airplane.

During three incredibly hectic days, they created a new flight plan, switching the path from a southern route to a more northerly route, and thereby incidentally cutting the total distance by 756 miles (1,210 kilometers). Mission control at Mojave would be in constant contact with the crew, providing *Voyager* with weather information gathered by three geostationary weather satellites that covered most of the route. Jack Norris and his mission control crew would be at their computers constantly to relay advice on fuel burn, power settings, altitudes, temperatures, and the many other factors that affect efficiency. Their calculations would confirm or deny that Rutan and Yeager had enough fuel to make it all the way around.

On the afternoon of December 13, the crew flew *Voyager* to Edwards Air Force Base. At takeoff the next morning, *Voyager* would be laden with more fuel than ever before, and would require every inch of Edwards's extra-long runway to get airborne. During the night, team members pumped 7,011.5 pounds (3,187 kilograms) of fuel into the 17 tanks, bringing the gross takeoff weight, with crew and 130 pounds (59 kilograms) of provisions, to 9,694.5 pounds (4,406.6 kilograms). The fuel-heavy wings

drooped until their tips touched the runway, so the fuel load was shifted to raise the wings one foot off the tarmac. By early morning, ice forming on the upper surfaces of wings and fuselage had to be laboriously removed and the wings covered to protect them from new ice.

To curb *Voyager*'s tendency to lift off during the takeoff run before it had enough air speed to be controllable, the ground crew shortened the nose landing-gear strut, which had the side effect of lowering the wing's angle of incidence, or the angle at which it meets the air. Still worried that the wing tips would scrape the runway on takeoff, the crew then pumped the main landing-gear struts higher to increase the aircraft's ground clearance by another seven to eight inches, which lowered the an-

gle of incidence even more. The full tanks in the tail booms twisted the wings, lowering the angle still more. If the angle of incidence of a wing is lowered, the wing will develop less lift; at some point, if it is lowered enough, the wing actually will drive itself down instead of lifting itself and the airplane up.

A few minutes before 8:00 A.M., Dick and Jeana were aboard, the engines were warm, and it was time to go. Slowly easing the power up on both engines, Rutan started down the 15,000-foot (4,575-meter) runway. Although *Voyager* began to accelerate at the predicted rate, the aircraft failed to reach the anticipated speeds as it passed preset checkpoints along the takeoff strip. That was when observers realized that the wing tips were dragging

On the morning of December 14, 1986, Dick Rutan and Jeana Yeager prepare for takeoff on their round-the-world flight. Voyager's fuel-laden wings droop under the weight of its full load, at 7,011.5 pounds (3,180 kilograms) the most it had ever carried. At right, Burt Rutan and crew watch a video of the airplane's harrowing, 14,000-foot, two-minute, six-second takeoff.

on the runway! The negative angle of incidence was driving the wings down so far that the tips were dragging. Perhaps mercifully, Dick and Jeana could not see the wing tips from the cockpit. Burt, airborne with Mike Melvill in a twin-engine chase plane, could see them, and he got on the radio immediately. "We were telling Dick to lift the nose earlier to raise the wings, but he was concentrating on the aircraft's slow acceleration. The tips were scraping the ground extremely hard the last 2,000 to 3,000 feet [610 to 915 meters]."

After using up more than 14,000 feet (4,270 meters) of runway, only a few seconds remained before they ran off the end. "Be smooth like you've never been smooth before," Dick told himself, "and, as Jeana called 87 knots, I eased back ever so gently on the stick, gradually starting the nose up to rotate, and the wings started to fly." As the nose lifted, the wings were pulled into a positive angle of incidence. They arced up off the ground, and *Voyager* labored into the air. But now came the real moment of truth: would the fully loaded aircraft be too unstable to control? "Within three or four seconds of take-off," remembered Burt, "there was great relief to see that it was controllable and would fly." They knew that if Dick could achieve 100 knots (192 kilometers per hour) of air speed, he could climb, and the airplane would have the margin of performance it needed. "It was almost like I didn't think it could happen, but it happened!" recalled

Burt. "We got 100 knots!" The relief didn't last very long.

Burt and Mike pulled up alongside *Voyager* to get a look at the wing tips. A good 12 to 18 inches (30 to 46 centimeters) of the bottom surface of each wing tip was severely abraded. Burt worried that the outer-wing fuel tanks had been damaged and might be leaking their precious gasoline. The winglets, small vertical fins rising from the ends of the wings to improve their aerodynamics, appeared to be almost severed from the wings themselves. After watching for a moment, he could see that no fuel was leaking from the damaged area, but "it was clear," said Burt, "that the right winglet was not going to stay on the aircraft much longer, and we were concerned that it might peel some top skin from the wing. We told [Dick] not to use any left rudder that might cause the winglet to tear inward and peel the skin back."

After talking it over, Mike Melvill and Burt and Dick Rutan decided that Dick should try to sideslip *Voyager* right and left to see if such maneuvers might break the damaged winglets off without causing further injury to the wing tips. To everyone's immense relief, each winglet came off with a clean break and fluttered away. Although loss of the winglets increased drag by 1.5 percent, if all went well the margin was acceptable. Had just one stayed on, however, *Voyager* would have been so out of trim that drag would have caused unacceptably high fuel consumption. As it was, extra drag caused by the loss of the winglets ultimately cost 115 pounds (52 kilograms) of fuel.

Dick and Jeana headed out across the Pacific Ocean, chased by Burt Rutan and Mike Melvill in the twin. Burt and Mike wanted to stay with them as long as possible, but, eventually, they had to turn back before fuel became critical. "I wondered," said Burt later, "when and under what conditions we'd see these people again, or if indeed we would. When we started the *Voyager* project, four years before, we thought we would find the money somehow and chase [*Voyager*] all around the world to keep an eye on them. Here, I went out two hours into the ocean, . . . said good-bye to them and they had 2,500 miles (4,000 kilometers) to go before they got to Hawaii. It wasn't planned that we would

PERIMENTAL

turn them loose like that. It was emotional, no question about it. We waved good-bye to them and they waved to us."

On board *Voyager*, everything looked great. The Omega long-range-navigation set had them right on course, with updates from a satellite global-positioning system (GPS). Both engines were performing flawlessly; the mission plan called for both engines to run until 4,400 pounds of fuel remained, at which time the forward power plant would be shut down. The weather was excellent; it would never be as good again.

Although mission control planned to relay weather information, Dick had insisted—against Burt's objections—on installing weather-avoidance radar. Something over a day out, *Voyager* came upon Typhoon Marge near the Marshall Islands. Snellman and his colleagues agreed that Dick and Jeana should head north and go around the storm, while hugging it as closely as possible to pick up favorable tail winds. As they closed with the storm, the air grew increasingly rough, until Dick was fighting severe turbulence. Jeana, lying down and unable to see outside, became airsick. However, the

substantial tail wind generated by the tropical depression boosted the aircraft's ground speed from 120 to 145 miles per hour (192 to 232 kilometers per hour). On the other hand, the turbulence around towering cumulus clouds continued to pound *Voyager* mercilessly.

In these rough flying conditions, Rutan stayed at the controls until, well over two days into the flight, he switched places with Jeana, who was still airsick but determined to do her part. Already, mission doctor Jutila and his nurse, Suzie Bowman, were not happy with the condition of their charges. As rough as it had been, something far worse had riveted the attention of both aircrew and mission control: the fuel consumption wasn't working out as planned. Dick's calculations of fuel consumption revealed that too much gas was being burned. Jack Norris saw that "fuel consumption from the engine flow transducer looked right, but gross weight and fuel remaining looked far too low, dead wrong!"

Burt thought Dick "was flying the aircraft sloppy and using too much fuel." In the air and on the ground, everyone studied the data, but tension in-

"It's dark as the inside of a cow up here," Dick remarked from Voyager*'s cramped cabin, above, during a July 1986 nighttime training flight. Here, Jeana flies the aircraft while Dick assumes the rest position; the cockpit is offset to the right. Both pilots wear nasal cannulas to access their high-altitude oxygen system.*

creased as the fuel seemed to be disappearing at an ever increasing rate.

Nevertheless, Dick managed to get about six hours of rest while Jeana flew over the Philippines. Mission control ordered another weather diversion as *Voyager* approached the South China Sea; massive thunderstorms were building. To avoid them, Rutan and Yeager would have to fly as far north as possible, but this route would put them right up against the coast of Vietnam, a nation that not only had denied *Voyager* permission to overfly its territory, but against which Dick had flown more than 350 combat missions. He worried that some form of retaliation might be in store for him should he fall into Vietnamese hands. Using guid-ance from mission control, he threaded a 20-mile (16-kilometer) storm-free corridor while staying just off the forbidden coastline.

As *Voyager* approached the Malay Peninsula, just short of three days aloft, Yeager's and Rutan's spirits soared. An aerial rendezvous with some of the support team was scheduled. No one had seen the aircraft since takeoff, and there was great concern over the condition of the wing tips and the possibility that fuel was leaking from damaged wing tanks. But, even more important, the two tired pilots needed to see a familiar face, as fatigue sent them into emotional highs and lows. Unfortunately, officials in Bangkok, Thailand, held the chase plane on the ground in Hat Yai, Thailand,

Voyager's instrument panel includes, at upper right, a King KWX-58 four-color radar screen and, beneath it, the monitor for the King KNS-660 VLS Omega navigation computer. Masking tape covers a broken deck-angle gauge to prevent it from distracting the pilot.

so no visual contact was possible. The crews of both aircraft had to content themselves with a radio conversation.

Over the Indian Ocean, into day four, 15-knot tail winds buoyed the crew's spirits again, although turbulence seemed to be a constant, unwelcome companion. The fragile craft responded to even the mildest changes in the air. They reached the halfway point over the Arabian Sea, short of Africa, where the worst weather of the trip was expected.

As *Voyager* approached the African coast, the missing-fuel mystery deepened until everyone was trying desperately to solve it. Then, a chance observation and shrewd analysis brought understanding and a measure of relief. Recalled Jack Norris, "Dick noticed bubbles in the fuel line flowing the wrong way and concluded fuel had been flowing back into the tanks. At the same time on the ground, checking with old friends, we established the six ways the turbine flow meters could read incorrectly." Checking all possibilities, the team discovered that the counters still counted forward, "even when the flow was backwards."

There was elation in the air and on the ground. Burt couldn't believe it. "We were sending fuel back to the fuel tanks that was not being measured. Now, wonderful news! We've got more fuel than we think we do! Bad news—nobody knew how much. We had spent three days . . . thinking that the airplane was lighter than it really was. That saved the flight. Because we thought we were lighter, we flew the aircraft slower, dangerously close to stall, but getting a little more efficiency." On paper, the team was able to "reclaim" about 1,000 pounds (455 kilograms) of fuel that they had thought was gone. Dick immediately increased the speed to correspond to a higher gross weight, and *Voyager*'s sick flight characteristics which were caused by flying too slowly, were cured.

But the confusion caused by the fuel-flow transducers had left the team with no way to know just what *Voyager*'s current gross weight was; no one knew how much fuel *Voyager* still had left, or whether a fuel leak was draining the precious supply, or even if the engines were performing properly. The only way to check all of these factors seemed to be to conduct an in-flight inspection and

performance comparison with another airplane. As *Voyager* neared Kenya, Doug Shane and four other team members left Nairobi in a twin-engine aircraft, and, this time, to the joy of both crews, the aerial rendezvous with *Voyager* was successful.

From his aircraft, Shane inspected *Voyager* for leaks or signs of other malfunctions. Everything looked normal. After a series of single- and twin-engine climbs and angle-of-attack-versus-air-speed tests, Dick and Jeana were convinced that the engines were running perfectly, and that the gross-weight figures indicated enough fuel on board to complete the flight. Relieved but exhausted, they waved good-bys to their escorts and climbed to meet a line of thunderstorms looming beyond Lake Victoria.

Stress and lack of sleep had exacted a severe toll from the pilots. Whenever mission control would check in with the *Voyager* crew, the team in California had no way of knowing what kind of response they would get. Dick's and Jeana's emotions were ragged, and ranged from elation to deep depression to anger to almost anything in between. Mission control found that trying to talk over the fuel problem could be tough, since Dick was in no mood for bad news. Burt recalled Doctor Jutila's straightforward advice. "Talk to them . . . they're bored to where they need someone to talk to . . . they need emotional support, they need encour-

Voyager *volunteers working in the flight control's radio room, above, include, from left to right: Stu Hagedorn, Mike Melvill, Glenn Maben, and meteorologist Len Snellman. Satellite communications enabled mission controllers to stay in radio contact with* Voyager *for most of the flight.* Voyager*'s planned course, plotted on map at right, flew mostly over water, and changed as constantly as the weather. Certain problem areas could not be avoided. As Jeana recalled one incident, "I began picking my way through the big storms that churned up from the Philippine Islands, great booming cumulus clouds that reached high above the airplane."*

agement . . . everybody get in there and talk to them."

Burt was often at a loss as to what to say. "They'd blow up when you mentioned something to them like, 'Hey, you've got to keep your altitude up.' Don't ask him for data because he was so fatigued he'd blow up instead of giving you the data . . . 'Get off my back!' There were times when the crew was crying [for] happiness."

Crossing Africa into the fifth day was a nightmare. Not only were thunderstorms popping up all over, but several countries had denied overflight privileges to *Voyager*. To avoid the weather and avoid violating forbidden airspace, Dick and Jeana were routed south over Lake Victoria and told to put on their oxygen equipment and climb to 20,000 feet (6,100 meters), which would put them above most of the weather as well as the tallest mountain peaks. As they neared Uganda, storms were build-

ing everywhere. Mission control could not offer much help in finding a break; only Dick could see the breaks in the towering clouds ahead. At one point, Dick saw a break in the weather; if he took it, he would have to fly through Uganda's forbidden airspace. He opted to use an old military tactic: he turned off the radios and pressed on. Just as he entered Ugandan airspace, the break closed in behind him; had he waited, he would not have made it. Needless to say, mission control was stunned when, with no warning, *Voyager* stopped transmitting. For over three hours they feared the worst: that the aircraft had crashed in Africa.

Meanwhile, at 20,000 feet (6,100 meters), *Voyager* weaved and dodged the giant thunderheads. Jeana failed to get enough oxygen and became semi-comatose, rousing into fitful wakefulness when Dick would take one hand from the controls to shake her violently, then lapsing back into uncon-

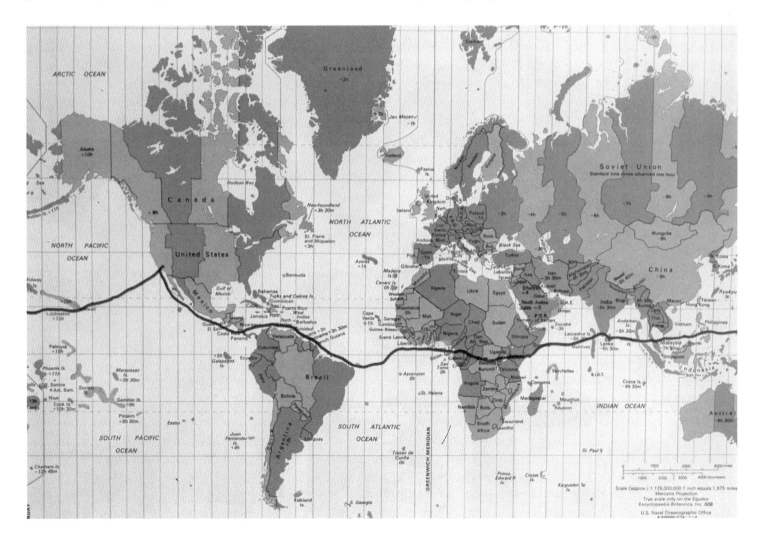

At sunrise on December 23, 1986, right, Burt Rutan and Mike Melvill, in the twin-engine chase plane, rendezvous with Voyager on the home stretch over Southern California. "Dick, time to land," said Jeana, finally, after Voyager had made several celebratory passes over the crowd awaiting its arrival at Edwards Air Force Base, opposite. "We're running low on fuel." She then began the difficult task of cranking the landing gear down by hand. Having completed the smashing of the last great aviation record, Jeana and Dick and Voyager touched down at 8:05 A.M., after 9 days, 3 minutes, and 44 seconds in the air.

sciousness. Later, Dick, starved for sleep, cut off from the world, lost in a sea of surging emotions, weaving through a nightmare-black sky of towering thunderheads, suffered a series of hallucinations, some euphoric, some terrifying. For a time, he became certain that Voyager was exploding, coming apart in a ball of fire. "The instrument panel was bulging out toward me, swelling and widening . . . . The radar screen was swelling into a big glass blister." Then everything returned to normal. No pilot in history had suffered from such extended sleep loss during a record flight. For the entire duration of the flight, Jeana was able to fly at times, but Dick flew all of the night and bad-weather legs, taking only brief rests.

When Dick finally turned the radios back on and called Mojave, he was over eastern Zaire, still 12 hours away from the Atlantic Ocean. Mission control, practically the scene of a wake, reacted to the reawakening radio as if the dead had come back to life. But the weather was still terrible. For hours longer, Snellman and his team tried to help the pilots avoid thunderstorm after thunderstorm with constant course changes. The intensity did not let up, with high mountains yet to come.

As the Atlantic came into view at last, Dick and Jeana broke down and wept. Dick radioed that he never wanted to fly across Africa again. There were tears and hugs in mission control. Their airplane and friends had made it through what surely would be the worst weather of the trip. As Voyager started out across the Atlantic, the weather team put them into clear air 100 miles (160 kilometers) south of a solid wall of thunderstorms. Not only was the air blessedly smooth, but a strong tail wind was pushing them. Then, halfway across, another adrenalin rush took over as a red oil-warning light for the rear engine came on. The oil was foaming, but they quickly transferred more oil to the engine, which settled the foam and doused the light.

As Voyager flew into day six, the coast of Brazil appeared ahead. The Atlantic had been merciful, and, though darkness enveloped the two pilots, they took comfort in knowing that a full moon soon would rise. Without warning, however, a group of thunderstorms grew, surrounding and towering over the frail machine and its stretched-to-the-limit crew. Mission control had given no warning of bad weather, since the satellite photos just 30 minutes before had showed nothing threatening. For its part, the on-board weather radar, Dick's gift to himself, painted wall after wall of severe weather. Helpless to do anything about these conditions, he had no choice but to bore into the boil-

ing line of convective cells.

The fragile plane was immediately tossed around like a toothpick in the worst turbulence Dick or Jeana had ever experienced. First one wing and then the other was slammed straight up until Dick was sure *Voyager* would be thrown out of control or torn to pieces—or both. Finally, as he recalled, the storm "spat us out at 90 degrees of bank. . . . We unloaded to a quarter of a G, added in full rudder, added aileron, and slowly recovered."

Voyager had not been designed to withstand forces that would heave it into a sudden, 90-degree bank. Rutan radioed Mojave, "We're in big trouble. We need some help, and that's a fact." Over the next 90 minutes, mission control took the latest satellite photos and vectored the pilots out of the storms and into the Southern Hemisphere. Once everyone was settled down, Dick radioed another strained message: "I damn near lost it." After the flight, he recalled this time as the most terrifying of the entire trip.

Although they had planned to cross into the United States at Texas, following the shortest route home, the weather was not going to cooperate, and the crew was in no position to argue. Following the South American coastline around the southern Caribbean, Rutan and Yeager headed for Costa Rica, picking up favorable tail winds with no turbulence. On the morning of December 22, they hit the Pacific again, just short of eight days out. With clear weather ahead, it looked like it was going to be all downhill if Dick and Jeana could muster what energy they had left.

Passing Guatemala City, the tail winds that had blessed the flight so far slowly turned into head winds, until *Voyager*'s ground speed bled from 105 to 65 knots (202 to 125 kilometers per hour). Jack Norris and his loyal band were faced with some sobering calculations. Over the Caribbean, they had figured that the fuel supply would be adequate, but if *Voyager* was slowed by head winds all the way home, most of the reserve would be used. At this point, Norris had to rely on judgment rather than a calculator and to trust that they had not picked the wrong way home.

Once again, stress became a constant companion, stretching already taut nerves close to the breaking point. As the crew coaxed *Voyager* up the Mexican coast off Baja California, Rutan started a slow descent to find better winds. Then mission control got an unbelievable radio call: "The engine has stopped!" One electric fuel pump had failed, and fuel would not gravity-feed from the forward-located canard fuel tank when the aircraft was in a descending, nose-down attitude. Only 700 miles (1,120 kilometers) from home, *Voyager* was now a glider.

Dick and Jeana went through every emergency procedure they could think of while calmly radioing their altitude every 30 seconds. Finally, Mike Melvill couldn't stand it any longer; he got on the radio. "Well, damn it, start the front engine." After four minutes of silence, Dick leveled out, fired up the front engine, and then got the rear engine

going again. Dick and Jeana decided they'd fly the rest of the way with both engines running, and they re-routed the fuel lines in flight to make sure the engines wouldn't quit again. Earlier, Jeana had climbed up behind the instrument panel to replace a gyro horizon and save the autopilot, without which the flight would have been in real jeopardy.

Both of them had regained some strength during the latest—and, as it turned out, the last—crisis. At least it had given them something to do, other than to sit and wait. Dick had flown 85 percent of the flight, averaging only two to three hours sleep a night over seven and a half days.

At about 4:00 A.M. on December 23, the Mojave team figured that *Voyager* had just enough fuel to make it home. Dick and Jeana were sucking small quantities of fuel from every corner they could

reach with the fuel-boost pump, managing to bring the level up to the magic 13 gallons (49 liters) needed in the header tank.

As the sun rose over Southern California on December 23, 1986, Burt and Mike, in the twin-engine chase plane, rendezvoused with *Voyager*, after talking their way to the meeting by counting down the miles from Long Beach. When they saw each other, recalled Burt, "we just all broke down in tears. All this hell we'd gone through for nine days and there they are! Dick was jovial, talking, excited. . . . Mike and I were crying. He was the guy who hadn't slept and we were just absolutely basket cases . . . couldn't even think straight." Burt Rutan cried for the 45 minutes it took to fly home with his brother.

When Dick and Jeana reached Edwards Air Force Base at 7:35 A.M., there were 50,000 people waiting to greet them. Test-center commander Major General Ted Twinting had grounded all aircraft on a usually busy morning. Edwards had been the site of too much aviation history to ignore the smashing of the last great record.

Dick made four passes over the lake bed to show off his airplane, as any decent fighter pilot would. Jeana pumped the landing gear down by hand. To make it an even nine days, they flew around the lake bed one more time. President Ronald Reagan, watching in the White House and frustrated with all the circling, blurted, "Land the damn plane!"

Melvill read off the altitudes to Dick as he came down on final approach. At 8:05:28 A.M., 24,986.727 miles (39,979.76 kilometers) after leaving the same spot, *Voyager* landed without having touched the Earth for 9 days, 3 minutes, and 44 seconds.

A total of 18.3 gallons (69.5 liters) of fuel remained (out of 1,190.1 gallons or 4,522.4 liters), hidden in various cubby holes throughout the 17 fuel tanks. Only five gallons (19 liters) remained in the header tank that fed the engines. The average tail wind for the flight had been 9.774 miles per hour (15.64 kilometers per hour). This boost had given *Voyager* the equivalent of more than 2,111 extra miles (3,378 kilometers) of flying time. The pilots had started with a reserve-fuel range of almost 2,400 nautical miles (2,880 statute miles or 4,640 kilometers), but had used almost all of it in flying more miles than planned and in flying on two engines for longer than anticipated. The estimates on weather and performance supplied by the meteorologists and the performance team had predicted just such an outcome. It may have seemed like a close call to outsiders, but the team had correctly made the calculations that had allowed Dick Rutan and Jeana Yeager to take a planned, premeditated risk. The flight distilled the essence of all that has made American aviation great.

Perhaps X-15 test pilot Scott Crossfield summed it up best: "The most remarkable people in aviation were the Wright brothers, who disdained institutions, solved all their own problems, paid for everything out of their own pockets, and brought the miracle of Kitty Hawk to us all.

"The Rutans and Yeager disdained institutions, mortgaged everything but their dignity, gave six years of their lives creating a most ingenious airplane, planned and flew the most ingenious flight against all kinds of hazards, all on their own. They subjected themselves to nine days of the most exquisite torture anyone has ever volunteered for in their life, and did an incredible job that no government could do—NASA couldn't do it, the military couldn't do it. There was no prize, no money, and they are still paying off their debts. Theirs is one of the most remarkable aeronautical feats in history."

Sitting atop Voyager, *Dick and Jeana wave to a welcoming crowd of some 50,000 people at Edwards Air Force Base. Jeana had lost eight pounds during their ordeal, Dick six. Fourteen days later, on its flight back to its home base at Mojave Airport, one of* Voyager*'s engine-coolant seals failed completely. The aircraft would never fly again.*

INDEX

Illustrations and caption references appear in bold.

PICTURE CREDITS

Legend: B Bottom; C Center; L Left; R Right; T Top.

The following abbreviations are used to identify the Smithsonian Institution (SI) and other organizations.

LC   Library of Congress, D.C.
NASA   National Aeronautics and Space Administration
NASM   National Air and Space Museum (SI)
USAF   United States Air Force

Front Matter: 1 Ed Castle, MD; 2-3 UPI/Bettmann, NY; 4-5 John Ricksen, FL; 6-7 Jeffrey Vock/VISIONS, NY; 8 SI (91-19563); 10 SI (85-10846); 11 SI/Lockheed Corporation, 1985.

Powered Flight: pp. 12-13 SI (A-38618-A); 14T SI (A-18881); 14B, 15 The Bettmann Archive; 16 LC; 17T The Bettmann Archive; 17B SI (11506); 18 SI (A-52375); 19 H. Armstrong Roberts, PA; 20 art by John Batchelor, England; 20-21 SI (26-767-B); 22 art by Paul Takacs, MD; 23 SI (A-42710); 24 SI (9620-A.S.); 25 SI (76-17482); 26 art by Keith Ferris, USAF Art Collection; 27T LC; 27B FPG International, NY; 28 The Bettmann Archive; 29T SI (78-3620); 29B SI; 30T FPG International; 30B SI (A-43064-A); 31TR FPG International; 31TL SI; 31B SI (43056-A).

Coast to Coast: pp. 32-33 SI (A-3495); 34T SI (47151); 34C SI; 35T SI (91-6115); 35B SI (31291-B); 36 SI (76-1826); 37T Charles H. Phillips, MD; 37B SI (44887-F); 38R SI (38497-H); 38L SI (A-48065-L); 39 SI (A-3491); 40 SI (86-20033); 41 SI (77-9038); 42-43 Ross Chapple, VA; 44, 45 UPI/Bettmann; 46 SI (47017-B); 47T SI (A-50818); 47B SI (49911); 48-49 Ross Chapple; 50 SI (76-15516); 51T SI (45881); 51B SI (A-42966-A).

The Atlantic and the World: pp. 52-53 art by Henry Farré, USAF Art collection; 54 SI (1132); 55 The Bettmann Archive; 56 SI (A-37585-B); 57 SI (10404); 59 art by Ted Wilbur, ASAA, VA; 60 SI (A 21393-B); 61 SI (21393-C); 62 SI (81-8960); 63 SI (44750-B); 64 UPI/Bettmann; 65 McDonnell Douglas Corp., CA; 66 SI (76-2796); 67 SI (79-2186); 68 SI (48828); 68-69 SI (A 2709-A); 70-71 SI (51479); 71 SI (77-7985); 72-73 Ross Chapple; 73B SI (43388); 74T UPI/Bettmann; 74B SI (86-985); 75 The Bettmann Archive.

USA to Europe Nonstop: p. 76 Ross Chapple; 77 Lindbergh Picture Collection, Yale University Library, CT; 78 The Bettmann Archive; 79T SI (90-

7468); 79B AP/Wide World Photos; 80T H. Armstrong Roberts; 80B Lindbergh Picture Collection, Yale University Library; 81 FPG International; 82 Missouri Historical Society; 83 AP/Wide World Photos; 84TL The Bettmann Archive; 84TR SI (83-14191); 84B UPI/Bettmann; 85 The Bettmann Archive; 86-87 art by John Batchelor; 87 SI (A12720-C); 88 Ross Chapple; 89 Lindbergh Picture Collection, Yale University Library; 90T UPI/Bettmann; 90B SI (A42065-A); 91T,BR Lindbergh Picture Collection, Yale University Library; 91BL SI (86-9656); 92T SI (92-2946); 92C Charles H. Phillips; 93 SI (86-13507).

Air Transport for All: pp. 94-95, 96 The Bettmann Archive; 97 UPI/Bettmann; 98 Michael Freeman, London; 99 SI (75-11398); 100T SI (72 8419); 100B SI (82-5412); 101 SI (83-8865); 102T McDonnell Douglas Corp.; 102B SI (76 2714); 103 SI (75-5031); 104T James A. Sugar/Check Six, CA; 104B SI (76 3132); 105T SI (76 3139); 105B McDonnell Douglas Corp.; 106 Mike Mitchell, DC; 107T SI (A 1070); 107B UPI/Bettmann.

Golden Air Frontiers: p. 108 The Granger Collection, NY; 109 The Bettmann Archive; 110T Terence McArdle, MD; 110C UPI/Bettmann; 111T National Museum of Science, London; 111B SI (76-18240); 112 UPI/Bettmann; 113 Carolyn J. Russo, NASM/SI; 114 art by John Batchelor; 115 Oklahoma Historical Society; 116 UPI/Bettmann; 117T,B FPG International; 118 Ross Chapple; 119 The Bettmann Archive; 120, 121 UPI/Bettmann; 122T Ross Chapple; 122B The Bettmann Archive; 124C FPG International; 124B, 125T UPI/Bettmann; 125C SI (A411H); 126TL UPI/Bettmann; 126TR,B The Bettmann Archive; 127T FPG International; 127B Mark Avino, NASM/SI; 128 (87-16237); 128-129 Michael Freeman; 130L SI (31758); 130R Carolyn J. Russo, NASM/SI; 131 UPI/Bettmann.

Rocket Power: p. 132 NASA; 133 Ross Chapple; 134T The Bettmann Archive; 134B AP/Wide World Photos; 135 The Bettmann Archive; 136L SI (A-624-B); 136R SI (A590-C); 137T Ross Chapple; 137B AP/Wide World Photos; 138L SI (A-4316-C); 138R SI (76-13636); 139T SI (77-4214); 139B SI (76-7559); 140L UPI/Bettmann; 140R SI (78-5935); 141 SI (79-13171); 142T UPI/Bettmann; 142B NASA; 143 Ed Castle.

Jet Power: pp. 144-145 SI (7910093); 146 SI (801896); 147T "The First Whittle Engine," by Rod Lovesey; from *Whittle: The True Story*, by John Golley and Bill Gunston, in association with Sir Frank Whittle, ©*1987* Airlife Publishing, Shrewsbury, England, and Smithsonian Institution Press, Washington, D.C.; 147B SI (80-2446); 148T art by John Batchelor; 148B SI (90-3248); 148-149 art by John Batchelor; 150 SI (90-8393); 150-151, 151, 152-153 art by John Batchelor; 153 SI (76-13231); 154T SI (79-

13826); 154B SI (78-17070); 155T SI (78-19068); 155B SI (78-18982 #10A); 156, 157 Terence McArdle; 158 From *Test Pilots: The Frontiersmen of Flight*, by Richard Hallion, 1981, 1988, Smithsonian Institution Press, D.C.; 159 NASA/Langley Research Center; 160-161 Ross Chapple; 161 UPI/Bettmann.

The Sound Barrier: pp. 162-163 The Bettmann Archive; 164 SI (81-3105); 165 SI (1241); 166 Ross Chapple; 167T NASA/Dryden Flight Research Facility, CA; 167B SI (83-2821); 168 UPI/Bettmann; 169T SI (A-5231-A); 169B AP/Wide World Photos; 170, 171 Terence McArdle; 172T SI (87-6747); 172B SI (88-9417); 173 SI (A-5346-B); 174-175 USAF Art Collection, NASM/SI; 177 UPI/Bettmann.

The Jet Airliner: p. 178 Terence McArdle; 178-179 The Boeing Company Archives; 180 SI (K8334); 181 SI (35955AC); 182, 183T George Hall/Check Six; 183B Tex Johnston collection, WA; 184T,B, 185 The Boeing Company Archives; 186T George Hall/Check Six; 186B Tex Johnston collection; 187 The Boeing Company Archives; 188 McDonnell Douglas Corp.; 189 The Boeing Company Archives; 190-191 art by John Batchelor; 191 The Boeing Company Archives.

The Threshold of Space: pp. 192, 194 NASA; 195 NASA/Langley Research Center, VA; 196 USAF, Edwards Air Force Base, History Office, CA; 197C Diagram by Julie Schieber/Phil Jordan & Associates, adapted from an original NASA illustration; 197B M. McCaffrey, USAF Art Collection; 198 UPI/Bettmann; 199 NASA/Dryden Flight Research Facility; 200, 201, 202 NASA; 203T,B, 204, 205 NASA/Dryden Flight Research Facility; 206 NASA; 207 Erik Simonsen, CA; 208-209 NASA/Dryden Flight Research Facility; 209 USAF, Edwards Air Force Base, History Office.

To Space and Back: p. 210 Terence McArdle; 211 art by Pierre Mion, VA; 212T SI (78-17215); 212B SI (A-4778-C); 213 SI (87-17009); 214T Chad Slattery, CA; 214B NASA; 215, 216T NASA/Dryden Flight Research Facility; 216B Diagram by Julie Schieber/Phil Jordan & Associates, adapted from an original NASA illustration; 217C AP/Wide World Photos; 217B, 218T NASA/Dryden Flight Research Facility; 218B Chad Slattery; 219T Terence McArdle; 219B, 220, 221T NASA; 221B NASA/Dryden Flight Research Facility; 222-223 art by John Batchelor; 224TL,TR, 224-225, 225T, 226T, 226-227, 227T NASA; 228 Roger Ressmeyer/Starlight, NY; 229 NASA.

The Last Great World Record: 230-231, 232, 232-233, 234, 235T,B, 236, 237T,B, Mark Greenberg/VISIONS; 238-239 Nyland Wilkins/VISIONS; 239, 240, 240-241, 242, 243, 244, 245 Mark Greenberg/VISIONS; 246 Erik Simonsen; 247 Mark Greenberg/VISIONS.

ACKNOWLEDGMENTS

Writing about the most famous air- and spacecraft as well as about their designers and pilots was somewhat intimidating, like approaching an icon. The icons of aviation are difficult to deal with: the hallowed mystique, the aura, that surrounds them is often so fixed in the public consciousness that any retelling of the story can be considered an assault. I have approached them with the same reverence, the same love, that I had for them as a boy who yearned to fly, emotions now tempered by the reality of a historian's research. The two are not, in my mind, contradictory, but rather, complementary.

I have tried to meld my 4,000 hours of flying time in more than 170 different types of aircraft with the history I have found. Mine has been a rich, exciting life as an aviation historian because I try to fly what I write about. Combining my experience with the stories of the people who designed and flew these machines should offer readers a chance to go beyond the nuts-and-bolts technical details to experience the tragedies and triumphs of those who made each of these a unique period in history.

Telling these stories would have been impossible without the selfless and enthusiastic help of so many people.

Tom D. Crouch, senior curator at the National Air and Space Museum, was immediately a mentor and a constant help. His Pulitzer Prize-nominated book about the Wright brothers, *The Bishop's Boys*, as well as his other books, are marks for any historian to shoot for.

Alexis "Dusty" Doster, my editor and an aviation historian to be reckoned with, sent a constant stream of reference books that were absolutely crucial to the completion of this project. Even more important, he encouraged me to keep bringing my pilot's viewpoint into each chapter—he wanted to know how these airplanes handled. This continual flow of positive reinforcement made me search that much harder for the humans behind the machines.

Patricia Gallagher, Editor-in-Chief at Smithsonian Books, never seemed to be worried about the deadlines I was missing. She wanted an adventure story full of personal drama and she was willing to give me the extra time to find it. The book is richer because of that upbeat support.

The National Air and Space Museum staff never seemed to tire of my showing up asking for something they had to work to find. Russ Lee did some real legwork in getting clearance for use of documents in the curatorial files. As usual, Dan Hagedorn, Larry Wilson, Tim Cronen, and Melissa Keiser dug material out of the library whenever I needed it.

John Honey, producer of the documentary filmed in parallel with this book, was more than willing to share his interviews with me.

Jack Norris, technical and performance director at *Voyager* mission control, was absolutely selfless in sending me a copy of his official log and flight analysis of the world flight, something he normally sells. The 72-page book is packed with information about the people who worked at mission control, with technical details, exact times and fuel states, a narrative of the mission, maps, graphs, performance charts . . . everything on exactly how the *Voyager* performed. And Jack took the time to scribble notes throughout for my attention.

Bettie Ethell, my lifetime companion and best friend, was absolutely crucial to getting the book done faster than it normally would have taken. She transcribed taped interviews hour after hour so I could keep writing, and then she proofread the manuscript with each rewrite. Regardless of how much or little technical detail I threw in, if she couldn't understand it she made sure I rewrote it. It wouldn't have happened without you, hon.

—Jeff Ethell

The Editors of Smithsonian Books would like to thank the following people and organizations for their assistance in the preparation of this book:

Mark Avino, Peter Jakab, Carolyn Russo, Mark Spencer, Michael Fetters, Timothy Cronen, Allan Janus, Brian Nicklas, Melissa Keiser, Archives, NASM/SI; John Batchelor, Dorset, England; Ross Chapple, VA; William Dana, Larry L. Sammons, Hunter Adler, Jim Ross, Ames Research Center, Dryden Flight Research Facility, Edwards Air Force Base, CA; Richard P. Hallion, Bolling Air Force Base; Mary Ellen McCaffrey, OPPS/SI; Alice Price, USAF Art Program; Judith Ann Schiff, Manuscripts & Archives, Yale University Library; John Sewall, Nell Sewall, Newport News, VA; William Sewall, Bill Taylor, Langley Research Center, Hampton, VA; Althea Washington, NASA; Pamela Vanneck, Network Group.

Suppliers:

Jerry Benitez, Stanford Paper Company; Anthony Collins, Dale Fries, Simon Gore-Grimes, Geraldine Nerney, Tim Norden, Steve Stewart, Colotone Graphics, Inc.; Cooper Direct, Ltd.; Stephanie Garber, Westvaco; Tracy Hoare, Steve True, Process Materials; Bob Jillson, Holliston; Phil Jordan, Julie Schieber, Phil Jordan and Associates; William Liddell, Creative Automation Company; John McGough, TempoGraphics, Inc.; Cliff Mears, Shirley Schulz, R.R. Donnelley & Sons Company; Robert J. Muma, Allen Envelope Corporation; Tom Suzuki, Tom Suzuki, Inc.; Robert Volkert, Calmark, Inc.

THE TELEVISION SERIES

"Frontiers of Flight" represents a collaborative venture by Discovery Productions and Network Projects. Originally conceived by Philip Osborn, a pioneer of Discovery Productions' popular "Wings" series, it is one of a number of aviation programs that Osborn, along with his company, Network Projects, has supplied Discovery since 1987.

In 1990, Network Projects and Discovery Productions approached the Smithsonian's National Air and Space Museum (NASM) with the idea of a television series celebrating NASM's unparalleled collection of significant historical aircraft. The concept met with great enthusiasm, but the NASM collection is vast: how could one series portray its range and breadth with unity and logical progression?

Series writer/director John Honey invented a title that held the answer: "Frontiers of Flight." Thirteen individual programs would address major aviation frontiers that had been challenged and conquered by airplanes in the NASM collection.

Discovery and the National Air and Space Museum agreed, and a three-way deal was negotiated: Network and Discovery became co-production partners; NASM offered special access to exhibits for filming, its curatorial staff for advice and research assistance, and its still photographs and film libraries for archival program material. Smithsonian Books, in collaboration with Orion Books in New York, began work on a book reflecting the title and structure of the television series. They commissioned noted aviation writer Jeffrey Ethell to produce the manuscript. The book and the television series began to evolve simultaneously and in a highly complementary fashion.

Network presented Smithsonian Books with program outlines, tapes of interviews, and access to Terry McArdle's location photographs, 10 distinguished examples of which appear in their book. A strong visual and textual relationship exists between the book and the television series, but each also pursues a path that best achieves the goals of its particular medium.

Network and Discovery received enthusiastic support from the staff of the National Air and Space Museum, with seven people from that institution deserving special mention: Wendy Stephens, who assisted the effort from the Smithsonian's first involvement; Patti Woodside, who also provided support and encouragement from the idea's earliest genesis; Don Lopez, a delightful and unfailingly resourceful contact throughout the production; Tom Crouch, who offered invaluable historical insight; Michael Fetters, who often achieved the impossible in organizing nighttime shoots of the museum's airplanes;

Mark Taylor, who orchestrated access to the NASM film archive, as well as to other film archives around the country; and Melissa Keiser, who transformed the daunting task of shooting still photographs on film into a straightforward and tension-free task.

Hundreds of other people—celebrated aviation pioneers and their relatives, the staff of aerospace companies, archivists, airplane buffs, and private individuals—have contributed generously to this project. Network, Discovery, and the National Air and Space Museum are sincerely grateful for their assistance.

Executive in Charge of Production
Clark Bunting
Executive Producers
for Network Projects, Philip Osborn
for Discovery Productions, Peter McKelvy
Writer/Director
John Honey
Director's Assistant
Maria Honey
Production Manager
Pamela Vanneck
Smithsonian Administration
Wendy Stephens
Director of Photography
Terence McArdle
Camera Assistant
Marcus Smith
Sound Recordist
Paul Rusnak
Gaffer
John Pacy
Offline Editor
John Honey
Online Editor
Larry Asbell
Edit Supervisor
Maria Honey
Sound Post Production
Eric W. Swartz, Steven P. Weber
Original Music
Lyall McDermott, Stewart Long
Performed by
Members of the Tasmanian Symphony Orchestra
Liaison for the National Air and Space Museum
Don Lopez, Tom Crouch
Research
Barry Cawthorne

Smithsonian

FRONTIERS OF FLIGHT

was designed and typeset by
Phil Jordan and Associates,
Inc., Arlington, Virginia.
The book was produced on
a Macintosh IIci using
Quark XPress. The text type
is Monotype Times New
Roman, with Univers 57 for
captions. Headlines are set
in ITC Anna. Colotone
Graphics, Branford,
Connecticut, provided
picture separation, type
output, and film prepara-
tion. R.R. Donnelley &
Sons Company printed the
text on a four-color web
press, printed the jackets on
a sheet-fed press, and notch-
bound the book at their
manufacturing plant in
Willard, Ohio. Text paper
is Consolidated 70# Con-
soweb Gloss, the endsheets
are Process Materials
80# Multicolor Antique,
and the bookcloth is
Holliston Kingston
Natural Finish.